OL
CLUB

Praise for *The Lost Shankly Boy*

A gripping story of a young man's quest to become a professional footballer, his fightback from a series of challenges – including a hair-raising brush with death in South Africa - and ultimately of a bond between player and manager that has spanned a lifetime. All of it told with an easy-going style that at times takes you closer to the history of the Shankly era than ever before.

Dave Usher, The Liverpool Way

An honest tale of the beginnings of the Shankly era at Liverpool, seen through the eyes of a talented yet humble boy. A brilliantly told story, with a stellar cast, yet the real star is George Scott and the impact that his short career at Liverpool had on the rest of his life. Jeff Goulding manages to encapsulate George Scott's incredible story and transport you so vividly into the fabled boot room, that you can smell the dubbin on the boots.

Stuart Horsfield, These Football Times

Parts of his book will make you howl with laughter while others will have you reaching for a box of tissues to mop up the tears. We can only be thankful that the 'Lost Shankly Boy' was eventually found and encouraged to tell us all about his amazing journey.

Christopher Wood, LFC History

George Scott was a Liverpool player for five years, but his extraordinary story shows how Bill Shankly managed his entire career.

Chris McLoughlin, Senior Writer, Reach Sport

George's book captures every emotion. You will laugh and you will cry as his story, so brilliantly written, takes you from humble beginnings to the heart of Liverpool's rise to world fame, both culturally and on the football field. It is a pleasure to read as George's inspirational story unfolds. Bill Shankly insisted on working with people of good character. This book illustrates why George Scott was part of Shanks' Red Revolution.

Kieran Smith, Liverpool FC Historical Group

The George Scott story fills in the gap between what life was like for the men who became legends and those who didn't quite make it. It illuminates what the life of reserve players was like and how they had to cope with life after Liverpool.

John Pearman, Red All Over the Land

The Lost Shankly Boy

George Scott's Anfield Journey

George Scott with Jeff Goulding

pitch

First published by Pitch Publishing, 2020

Pitch Publishing
A2 Yeoman Gate
Yeoman Way
Worthing
Sussex
BN13 3QZ

www.pitchpublishing.co.uk
info@pitchpublishing.co.uk

A CIP catalogue record is available for this book from the British Library.

ISBN 978 1 78531 678 4

Typesetting and origination by Pitch Publishing

Printed and bound in India by Replika Press Pvt. Ltd.

Contents

This book is dedicated to:

My beautiful wife Carole
thank you for 54 years of happiness
without you I would have achieved nothing

Also, to our amazing family
Gavin and Diane Scott
Callum Scott
Charlie Scott
Craig and Joanne Scott
Cameron Scott
and
James Scott

Finally, in loving memory of
my mother Agnes Braik
my father George Edward Brown Scott
my stepfather John Livingstone Braik
my grandparents Bill and Jean Fiddes
my brother-in-law Billy Kneale

Acknowledgements

MY GRATEFUL thanks must go to Ian Callaghan MBE for writing such a lovely foreword to this book and to my co-author, Jeff Goulding. Thanks also go to Chris Wood, whose encyclopaedic knowledge of Liverpool FC and football in general have proved invaluable, and to Jonny Stokkeland for providing me with valuable information and statistics from the Liverpool FC archives.

I would also like to express my gratitude to my great friend, Gordon Wallace. Thanks for the many brilliant experiences we have shared on the football field and on the golf course in the past 60 years. To all the players I have played with during my football career and all the wonderful people I have worked with in my life after football.

And to Bill Shankly, for setting the standards I have lived by.

Some are dead and some are living
In my life I loved them all

Lennon and McCartney, 1965

Foreword

By Ian Callaghan MBE

GEORGE AND I arrived at Anfield via different routes. I was obviously a local lad and had already been training at Melwood as an amateur for a couple of years when George arrived in 1960 from Scotland. George signed on as an apprentice and I can vividly remember watching him and the other lads that Shanks had brought down from Scotland having to do all these chores around the stadium.

They'd be cleaning the first teamers' boots, picking up the rubbish from the Kop after a game and forking over the pitch. Let's just say it didn't look like pleasant work. I'd feel sorry for them, but at the same time I was relieved that I didn't have to join them.

I played several times with George in the reserve team during the 1962/63 Central League season. George was a hard worker. He was also a talented attacking midfielder, with an eye for goal. I always knew that if I found him with a pass, he would know what to do with the ball and I'm sure I set a few goals up for him during that season.

Shankly wanted players who could fight, had skill and ability and who could stand up for themselves and their team-mates on the pitch. You had to have a work ethic, and George had all of this in abundance. The problem for him was that Bill had assembled a first team full of established internationals, players who, for the most part, were the finished article.

Back then, there was the first eleven and the reserve team. That was it. No substitutes and, unless a player was injured, the opportunities were very few and far between. I feel blessed to have been given my chance and to have taken full advantage of it. But I always felt that George was forever on the cusp and very unlucky not to make the breakthrough.

There was no questioning his work ethic, or his consistency, and his goal-scoring record spoke for itself. He was also very vocal and expended so much energy on the pitch. That wasn't me though. I was a quiet player who liked to just get on with the game. I know the boss thought very highly of George, probably because the one quality he admired most in any player was enthusiasm. Unfortunately, for George, the road to the first team was blocked by players who went on to be legends for the club and who won many honours.

George and I never had a cross word in all the time we played together and in all the time since our playing days ended. I was especially pleased that he had managed to play for his boyhood club back in Aberdeen and thrilled that he became a player of some renown in South Africa. He deserved to have that success.

Today, George and I stay in touch and support each other with the various charity activities we are involved in. Both of us are so blessed to have been at Anfield during the birth of what became one of the biggest footballing institutions on the planet.

George remains as passionate about the club today as he was 60 years ago. That he still speaks so highly of a manager and a club that let him go, speaks volumes about the man. He was a loyal servant of Liverpool Football Club and has remained a supporter ever since.

George and I witnessed the first building blocks of the modern Liverpool being laid, and we saw at first hand the hard work and dedication of the men who dragged the club from the Second Division and drove it to the top of the game. I know George has many great stories to tell about those five years he spent at the club and his life after Anfield. They were truly the best of times for both of us.

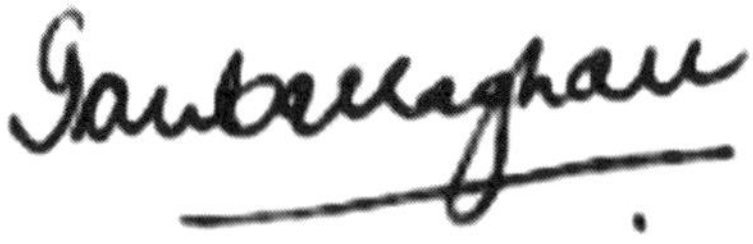

Ian Callaghan MBE

Introduction

BILL SHANKLY had a million quotes, he taught me so much. You will find his sayings and lessons littered throughout this book. But one of his mantras has stayed with me more than any other, 'You are nothing without enthusiasm.' So as I sit down and prepare to write my memoirs, I hope that every word you read will embody this spirit. Even though, as I write this, I find myself contemplating the loss of so many wonderful people, the challenges I and my family have faced and, to be truthful, my own mortality.

As I look back on my life, I realise that I have been blessed to have met, known, worked with and loved so many great people. I hope I haven't taken any of them for granted, but perhaps I did a little. In my latter years, looking ahead to turning 76 and facing the challenges that come with age, I have come to reflect more on what I now realise has been a remarkable life. I believe it's a story worthy of telling, but unknown to so many. I have crossed paths with some truly inspiring folk. Their stories have lit up my life. So, before I get too old to record them all for posterity, I have decided to share it all with you.

I'll start, somewhat oddly, you might think, by taking you to an operating theatre, at Arrowe Park Hospital on

Merseyside. August is giving way to September and the year is 2019 and I'm about to undergo an operation for skin cancer.

As I suppose many people do in times like these, when we are faced with our own mortality, we reflect on how we got here, on what we have achieved in life and what we will leave behind. So, it was during those moments, as I waited for surgery, that I began to think about my journey and my legacy.

Mine has been an extraordinary life. Yet, here I was at the age of 75, forced to contemplate an uncertain future and placing my life in the hands of someone I barely knew, and who knew nothing of me; or so I thought.

I'd had this tumour on my head for at least three months. I'm fair skinned with blue eyes and have had a history of pre-cancerous lesions on my scalp. They had now turned cancerous and progressed to the point where I needed surgery. I was desperately hoping they had caught it in time.

So, I'm lying there, and the medical staff are busying themselves with kit and equipment, and I can hear them chatting to each other, but I'm not really with it. Instead, my mind drifts back to playing football in South Africa in the late 60s. I was there from 1966 to 1968. I remember travelling with my team, Port Elizabeth City FC, across the country to Durban, Cape Town, Pretoria and places like Johannesburg – 6,000 feet above sea level.

I'm sure playing football for 90 minutes in the hot sun without suntan lotion did me no favours. However, sunburn would prove to be the least of my worries back then. More of that later though.

I had only ever been a visitor to hospitals, never really a patient. So, inevitably, my thoughts drifted back to the times I had spent visiting my wife, Carole, in this same hospital, back in 2004 and again in 2009. That had been one of the most difficult periods of our lives.

On 26 December 2004 the news was filled with horrendous tales of people fighting for survival after the catastrophic tsunami, which had struck South East Asia. Thousands had been swept to their deaths over there. Meanwhile, back on Merseyside, my wife Carole had been admitted to a local hospital for routine surgery. She had always been in the best of health up to that point and we had been very happily married for 38 years. So, it had been with little sense of trepidation that I kissed her goodbye and told her I would see her in a few hours, after the operation.

I then went home for lunch. There was really no sense in hanging round the hospital. However, when I returned, fully expecting Carole to be in the recovery ward, I was instead greeted by a nurse who advised me she was still in surgery. All I could do was wait – and what a long wait it seemed.

Eventually, the door of the waiting room opened, and Carole's surgeon came into the room accompanied by a theatre nurse. I could tell by their demeanour that something had gone terribly wrong. I was right. There had been complications during the operation, and she would have to be transferred urgently to Aintree Hospital in Liverpool to undergo emergency life-saving surgery. Time was of the essence.

I'm not an overly religious man, but I have often felt what I believe is the hand of destiny on my shoulder. I'll come back to why that is, later. Suffice it to say, I certainly felt it in the case of my wife's emergency surgery. Call it good fortune or the fates smiling upon us or whatever, all I can say is to this day we will be grateful that one of the top liver surgeons in the UK, Professor Graham Poston, was on duty over in Liverpool just when Carole needed him.

As Carole raced through the Mersey Tunnel in an ambulance, its blue lights flashing, I followed behind. All I could think of was how I would tell my two sons, Gavin and Craig. They would meet me at Aintree, and there we would wait together, for many hours.

Just after midnight, the waiting room door flung open and we saw Dr Poston walking towards us. The image of him doing up his tie as he crossed the floor has never left me.

'Hello Mr Scott. Are these your two boys?'

The mundane greeting was a prelude to the news that Carole's case had been his third operation that day, but he had still managed to repair the damage and although she would need to spend considerable time in the intensive care unit, the six-hour procedure had been a success.

'You can go in and see her now,' he said, 'though it may upset you. But trust me she will recover well; I have done an excellent job.'

His confidence put me in mind of my old boss, Bill Shankly. 'You have to tell everyone you're the best, every day. Then go out there and prove you are.' I hoped Mr Poston was, and so he proved to be.

Carole was in intensive care for several days and was very poorly. But she went on to make a full recovery. Her surgeon had indeed done an excellent job. We will always be grateful to destiny, that this gifted surgeon was there that day to save her life.

I closed my eyes briefly as the memory faded. Then my mind raced forward five years, to August 2009. Things were going well for us again. I was honoured and delighted to have been elected captain of Bromborough Golf Club, in Wirral, Merseyside.

I was loving my year as captain of the club and had played lots of golf that summer. So, I was delighted when my friend, Terry Keenan, offered Carole and I the use of his villa in Spain. A week's break in the sunshine sounded perfect. We were having a great time, when towards the end of the week she discovered a lump in her neck. We were both troubled by it and decided we would have it looked at on our return.

The initial consultation had reassured us that it was a minor issue, but the problem didn't go away and this lump continued to grow. Soon she was having headaches so bad she was prescribed morphine by the doctor.

I set off to collect her prescription one day, having left Carole with her sister Eileen. When I got back, I thought I would prepare it for her and take it upstairs with a cup of tea. As we walked into the room, we saw her standing next to the bed and then she just collapsed to the floor, right in front of Eileen and me.

You can't imagine the horror of something like that until it happens, and even then, it's hard to describe it. I immediately phoned the emergency services in a panic, as it looked like she wasn't breathing. The wonderful lady in the control room guided us through what we needed to do. Still for all of that, the thought of doing chest compressions on my own wife filled me with terrible anxiety.

Nevertheless, Eileen and I gritted our teeth and got ready to attempt resuscitation when there was a loud banging on the front door. By some miracle the paramedic had arrived within five minutes of Carole's collapse.

I'll never forget him; his name was Brandon. He was such a young lad, but he worked so quickly and revived Carole, although her blood pressure was so low, she kept blacking out. Eventually, after around half-an-hour, she was stable enough to be transferred to hospital.

We later found out that Carole had an aggressive form of non-hodgkin's lymphoma. She underwent surgery under Dr Galvani at Arrowe Park, followed by six months of chemotherapy. She did so with so much grace and positivity. We are eternally grateful to the team there for all they did.

In my life, many people have been sources of inspiration to me. You will hear about them all in due course. Bill Shankly was certainly one of them, but my wife Carole and her brave and ultimately successful battle with cancer will always be my greatest source of inspiration. We have been so happily married for 54 years now and she is not only the most beautiful but also the kindest and most heroic person I have ever known.

So, perhaps because of all of that, or maybe despite it, I felt strangely relaxed as I was wheeled into the operation theatre. I was greeted by my surgeon (a lovely girl called Kristina) and her colleague, the plastic surgeon.

They were both smiling at me, reassuring me as I was placed into my surgical gown. Then some dark glasses were placed on my face to shield my eyes from the bright light above. I became aware of the fact that there were quite a few support staff standing around and it distracted me for a moment. Kristina began to apply an antiseptic solution to my head, followed by a brace which would keep it still for the procedure.

They were a team, working in harmony. Each was individually gifted, but together they were greater than the sum of their parts. I remembered a great Scotsman, who I worked with for five years and grew to admire and respect for my whole life, for whom this ethos was a guiding principle. It had served him and me very well over the years. I hoped it did the same for the surgical team in the room that day.

Then, from the constant white-noise-like murmur of the operating theatre, I became aware that someone was talking to me. A voice was saying, 'George, I believe you played for Liverpool once?'

'Yes, I did. A long time ago. It was between 1960 and 65. I played under Bill Shankly.'

There seemed to be an interested buzz about the room. Other people joined in and I heard someone say, 'Look, I've Googled him. Hey, you had hair then George. Look at Shankly coaching you at Melwood. Wow, is that a reference Bill Shankly gave you? That's fantastic.'

They had come across some of my mementos, photographs and stories from that era, and it felt reassuring that they knew who I was. Not because of ego, although recognition is always welcome. More because, well, if you're about to have an operation, it helps if the team performing it see you as a person, with a life, and not just as a number.

Then I heard another voice, somewhere in the distance.

'You'll love this piece of music, George. Just relax and have a listen.'

The next thing I heard were the strains of Gerry Marsden and the song I had first heard with a former Liverpool legend, Peter Thompson, in comedian Jimmy Tarbuck's house way back in 1963 – 'You'll Never Walk Alone'.

I smiled and a wee tear filled the corner of my eye. Then I heard, 'Scalpel please,' and I swallowed hard.

One hour-long operation, 20 staples, 14 stitches and then some painful chemotherapy treatments later, I was finally declared 100 per cent clear. Destiny was once again on my side. It has felt that way my whole life. I don't know what it is, it sounds ridiculous, I know, but it helps me to believe it's true.

My life has been an amazing one, filled with hope, disappointment, struggle and, ultimately, happiness. I have met some incredible people and travelled the world. But it all began in 1960 when I met a craggy Scotsman from a mining village called Glenbuck, at Anfield. I was just a 15-year-old boy from Aberdeen then, and as I boarded a train to Lime Street station, Liverpool, I had no idea of the adventure I was taking.

I'm George Scott, I was a lost 'Shankly Boy', but you will find my story in these pages. I hope you enjoy reading it as much as I love living it.

Chapter One

Life in Aberdeen and the Call of Anfield

THE JANUARY cold wrapped itself around me and despite my coat being buttoned up to my neck, its icy fingers reached inside and caused me to shiver. At my side on the platform of Aberdeen Station – or the Joint as I remember calling it back in 1960 – stood my grandfather, Bill. I was just 15 years of age, with a small brown suitcase in one hand and a £20 note in my pocket (a king's ransom back then). Ahead of me was 353 miles of train track and, ultimately, Anfield and Bill Shankly.

I had already undergone a successful week-long trial at Liverpool a few weeks earlier. To be honest, I had never heard of the place, much less the team, before my trial. Liverpool Football Club sat in the Second Division. Though I had long dreamed of being a professional footballer, Anfield wasn't on my radar.

My long-held ambition had been to play for my local club, Aberdeen. As the fates would eventually decree, I would get my wish. But there was a fair bit of adventure to be had before then. Most of my childhood, for as far back as I can remember, involved playing football.

I had grown up in the romantically named China Cottage, situated on the shore of Aberdeen Harbour. An old Aberdonian, returning from a trip to the Far East had named it, along with the house next door (Putong Cottage). I lived with my mum, Agnes Fiddes, and my grandparents.

My mother had been just eight years old at the start of the great depression of the 1930s. She lived with her parents, Bill and Jean, in that rented two-room flat until 1950.

During the war, German planes would brave the anti-aircraft guns of the Torry Battery, which was situated opposite the entrance to the harbour just around the Bay of Nigg, less than a mile from China Cottage, as they flew over to drop bombs on the shipyards and the city beyond.

Today, the remains of the battery fort are still there. It's a tourist destination now and visitors can pose next to the remains of the battery barracks or photograph the schools of dolphins swimming close to the breakwater.

I still recall my grandad Bill's portrait, hanging on the wall above the bed. I can still see him, resplendent in the uniform of the Seaforth Highlanders, his red-and-white checked hat perched on his head. He had served with distinction in the First World War, surviving a bullet from a German sniper and suffering from gas inhalation in the trenches.

During the Second World War, he worked in the Hall, Russell and John Lewis shipyards on the Aberdeen docks as a plater and welder. He once told me of how, during one shift, he had gone for a break across the road to the little café. As he sat there, drinking tea, a German bomb hit the yard where he had been working only moments before, killing many of his workmates.

It no doubt would have devastated him, and who knows what guilt he felt at surviving such a horrible tragedy, while others perished through sheer chance. Nevertheless, his stoicism shone through as he would relive the story for me. 'Never worry during your life George, it is all to do with destiny. If your time is up your time is up.' I realise now that I took those words to heart, and they have guided me for much of my life.

Despite the beautiful location, at the bottom of St Fitticks Road overlooking the Bay of Nigg and Aberdeen Harbour, living conditions were so hard for my grandparents and my mum. Their cottage faced out towards the often-stormy North Sea and the winters were cold and harsh.

Post-war austerity meant money would be scarce and people learned quickly that unless they rallied together as a community, life would be grim. That created a great sense of camaraderie and formed the basis of my philosophy on life as I grew up.

It's why I could identify with and be inspired by the likes of Bill Shankly, whose entire ethos was based on these principles. There are no hardships so great that can't be faced, when everyone works together for the greater good.

Throughout all that hardship, I was spoiled rotten by my mum and my grandparents. I idolised them. And, although we lacked the material things that we take for granted today, I never felt deprived.

A great motivator for my mum and her parents, I think, was a desire to compensate for the fact that I never knew my father, who had died in Normandy during the war. My mum had been only 16 when war was declared. She was academically bright but the conflagration in Europe would cost her the remainder of her education.

With many of the men off to fight, she and others like her would have to find work to support their families and the community. She started work as a box maker in Fiddes's Ltd in Torry, making the boxes for ammunition, which was being shipped to the forces.

It was there that she met my father, George Edward Brown Scott. They soon fell in love, working side by side at the factory, and were married at the start of 1944. The pair were just 20 years old.

Sadly, it would prove to be a short-lived marriage. My dad was called up to join the 2nd Battalion of the Gordon Highlanders and was killed in France in August 1944, just three months before I was born in October.

One day he was just a young boy who fell in love with my mother and was looking to enjoy a happy future life building a family together, then a few weeks later he was being trained to use a rifle and preparing to kill or be killed. Sadly, his fate was to be the latter.

To me, he was, and always will be, a hero. He gave his life in the service of his country. His sacrifice meant that we could be free. His spirit and his name live on through me and his two grandsons, my sons, Gavin and Craig, and his four great-grandsons: Callum, Cameron, Charlie and James.

I would later discover, from the mother of a fellow soldier, that my father had volunteered for the mission that cost him his life. He died when the boat they were in was hit by a shell as they crossed a small river. My dad was thrown overboard, but despite trying valiantly to get hold of his hand, the lad couldn't hold on and my poor father slipped beneath the waves. His body was eventually recovered, and he is buried in a beautifully maintained war grave near Bayeux in Normandy.

We still have a letter he wrote to my Aunt Lena (his sister) from France, just two days before he was killed. Strangely, I can see something of myself in his words.

He spoke of his love of home, and of music and how he was missing my mother. He valued family life in Aberdeen more than any medal. However, his reassurances that he would be home 'in no time at all' were the most poignant.

I would visit his grave, on the 50th anniversary of D-Day, with my two sons. I recall being struck by the fact that none of the boys lying in those graves were over 21 years of age.

It also made me reflect on how tough life would have been for my mother, widowed so soon after her wedding. Then having to bring up a young child during the most difficult of times. She once told me that as others danced in the streets on VE Day at the end of the war, for her it felt like the saddest day of her life. Her husband wouldn't be returning home.

After the war, life somehow went on. Despite the rationing and other privations, Mum and her sister Lizzie would go to dances and all the usual places where young people meet. It was at one of these social events that she met Johnny Braik, a wonderful man with whom she was destined to enjoy a long and very happy marriage. They would remain together for 41 years until his passing in 1991.

I would have been just four years old when they got together. It would have doubtless been a challenge, especially listening to me yelling, 'You're not my father,' at every attempt of his to verbally discipline me. I'll always be grateful that he didn't give up on me, and he and my mum were married within a year of their meeting.

Their marriage was to be blessed with the birth of two sons, my brothers Ian and Alan. Ian was born in December 1950 and Alan in April 1952. I was delighted that I would no longer be an only child.

The greatest tribute I could pay Johnny was that never once throughout his life did he ever treat me as anything other than his own son. He loved the three of us equally, and we felt the same way.

Ian, Alan and I grew up as the closest of brothers, and we still are to this day. I remember how thrilled my mum was the first time she heard me shout to Johnny, when I was seven years old, 'Can I go out to play now Dad?'

I'll always treasure the memory of my own father, who like so many other young men made the supreme sacrifice in the service of his country, but Johnny became the only father I ever really knew. And, in the years ahead I grew to love and respect him. He was a wonderful father to myself and my two brothers.

Johnny had been called up at the outbreak of war and served in the Queen's Own Cameron Highlanders. He was captured in the first year of the war. He once told me of a terrifying brush with death when, along with a group of his comrades, he was lined up against a wall at machine-gunpoint. Fearing the end was at hand, and watching his short life flash before his eyes, he prepared for death. Then, miraculously, a German officer barked a command and the guns were lowered.

They were asked to empty their carbine rifles, and the Germans examined the bullets. They were looking for 'dum dums' (these were bullets which had the pointed front removed, ensuring they would inflict terrible wounds, even if the victim survived). Fortunately for Johnny and his mates, they had none and they were spared summary execution.

Instead, they faced a long march to a prisoner-of-war camp, where he would see out the remainder of the war. There he faced forced labour in the salt mines. Conditions were awful and he suffered terrible hunger at times, but told me that in time he developed reasonably good relations with his captors, even learning to speak some German and to play the harmonica.

These two men, my father and stepfather, were the benchmark for me growing up. I always felt that if I could be as good a man as they were, if I could show the same level of commitment to anything I tried throughout my life, then that would be very much an objective to aspire to.

As a child, growing up in the district of Torry, overlooking Aberdeen Harbour, there was plenty to keep me entertained and out of mischief. I would fish from the harbour wall and watch as, on the fourth Monday of every month, the fishing trawlers left the harbour in unison, bound for the North Sea fishing grounds. This was Aberdeen's major industry, its bread and butter. I can remember standing on Banana Pier or Skates Nose Pier, waving to the crews as they sailed away. These are happy memories.

These trawlermen were a hardy breed. Many times, especially in the winter, the waves would hit the breakwater at the exit from the harbour and bounce high over the lighthouse.

They were the bravest of men, risking their lives to put bread on the table for their families. Their wages were determined by the size of their catch and how much it sold for at Aberdeen Fish Market.

After my mother remarried, we moved out of China Cottage, with its picturesque views over Aberdeen Harbour and the Bay of Nigg, and into Aberdeen city centre and 85 Spring Garden. It was a less than glamorous tenement building, shared by five families.

I would still go back to see my beloved grandparents in China Cottage by the sea. I also had many friends in that part of the city and some of my earliest memories of playing football stem from these times. We would go around to the salmon fishing depot round the bay and 'borrow' some of their fishing nets in order to fashion football goals in the field opposite my grandparents' house. There, we would play football all day long.

My first representative match came when I was selected for the St Paul Street Primary School team, at the age of eight. I was the youngest in the team, with most of the other lads being around ten years old.

The game was against the best team in the league, Woodside Primary School, and they had a fearsome reputation. They played in white and were known as 'The Ghosties'. The venue was Links Field and the scoreline was a very unflattering 16-1 to Woodside, not that I told my parents that. When they asked me how I had got on, I said we had won 2-1 and that I scored the winning goal. They were so thrilled for me, until the true score appeared in the school football results section of the evening sports paper, the *Green Final*. I was grounded for two days for lying.

Little did they know what a miserable experience the game had been. The teacher had told me to stay out wide on the wing, which I had hated. It was so lonely out there in the cold, with no one passing the ball to me. Not the most auspicious of beginnings.

Somehow, I soldiered on though, and my Uncle Pat became the first to notice my football ability. He knew I was really determined to eventually play professionally and would use it to keep me in line. I remember my mum would plead with me every day to eat the crusts on my bread, something I steadfastly refused to do. With rationing still in effect after the war, people of my mother's generation abhorred waste.

One day, I recall my mother was telling me off as I was about to leave the house. I had left behind a pile of uneaten crusts on my plate. Uncle Pat quickly interjected. His tone was serious and stern.

'George, son, if you don't eat your bread crusts you will never be a footballer.' That was all the convincing I needed, and I gobbled up every crumb on that plate.

In 1956 my mum and Johnny moved to a new three-bedroom council house in the suburb of Mastrick on the outskirts of the city. To my parents, and to us kids too, it was like winning the football pools. It had a lounge and a kitchen downstairs and upstairs was the sheer luxury of three bedrooms, a bathroom and a toilet. It was also a corner plot and had a large garden area, which Johnny loved. In no time he had it immaculate and even grew vegetables in it.

Things were beginning to improve as the country was being rebuilt and with it came improvements in our quality of life. My first experience of this came one day, when I got off the bus from school and immediately noticed a metal object attached to the chimney of our house. Bemused, I walked through the door and into the living room and was amazed to see in the corner what looked like a cupboard with a round screen on it. It was, of course, a television and the programme showing was *Six Five Special,* hosted by Pete Murray.

I sat there, transfixed, watching one show after another; *Juke Box Jury* and *Drumbeat* are two that come to mind from that period. Though the pictures were grainy black and white, I was amazed that we now had a television in our house.

The only other one I had seen up until then was at my Uncle Bob and Auntie Betty's house. They had won on the football pools and immediately rushed out and bought one. I recall the whole family congregating at their house, whenever there was a major programme on.

Aside from watching music on our new TV, I would keep myself entertained during the long summer holidays at the Aberdeen Lads Club in the Gallowgate area. This was a wonderful boys club and there I would meet with my friends and play endless hours of indoor five-a-side football, table tennis, snooker or even the old table game of push penny.

It was a wonderful facility for us youngsters where our parents knew we were safe and enjoying ourselves. The Lads Club had two football teams for various ages between 11 and 14. They were ALC Hearts and ALC Spurs, and as I began to develop more physically, I would turn out for either of them.

Kick-off would be at 3pm on Saturday, and I would already have played twice in the morning for my school team in two different age groups. Those games started at 9.30 and then 11am. Football was becoming my life.

Some very famous players emerged from the ranks of Aberdeen Lads Club, including Denis Law and Ron Yeats, both of whom were there roughly six years ahead of me. It was a good facility and even had its own playing fields where their home games were played.

Back then, my team was Aberdeen, 'The Dons', who played at Pittodrie. A group of us would sometimes go to see them. We idolised them and, in those days, they would attract crowds of over 30,000.

There was no way we could afford to pay to get in, of course. So, we used to make our way into the ground via the gasworks at the King Street end. Once there, we would run across to the high wire fence. Then, as soon as the patrolling policemen at the top of the terrace turned their backs, we would dig under the fence and run up the embankment where we would be dragged in by the men in the crowd.

This became routine practice for me and my mates. I recall one Wednesday afternoon, in the spring of 1955, my friend George Stables and I bunked off school to see a Scottish Cup quarter-final replay with Hearts.

We had drawn the first game 1-1, and the sense of anticipation for the game was huge, with over 40,000 turning up at Pittodrie Stadium.

Unfortunately, we were nabbed by the 'Bobbies' just as we reached the crowd at the top of the embankment and couldn't take our places amongst the vast throng of spectators. We must have looked absolutely devastated, because the policemen took pity on us. And, instead of throwing us out altogether, they arranged for us to be hoisted on top of the Pie Hut, where we had the best view of the game.

The Dons ran out 2-0 winners thanks to goals from Patrick (Paddy) Buckley and Harry Yorston. Buckley was a vital part of the Aberdeen side that took the Scottish League title in 1955. He had pace in abundance and had joined Aberdeen from St Johnstone, where he had scored 104 goals in 140 games, in 1952.

The transfer fee was £7,500, of which Paddy pocketed £600. He was capped for Scotland and played in the Scottish League during what were the glory days of the mid-1950s. Sadly, his Aberdeen career was ended by a terrible knee injury in 1957, although he did unsuccessfully attempt a comeback with Inverness Caledonian in 1958.

Harry Yorston joined Aberdeen from St Clements, a local junior team, in 1946. He would go on to become one of the Dons' greatest forwards. He came from a strong footballing family, and his uncle, Benny, had been an Aberdeen legend. Harry's goals, along with Buckley's, would prove vital in the run to the championship.

Harry retired from football at the age of just 28 to take a lucrative job as a fish market porter. He worked in Aberdeen Fish Market until 1972, retiring after winning £175,000 on Littlewoods Pools.

I still have vivid memories of running around the empty terraces after watching Buckley and Yorston play and collecting empty glass beer bottles. We would make tuppence per bottle when handing them back to the local shop on Merkland Road.

Alas, the Dons crashed out of the cup in the semi-final to Clyde. Buckley had scored both goals in a 2-2 draw, but Aberdeen lost the return game 1-0. It would rob them of a possible league and cup double. Just a month later they would be crowned league champions, pipping Celtic to the championship by three points. Buckley had been something of a hero that year, scoring 29 goals in all competitions.

The greatest dream of my young life, therefore, was to be wearing that red shirt and playing for my hometown club. I would go on to live that dream, but before I could, I would first wear the red shirt of another team. And they played their football on the banks of the River Mersey.

By the time I reached 15 years of age, I was already showing considerable talent as a schoolboy footballer. I had made a record number of appearances for the Aberdeen Schools select teams and was eventually picked for the Scottish Schoolboy trials. It looked odds-on that I would be selected for the first Home International match against Wales.

Unfortunately, I sustained an injury in the final trial and had to miss out on all three of the Home Internationals. That would prove to be the first of several disappointing injuries that undoubtedly curtailed my career. We will hear more of that later.

I was unaware at the time, but my footballing ability had been spotted by former St Mirren goalkeeper, Jim Lornie. He was now caretaker at my school but led a double life as a scout for Liverpool FC. He approached me and wanted me to travel south for a trial with the Anfield club.

I told Jim that I had no thoughts of signing for anyone other than Aberdeen, who at this time had already made my parents an offer of £6 per week to sign for them as an apprentice professional. And, as my stepfather Johnny was earning just £9 per week, to provide for a family of five whilst working for Aberdeen City Council, that seemed a hugely significant amount of money for a 15-year-old lad.

Besides, the furthest I had ever travelled from Aberdeen was the 60 miles to Dundee with my mum and brothers to visit Johnny at a Territorial Army camp. Jim was very persistent, though, and persuaded my mother to let me travel to Liverpool for a week's trial.

I thought it would be a great adventure, even though I knew nothing about Liverpool FC, who were a Second Division team in England and seemingly going nowhere. At least that's what I thought.

I did know of Bill Shankly, though. He had taken my big idol and fellow Aberdonian Denis Law from Aberdeen schools football to Huddersfield Town a few years earlier, where he had turned him into a star.

I completed the week's trial playing in a trio of games for the club's C team against Blackpool, Everton and Preston along with a lad called Gordon Wallace. That was the start of what would prove to be a lifelong friendship.

Gordon and I notched goals in all three games. Then he went back to South Wales and I got ready to return to Aberdeen. Despite a successful trial, I was still determined to sign for my hometown team.

I was called into Bill Shankly's office at the end of the week. I recall Bill was in there, sitting behind his desk. Alongside him, and standing up, was team coach, Reuben Bennett. Shankly said he wanted to sign me for Liverpool. He had been a huge admirer of Matt Busby and the young side he had constructed at Manchester United. Bill wanted to create his own 'Busby Babes', the 'Shankly Boys'.

He already had Chris Lawler and Tommy Smith, who Busby had attempted to sign earlier, and to those two he wanted to add Gordon Wallace, Bobby Graham and me. I was a little bit in awe of him, and Reuben. Nevertheless, I told them both that I was already committed to sign for Aberdeen.

I really laid it on thick, telling them both that my family, especially my grandmother, would miss me. I would be homesick. I was too young to leave home, at just 15 years of age. Bill and Reuben were having none of it. They worked really hard before letting me leave Liverpool and did everything they could to get me to sign apprentice professional forms for them.

Bill's pitch was that Reuben was from Aberdeen and so he would make sure I was looked after. He even went to the extent of promising to arrange evening classes at Childwall County College for me, so I could keep up my education. My response was that my family just wanted me to stay in Aberdeen and my grandparents would be heartbroken if I left home.

I said my grandmother in particular was very worried about me travelling all the way to Liverpool. I could see that I was getting nowhere, when in desperation I blurted out, 'My granny doesn't even know where Liverpool is.' Shankly leaned forward in his chair, elbows on the desk in front of him, hands clasped under his chin. His brow creased, and I noticed a twinkle in his eye, as he growled,

'Son, you go home and tell her that we are in the Second Division at the moment, but we will be in the First Division next season for sure. Soon, everyone will know where Liverpool is.'

Those words stirred something in me. His wit, his confidence, it was enthralling, captivating. He made such a huge impression on me. This was no ordinary mortal. In that instant, my mind was made up. There was only one club I could join, Liverpool.

My family were stunned at my decision. I don't think they could believe that I would ever want to move so far away, at 15. Nevertheless, they supported me to make the trip.

So, just a matter of weeks later, I was standing on that frosty platform at Aberdeen station with a head full of dreams. With my stepfather working, my mother in hospital undergoing minor surgery and my brothers at school, it had been left to my grandfather Bill to see me off.

I knew it was breaking his heart, and I saw tears glistening in his eyes as he waved me off. For almost all of the 100 yards or so that the train travelled away from the station, he continued to wave to me as I frantically waved back. Then the train turned the bend and he was gone from my view. I had no idea then that this was to be our last goodbye.

Six weeks later, Bill Shankly gently broke the news to me that he had passed away having collapsed suddenly with a brain haemorrhage. I tried to act like a man in the boss's office, but the sobs were uncontrollable. My grandad's words echoed around my head:

'Never worry during your life George. It is all to do with destiny, if your time is up, your time is up.'

Sadly, only a few months later, my beloved grandmother also passed away. I think she probably died of a broken heart having lost her husband and seen her grandson leave home at such a young age, leaving her all alone in China Cottage. I carried the weight of all that back with me to Liverpool. And, I have always tried to live a life they would be proud of.

Chapter Two

High Hopes and Great Expectations

TODAY, LIME Street station in Liverpool stands as a gateway to a global city, a threshold to the rest of the world. Visitors alighting its grand stone steps in the 21st century are treated to clean open vistas, taking in a huge LED screen, carrying commercials for all sorts of products. To their right, they have the majestic and visually stunning St George's Hall. This is a city that punches above its weight in so many ways: architecturally, in terms of the arts and, of course, football.

None of that's by accident. That the word Liverpool exists in the collective consciousness of billions of people, despite boasting a population of under half a million and covering an area of just over 40 square miles, is testament to its people. And its people are from everywhere.

At the dawning of the 1960s, I stood at that grand old station alongside two people who would become good friends and who, like me, were about to embark on an amazing adventure. My companions were Gordon Wallace and Bobby

Graham. We were all just 15 years of age and were meeting for the first time. A little shy of three miles away stood Anfield and residing there was a man who held our destinies in his hands, Bill Shankly.

Shankly had tremendous ambition. His vision for the club was every bit as bold as the city's founding fathers were in previous eras. Just as those people had constructed colossal edifices, such as the Walker Art Gallery, the Museum of Liverpool, St George's Hall and later the 'Three Graces' at the Pier Head, buildings that wouldn't be out of place in any world capital, Shankly wanted to build a team that could compete with the best on the planet. In this sense, and in so many other ways, he was a perfect fit for this city and its people.

So, as we awaited our transport to Anfield, our bellies full of butterflies and chatting excitedly, we couldn't possibly have truly understood the magnitude of the challenge ahead of us. The standards we would have to reach and then surpass would be huge. We were coming to sign as apprentices, but we would soon learn that the man who had courted us had much grander aspirations.

The club were in the Second Division of English football. Shankly had assumed the reins a month or so earlier. His first game in charge, a 4-0 home defeat to Cardiff City, had given him an insight into the challenges that lay ahead. The Reds, who were still wearing white shorts back then, sat in tenth place. Still, undaunted he pressed on. He had a vision for the club and the way he wanted it to play, and nothing would divert him from that.

Talking to the waiting press after the game against Cardiff, he would only say, 'Naturally I'm disappointed.

But it's just as well that I've seen the team give an off-form display in my first match. I've learned quite a few things this way.'

Those few lines gave away so much and those who cared to read between them would be left in no doubt that a revolution was on the way. Shankly had been a great admirer of the work Matt Busby had undertaken at Manchester United. He shared Busby's desire to build a side based on the enthusiasm and the raw talent of youth. I have lost count of the number of times I heard him tell us, and reporters alike, that 'without enthusiasm you are nothing'. Shankly also had an eye on European conquest, but more of that later.

Gordon, Bobby and I had no idea on that morning that we were being invited to become Liverpool's own version of the 'Busby Babes'. If we had known that we were about to join a group who, years later, would become known as 'Shankly's Boys', we would have been brimming with pride.

Liverpool Football Club had arranged lodgings for us with an elderly lady called Mrs Jones, in Skerries Road, next to the ground. Mrs Jones had a son called Alwyn, who barely said two words to us. Then there was the budgie and the family dog, called Peter. We swore the animals were better fed than we were.

Gordon and I would often go to the café on Walton Breck Road for extra food, as Mrs Jones was very sparing with her portions. It's fair to say I missed my mother's home cooking greatly for a very long time.

A couple of days after we had settled in, we were taken up to the stadium to meet the rest of the young lads who had been brought to Liverpool by their army of scouts. It was just a short walk, of course, and I remember how excited I was to be getting started.

Anfield was a very different place back then of course. There was no Paisley Way or Shankly statue. Bill would eventually earn his eternal place in front of the Kop, but in 1960 he was just getting started. There was also no hint of commercialism, with no club store or museum.

You entered the ground via the players' entrance located behind the old Main Stand. The old doorway is now covered by giant stone steps, leading to the incredible concourse of the new 2017 construction, which in turn sits on 96 Avenue, a stone pathway that stretches away from the stadium and disappears into Stanley Park.

Today, supporters walk along this tree-lined avenue, perhaps pausing for reflection on benches in front of the Hillsborough memorial, or on those dedicated to former club legends and icons. Back then, the area in front of the players' entrance was a car park encased by a brick wall, overlooked by terraced houses. Their occupants, staring from the bedroom windows, could watch the comings and goings of the club at will.

Once inside the players' entrance, you would then navigate your way down a long passage before turning left. There you would be confronted by the home team dressing room, which was the first door on the left. The image of that old dressing room is still vivid in my mind and will stay with me forever. On first seeing it, I remember being a little in awe of it. It seemed huge to me, a large square area with wooden benches around its perimeter.

However, today's facilities dwarf the original by some distance. Above the old benches were 11 pegs for the players' shirts (no substitutes in those days). The rest of the kit would be folded neatly beneath it. The boots, made clean and shiny by the apprentices, lay on the floor. Only black boots were allowed back then. To the rear lay a doorway that led to the washing facilities and toilets.

There were no showers in those days, only a large communal bath. Ex-trainer and handyman, Albert Shelley, would make sure it was filled with hot water at the end of the game. There were no ice baths in the 1960s; instead the players would leap into the hot bath immediately after the match. There would be lots of larking about and much laughter, especially after a victory.

In the centre of the dressing room was a large massage table where, before the kick-off on matchdays, Bob Paisley and Joe Fagan would rub wintergreen and oil into the players' legs and massage their muscles. I can still smell the wintergreen today. If I close my eyes, I can still see Reuben Bennett, simply looking on, deep in thought. Sometimes he would be barking at the players, motivating them and calling them to action.

Then, if I cast my mind's eye to the doorway, I can see Shankly sweeping into the room. Suddenly, all falls silent, there is no more chatter, only his voice can be heard, and there is electricity in the air. Shanks then delivers his final instructions. Beyond the doorway and the corridors outside it, a vast crowd can be heard; it's like a symphony calling the players to glory.

Back outside, in the passageway under the Main Stand, two left turns and a 20-yard stroll took you to another wooden door on the right. This was the entrance to perhaps the most famous door of any football stadium in the world. This, of course, was the iconic Boot Room; a place that has taken on almost mythical status.

It's really just an oversized cupboard, though, about the size of a living room in a terraced house in Anfield. In there, a strategy would be cooked up by a socialist cabal, consisting of a manager and his coaches that would one day 'conquer the bloody world' (as Shanks would put it). However, its appearance was far less glamorous than its legend suggests.

Along one wall were rows of numbered pegs with black football boots hanging on them. On the opposite wall was a large wooden work bench topped with hammers, nails and shoemaker's tools. There would also be black shoe polish and lots of football studs would be scattered all around the place.

Large wicker baskets filled with clean and dirty training gear and kits lined a third wall. Shanks and his backroom staff would sit on top of them and hatch their plans for world domination. Finishing off the decorative motif would be cans of paint, brushes for sweeping and other assorted implements.

This place was the domain of Bill Shankly, Bob Paisley, Joe Fagan, Reuben Bennett and Albert Shelley. As apprentices, we were allowed in there as 'ground staff', but only to clean the first team players' boots. This of course changed when you reached the age of 17 and signed your first professional contract; then your boots were cleaned for you.

Leaving the Boot Room, you would take a right turn, walk a few more yards and arrive at yet another door. This was the treatment room. It was a decent-sized room. This, of course, was where the players would receive the very best treatment available, which in those days usually amounted to oil, liniment and a good massage. That was until Bill Shankly invested in a magic machine from Germany, which put electric currents into the leg muscles. Shanks and Bob first tried it out on Jimmy Melia and almost electrocuted him. (But that's another story for later.)

Outside the treatment room and walking back on yourself, past the Boot Room and home dressing room, you reach the players' tunnel. The away dressing room is located just before the entrance to the arena, on the left-hand side of the passage. Once inside, you're immediately struck by how cramped it is. It's roughly half the size of the home team facilities, and the bath is much smaller too. This was of course quite deliberate. Shankly didn't want to allow the opposition even the smallest crumb of comfort. Subtle psychology was alive and well in those days.

Wasting no more time in here, you come out and avoid the players' tunnel for the moment, instead you walk back down the passage. On your right there is a sign on a door that simply declares, 'The Manager'.

This is a sacred place. You dare not enter, unless invited. If you were ever asked into this space, it would be for one of two reasons. You would either be built up and made to believe you could take on the world, or you would be chastised for stepping out of line. There would be no middle ground.

Beyond Shanks's lair, at the far end of the passage, is a final door. This is a sort of recreation room. Inside, a large snooker table sits in the middle of the floor and surrounding it is a set of leather benches. Fitted to the wall is a scoreboard and a rack for the snooker cues. This was a place to relax and bond with team-mates after training.

Again, if I close my eyes for the briefest of moments, I can still hear the laughter and the mickey-taking, the clatter of the balls as they drop in the pockets. I can see players, young men in their prime, placing bets on games of snooker or pool.

This room also doubled as a space to hold crisis meetings, like when we lost a home game. Such things were never tolerated lightly, and we would all come to realise that a defeat on home soil would be viewed as beyond the pale. It was an attitude and philosophy that would turn Anfield into a fortress.

Once outside the snooker room, you would come to a staircase, which led to the inner sanctum of the old Main Stand. This is where the canteen was located. There, the players would have lunch together every day on their return from training at Melwood.

Bill Shankly could occasionally be seen, sitting at his special table in the corner by the door. He would be drinking some concoction contained in a silver teapot and preaching, as only he could, to a member of the press who would be furiously scribbling down every word that he said.

The directors' room was located a little further along the same corridor. We never saw what went on in there. Their monthly meetings were held at times when the players weren't around. Shankly would attend them, but the goings on in that room were never divulged to us.

By now you may be wondering where the trophy room was. Today the Reds are the most successful football club in English football history. However, at the time of Shankly's arrival, some 68 years after the club's inception, Liverpool had accrued just five First Division championships. The last one had been secured 13 years earlier, in 1947. They had of course won four Second Division titles, but the club had so far never seen fit to build a room to host them.

It's incredible to think that today the club has amassed 46 major honours (hopefully 47, when football resumes after the Covid-19 lockdown and they can snatch those priceless six points). However, it's even more remarkable to me, that 41 of those trophies arrived in the 60 years after Bill Shankly's time, and that just five were won in the 60 years before his arrival. If there is a greater illustration of the fact that it was him who built the foundations of the modern Liverpool, his 'bastion of invincibility', then I'm yet to see it.

Now, back down those stairs and into the narrow passage that leads to the tunnel that opens out on to the pitch. Back then, the sacred turf wasn't the manicured affair we see today. Instead its centre circle and goalmouths were muddy and uneven.

There is no 'This is Anfield' sign yet for the players to touch in order to remind our lads who they play for and the opposition who they were up against, that would come much later. In fact, when I arrived in 1960, the stadium looked dilapidated and in desperate need of a coat of paint.

Once on the pitch and looking up to the Main Stand above the paddock (a standing area that ran alongside the pitch) beyond the directors' box and the wooden seats behind it, you would see a round arch-like feature in the centre of the roof. Emblazoned in gold letters, under a flawless wintry blue sky, were the words LIVERPOOL FOOTBALL CLUB.

In the centre of the stand, down at pitch level, is the dugout. This is a hollowed-out area with a stone roof, where the manager and trainers sat on matchdays. Next to that is the old Band Box. From there you can survey the Kop (home to 28,000 fanatical supporters) to your right, and the Anfield Road stand to your left. In front of you, across the pitch, is the Kemyln Road Stand (now the Sir Kenny Dalglish Stand). Both the Kop and the Anfield Road end are littered with red steel crowd barriers, dispersed at intervals across their vast terraces.

High on the top-right-hand side of the Kop as you view it from the dugout, there is a mini prison with bars separating it from the rest of the terrace.

This space was the soprano section of the Kop Choir. I'm of course talking about the 'Boys' Pen'. In there, Kopites would serve their apprenticeship before graduating on to the famous old terrace, as men.

It would be three years before the occupants of that end of the ground would sing 'You'll Never Walk Alone'. Gerry Marsden and the Merseybeat sound was still in its infancy. The Beatles had only got together at a garden fete in Woolton 12 months earlier. However, in no time we would be catching the 26 bus, or the 17D into town to watch them play live at the Cavern.

As we assembled in the manager's office, in January 1960, six of us boys were Scottish; Bobby Graham came from Motherwell, Gordon Wallace was born in Glasgow (although he was living in Llanelli in South Wales) Phil Tinney arrived from Dundee, James (Hamish) McKenzie was from Denny, Alex Totten came from Dennyloanhead near Stirling and, obviously, I was from Aberdeen.

The room was a spartan affair. Bill liked it that way. There was just a desk, with an old Olivetti typewriter sitting on top of it. He would use this to personally type many of his now legendary replies to supporters, who had written to him about all manner of things. Behind the desk was a filing cabinet next to the wall, upon which a few pictures were scattered. There was a ruthless simplicity and minimalist approach to Shanks. He didn't have time for clutter, or anything that could distract from the important stuff, football.

So, we waited there, patiently. I admit to a real sense of nervous excitement. From the moment I had met the man he'd had a real impact on me, and when I remembered him telling me that 'soon everybody would know where Liverpool was', I shivered.

Later, when my stepdad (who I had now started calling Dad) visited me at Anfield, I recall standing in the centre circle of the pitch with him, surveying the empty stadium. Shanks had looked me dead in the eye and said:

'Son, this place will become a bastion of invincibility and you are a very lucky young man to be here. They will all come here and be beaten.'

He was talking to me, but I could tell the words were also for my father's benefit. I'm sure he was as moved as I was by what Shanks said. The boss then turned to Dad, and asked, 'Who are you with Mr Scott?' My dad (who worked for Aberdeen City Council) replied, 'I work for the city Mr Shankly.'

Shanks looked puzzled for a second, then smiled. 'What league do they play in?' He asked with a twinkle in his eye.

The door to the office swung open, and I jumped, stirred abruptly from my reverie. There was a shuffling of feet as the boys and I all waited nervously to hear what he would say.

That was the Shankly effect. There was an aura about the man. When he spoke, the room fell silent. I swear you could sense his presence, even if you couldn't see him.

He breezed past us all and took up position behind his desk, and we all held our breath. Bob Paisley walked in behind him accompanied by two young local boys. They all stood at Shankly's shoulder. One of the lads looked much older than his fifteen years. He had a gruff Scouse accent. The other was tall with dark hair and seemed a little shy.

Bill said, 'I want you all to meet Tommy Smith and Chris Lawler, boys. You're all going on a journey together.' With those simple words, our adventure began. We would all sign as apprentices later that same week.

Our accommodation would be upgraded to permanent lodgings too. Phil, Hamish, Alex and I were taken to 258 Anfield Road to be introduced to our new landlady. This was the big white house which faces down Utting Avenue, and opposite the famous Arkles pub. Our landlady was Mrs Murphy. Her husband, Bill, was disabled and rarely left his bed.

That didn't interfere with his keen interest in horse racing though, and I can recall us all nipping down the road to the local betting shop to put his bets on; not ideal, given we were all underage.

The couple had a son called Gerry, a heavy-set lad who rarely moved out of the armchair next to the fire. We never did find out what his job entailed.

The two lads with whom I had stood at Lime Street station the morning we arrived in Liverpool, were moved to different accommodation. Bobby lived with a woman called

Mrs Griffiths, just a little further down Anfield Road and Gordon took up residence with a Mr and Mrs Clare in Harrow Road, just off Anfield Road. So, we remained close and these friendships have lasted a lifetime.

At 258 Anfield Road we would each give Mrs Murphy £3.50 per week, which covered our board and lodgings, including food, washing and ironing, and of course bed, breakfast and evening meal. In 1960, that meant she was doing quite nicely, with an income of £14 per week.

I remember thinking about my stepdad, Johnny, back home. He was only earning just £9 per week, and with that he had to keep his wife, himself and my two brothers in food and clothing and maintain a roof over their heads.

My first wage as an apprentice professional footballer was £7.50 per week. Out of that, I would pay for my lodgings. I would also place £2 in an envelope and send it home to Mum to help the family out. That left me with £2. To be honest, that was ample in those days for a young man to have a great time in Liverpool. It meant I could watch the Beatles start their career, playing live in the Cavern in Mathew Street.

Phil, Alex, Hamish and I would often meet up with Bobby Graham and Gordon Wallace and challenge the local English lads to five-a-side matches in Stanley Park. They were hard-fought games with no quarter given. Shanks would have been incandescent if he knew we were risking injury in this way.

One of those young English lads was Steve Peplow, who later went on to play two games in Liverpool's first team before going on to have a successful professional career. Steve featured for a number of clubs, including Swindon Town and Nottingham Forest and latterly Tranmere Rovers, for whom he made 248 league appearances and scored 44 goals between 1973 and 1981.

We were all just young lads though, and a long way from home. Out of our comfort zone for the first time in our lives, we would seek adventure and push the boundaries at every opportunity. And, of course, there was no better place on planet earth to do that than in Liverpool in the 1960s.

The city was in the throes of the 'Merseybeat' explosion. There were new groups being created weekly and the pubs and clubs, which seemed to be on every corner, provided the perfect backdrop for this musical revolution.

City centre venues that come to mind include: The Iron Door, The Mardi Gras, The Odd Spot, The Blue Angel, The Royal Tiger Club in Manchester Street and of course the most famous of all, The Cavern Club in Mathew Street. We loved bands like, The Merseybeats, The Searchers and Gerry and the Pacemakers.

They were all incredible acts, but there was always one group that stood head and shoulders above them all. They were four lads with these really unusual haircuts. They called themselves The Beatles.

We would often look forward to the end of training, when we would then race through our chores around the stadium and jump on the bus into town. There, we would take in the sessions at the Cavern.

I saw the Beatles many times. One performance stands out over all the others though, and that was when I saw them in the Odd Spot Club in Bold Street. They played 'Love Me Do' that night, and I couldn't believe it when I heard the same song on the radio. It was their first hit, and the rest, as they say, is history. It seemed like they were releasing a new song monthly, and all of them would soar to the top of the charts.

I also have memories of the Beatles wearing leather and their drummer being Pete Best. Ringo would obviously join later. The lads and I would watch them a lot back then. You just knew they were something special, musical genius at work. Liverpool was something special.

Along with the renaissance going on at Anfield under Shankly, and Everton doing well under Harry Catterick, Merseyside was quickly becoming the epicentre of the 60s cultural revolution. To be a young man, in the prime of your life and a footballer, in the middle of all of that was simply incredible.

Just as Shankly's footballing juggernaut had rolled out of one of the humblest and seemingly unimpressive spaces – Anfield's Boot Room – so too did the Beatles' musical phenomenon. The Cavern Club was a dingy cellar with brick pillars separating the space into different sections. The stage itself was very cramped and backed on to a grubby brick wall.

However, that created an amazing atmosphere and the acoustics in that confined space were great. It really raised the hairs on the back of your neck. That is, when you could hear the bands through the din of screaming women and girls. It could get uncomfortable at times though, and it was really warm when it was packed out.

The brick walls seemed to glow with damp, sweaty condensation. The dance floor was as crammed as the stage and there was little space for dancing. It will probably surprise people, but there was no alcohol on sale at that time either, with only Coca Cola on offer. The doormen outside would ensure that customers could bring nothing in with them either.

One night, I was standing close to the stage. The Beatles were setting up and tuning their guitars, chatting to each other as they did. I was sipping my drink and waiting for them to get started, when John Lennon looked over at me and called out, 'You got the time?'

It wasn't much. Just the briefest of interaction, but as far I was concerned, I had been chatting to a Beatle. I would dine out on that story for a good while, especially with the girls back at the Anfield Youth Club.

The place to be for Merseyside's footballers, though, was the Royal Tiger Club in Manchester Street next to the entrance of the Mersey Tunnel. Sadly, it's now long gone and has been replaced with the Premier Inn Hotel.

If you went there after a match on a Saturday night, and if you could get in (the queues would stretch down the street) you would be sure to rub shoulders with some of the greatest Liverpool and Everton players, including Brian Labone, Alex Young, Dennis Stevens, my namesake Alex Scott and Roy Vernon.

Vernon would be puffing away on a cigarette and always used a black-and-gold cigarette holder to avoid getting the nicotine on his fingers. The Everton lads would mix happily with ourselves and the likes of Ian St John, Peter Thompson and big Ronnie Yeats.

The queues were policed by Bill Gregson who owned the club, as well as the Home James bus company. He would later become the owner of Skelmersdale United, who won the Amateur Cup at Wembley in 1971. I remember Bill had the most spectacular hair piece we had ever seen.

It was in the Royal Tiger that I had my first alcoholic drink. It was given to me by Billy Stevenson who told me 'Don't worry Georgie, it is only Coca Cola with ice.' After a couple of these 'iced colas', I felt a little unusual.

Worried, I turned to Ian St John and said, 'Saint, do me a favour, taste that. Tell me what this drink Billy has bought me is, it tastes funny.' The Saint obliged, smiled and said, 'That's Bacardi and coke, Georgie. Son, you shouldn't be drinking that at your age.'

I had just turned 17. It was at about this time that Shankly issued his little red book of rules, which we all had to adhere to on pain of death. We will come to this later, but one of his big commandments was, 'No player shall frequent any establishment where alcoholic beverages are available after Wednesday of any week.'

He did, however, tend to close his eyes to us enjoying ourselves on Saturday nights after games unless there was a match on the Monday.

That reminds me of another story. Shankly had this habit of getting the odd word mixed up. One day, he had heard on the grapevine that there was a nightclub on Walton Breck Road called The Wookie Hollow. All the big cabaret stars appeared there in the 60s. So, Bill called Bobby Graham in to see him in his office, to discuss some of the rumours he had heard about his players and their nocturnal habits.

Bobby was really nervous and told me that he had a bad feeling about what the boss was going to say. We were all on edge and it seemed like he was in there for an eternity. We knew that Shanks had eyes and ears everywhere, and if Bobby was in trouble, we probably all were.

After what seemed like an age, Bobby came out and recounted what the manager had said, while we struggled not to laugh. Shankly had given him a real hard time, saying with a completely straight face:

'My spies have seen you in the Hooky Wallow on Thursday night, laddie. Who do you think you are son, Errol Flynn? If I hear you've been anywhere near that den of iniquity in future son, you will be fined a week's wages.'

We all rolled about the place laughing. It was as much out of relief as it was hilarity.

In the beginning we were all just determined to show Bill Shankly, Bob Paisley, Joe Fagan and Rueben Bennett that we were made of the right stuff, but boy, homesickness was a real problem and it took a fair bit of time to settle down.

A few of the lads I met in those early days went on to become legends of the club. Tommy Smith went on to captain Liverpool. He made 638 appearances in the first team and scored 48 times. Many people think of him as simply a tough-tackling hard man (and he was of course); that's after all what earned him the title 'Anfield Iron'. But Tommy could play football too. You don't get to play in four FA Cup finals, and win two of them, if you can't play football.

Of course, another one of Tommy's huge achievements was the wonderful header he scored in the 1977 European Cup Final against Borussia Mönchengladbach, in Rome. Shankly had dreamed of winning that trophy, and it is fitting that one of his boys helped to deliver it, albeit under Bob Paisley, not Shanks.

I loved Tommy Smith; even at the age of 16 he was a boy in a man's body. He was totally fearless and always 100 per cent positive and confident.

I must have played well over 50 games alongside Tommy in the Central League (reserve team) and I wasn't the biggest of players at only five feet six inches. However, I was aggressive, quick and good on the ball. This meant that I suffered quite a lot from heavy tackles, especially from behind.

Tommy took it upon himself to be my minder in the reserve team, and very often a quiet word in the ear of an opponent seemed to result in my somehow finding that extra bit of space. He was always brilliant with me and I had no doubt he was going to be a huge player for the club.

Chris Lawler was beginning to establish himself in the first team. Meanwhile, Tommy had yet to make the breakthrough, despite regularly hammering on the boss's door to ask why.

I remember one day at training, we were playing a five-a-side game when Tommy mistimed a tackle on Chris Lawler, leaving him with a huge bruise on his ankle. Tommy and Chris were the best of mates, and even roomed together on away trips. Tommy was genuinely remorseful and couldn't stop apologising to Chris.

Shankly, who was conducting proceedings, asked Tommy to help him take Chris across to the pavilion as he was obviously unable to continue playing. The lad's ankle was swelling up fast by this stage.

As they were making their way across the pitch, Chris with one arm around Shankly's neck and the other around Tommy's and limping badly, Tommy said to Shankly:

'Does this mean I will be in the big team on Saturday boss?'

That summed up Tommy for me. He was loyal and fearless and would put his own body on the line for a team-mate. However, he was utterly ruthless. Exactly the qualities needed to play for Shankly's Liverpool.

Chris Lawler made 549 appearances for Liverpool, scoring 61 goals from right-back. In one period he only missed three games in seven seasons. Chris was known by us as 'The Silent Knight' because he was quite economical with words.

I recall one occasion between Chris and Bill Shankly that still makes me laugh to this day. It sums up the pair perfectly.

As apprentice professionals, after cleaning the first team's boots, painting the stands and clearing the rubbish from the Kop, we would play five-a-side games in the car park behind the Main Stand every Monday morning. The opposition in these games would usually be Bill Shankly, Bob Paisley, Joe Fagan, Ronnie Moran and Reuben Bennett. On our side was Bobby Graham, Gordon Wallace, Tommy Smith, Chris Lawler and me. We never ever won those games because Shanks and company would have played until dark to make sure they got the result.

During one hard-fought match, Chris Lawler was injured and watching from the sidelines. As we only had four men to their five, Shankly tried a long-range effort to the unguarded goal, which skidded over the shoe that we had laid down as a goalpost.

He immediately shouted, 'Goal! We've won, times up, go and get a bath, boys.'

As you can imagine, this was a hotly disputed goal. Of course, our anger was exactly the response Shanks was keen to induce. He wanted us all to hate losing as much as he did.

The boss immediately noticed that Chris Lawler had been watching the whole time, and shouted to him, 'Son, you are in the perfect position to judge. Was that a goal or not?'

None of us expected Chris to go against the boss. He was such a quiet lad and it just wasn't his style. To our complete shock, he replied, 'No.'

There was a moment's pause, as all of us got ready for the boss's reaction. Then, without a hint of irony and in complete seriousness, Shankly shouted:

'Son, we have waited a year for you to speak. And your first word is a bloody lie.'

At Anfield, I was living the dream. For as long as I could ever remember, there wasn't nothing I wanted more than to be a professional footballer. Of course, I knew that hundreds of kids had the same ambition, and that very few ever managed to make it. But I was determined.

Growing up we all get asked, 'What do you want to do when you leave school?' My stock answer was always, 'I want to be a compositor [a print worker].' That was just for my parents' and teachers' benefit though. Football was my one and only ambition.

Years later my youngest brother, Alan, actually became a compositor. He went on to have a wonderful and successful career in the printing industry, until his retirement in 2018. It does make me wonder though, whether my constant references to the trade influenced him to choose that path.

If I ever confessed my true ambition, people would say, 'But you must have something to fall back on. What if you don't make it?' For that, I had another ready-made answer, 'Okay then, my second choice would be to be a journalist,' I would say. In truth, writing essays was the one academic activity that I enjoyed and excelled at.

My mother once told me of how my headmistress, Miss Tuenon, had told her that I was 'the most frustrating boy' she knew. 'He has the ability,' she continued. 'He should do really well, even go to university. But I'm afraid, all he wants to do is kick a football all day.'

I had been top of the tree, in terms of footballing ability, playing in the Aberdeen schools set-up. However, I had now moved into an environment where all the lads alongside me had been the best of the best in their own local environments.

We had all now entered the highly competitive and ruthless environment of the professional game. This was a completely different world to the ones each of us had been accustomed to back home.

Today, children as young as eight are scouted and brought to academies like Liverpool's at Kirkby. A few years ago, I went to Kirkby and observed that they have individual dressing rooms for the different age groups. The kids are all coached by highly professional staff, and introduced to 'The Liverpool Way'.

Photographs of the great players of the past, such as Steven Gerrard and some of those who I played with, adorn the walls. It must be such a wonderful feeling for these young boys to have been selected to train within the Liverpool FC youth system. Their families and friends must be so thrilled. I once overheard a woman say proudly whilst on the phone to someone else, 'Our Sean has signed for Liverpool.'

I couldn't help but reflect upon the fact that this whole set-up at Kirkby and the ethos that guides the club today, from the lowliest ranks all the way to the first team, owes its origins to those humble beginnings in 1960. More than that, they have their roots in Glenbuck in Scotland, and a man whose philosophy has endured for six decades.

Many of these kids, playing in the academy today, are envied by their friends at school. And, for the next few years at least, they will revel in the fact that they are training and playing for Liverpool. Then, for so many of them, reality bites. Time passes without any meaningful progress. A few years later their dreams are shattered, as it dawns on them that the step up from being a promising schoolboy footballer to becoming a Premier League star is a massive one. It can be as heartbreaking today, as it was in 1960.

For every Steven Gerrard, Trent Alexander-Arnold and Jamie Carragher, there are hundreds of young Sean's who end up broken-hearted at the age of 12. That's the other side of the glamour.

Just as today nobody can tell a young enthusiastic kid, eager to learn and seemingly at the threshold of achieving their life's dream, that they might not make the final cut, absolutely nobody could have told me that either. I believed; I knew I had what it took. And although I would taste bitter disappointment, I still believe that this inner self-belief is crucial for anyone to make the step up.

That was what Shankly preached every day. 'You must tell yourself all the time that you are the best in the world. Then, you must go out there and prove that you are,' he would declare. Whether you were successful or not was immaterial, you just had to believe and give all that you had in order to realise your dream. As far as he was concerned, there was as much reward in the journey as there was in the destination.

Chapter Three

The First Shankly Boys

SHANKLY ARRIVED at Anfield in 1959 with a vision and a plan. As we stood in his office, barely a month later, trembling with excitement and yearning to just get going, none of us would have had an inkling that this club, labouring in the Second Division of English football was about to become one of the greatest sporting institutions on the planet. And, that no matter how small a role each of us would eventually play, we were all there at the start of it. We were witnessing the birth of a footballing dynasty and of course we didn't have a clue.

One of my reasons for writing this book is a desire to preserve all these moments for posterity. To document the lives of a group of people, some of whose names may have been lost in the murky waters of time. I include myself in that category, and the title of the book reflects the fact that while there are many who know our story, there are far more who don't.

There will come a time, when I'm no longer able to recall these great stories from a life spent devoted to family and football. I don't want that day to come before I have committed them to paper. However, before I go any further with my own story, let's pause for a moment and talk about the other Shankly Boys.

Bobby Graham

More than four years on from that incredible moment in the office of Bill Shankly, his vision was beginning to take shape. The club had earned promotion to the 'big league', as he had put it, in 1962. By 1964, Shanks had assembled a side capable of dominating domestic football and already had his sights set on Europe.

The Reds had won their first league title under Shankly in 1964, four points clear of their nearest challengers, Manchester United. It was a remarkable feat and it meant that Shankly would be pitting his wits against the best in Europe.

First up, though, was a little-known team from Iceland called Knattspyrnufélag Reykjavíkur, in the preliminary round of the European Cup. We had won the first leg comfortably. The score had been 5-0 and my good friend Gordon Wallace (more of him in a moment) had bagged two of the goals.

The return leg at Anfield came a month later, on a Monday night. We had played Sheffield Wednesday at Hillsborough a little over 48 hours earlier, losing the game 1-0. Shanks would have been furious and continental opposition offered the perfect opportunity for the lads to appease the boss.

Gordon Wallace was injured and that meant Shankly would hand a debut to Bobby Graham. That debut came on 14 September 1964, and although he scored one, set up a penalty and hit the bar with a header, the night would be remembered for the quite remarkable behaviour of the Spion Kop.

The welcome they afforded the Reykjavik team, which was already vanquished from the first leg, was something I had never seen before and I'm sure will never be witnessed at any club again. Instead of rubbing salt in their wounds, Kopites adopted the Icelandic champions as if they were their own, and immediately took to barracking their own players.

Billy Stevenson's and Ron Yeats's faces were a picture when they were roundly booed (ironically of course) by Liverpudlians determined to make an entertaining night out of what was, in reality, a formality. The Icelandic players would leave the field to thunderous cheers and applause, despite their heavy 6-1 drubbing.

I hope it didn't spoil Bobby's debut. He had a great game and would have really impressed the boss with his performance. There were even greater things to come for him, though, as he would smash a hat-trick in a 5-1 thrashing of Villa in his league debut, just 12 days later.

Bobby was a tremendous player, and in the 1969/70 season he became an ever-present, making 54 consecutive appearances. He was eventually sold to Coventry two years later, as Bill Shankly brought in Kevin Keegan and John Toshack. Such is football, I suppose.

I had many great times with Bobby and one of the funniest experiences involved an evening in the front room of the couple who lived next door to our digs in Anfield Road. They were both lovely people; I remember they were called Mr and Mrs Horne.

After every home game they would lay out the table in their front room with sandwiches, tea and cakes for friends to come in and enjoy after the match. They were so kind and did a lot of work in the local community. Anyway, they would feel sorry for us youngsters, being so far away from home, and would open their door to us frequently. They had a daughter called Anita who was around our age, and often she would have her friends around too. Bobby had taken a shine to one of these girls; I'm sure her name was Rita.

One evening, Bobby Graham, Gordon Wallace and I were chatting with Anita and a couple of her friends in the front room, when Mr and Mrs Horne came in with some Coca-Colas for us. Bobby noticed that Mr Horne had a large badge on his lapel and asked him what it represented.

'We are members of the League of Well-Doers, and I'm this year's chairman,' he replied proudly. Bobby nodded approvingly and, with a completely straight face, replied, 'I would have been a member of that too, if I had stayed in Motherwell. I would have had a job working in the Motherwell Bridgeworks.'

Nobody had the slightest clue what he was talking about. We just looked at him, open-mouthed. Eventually Gordon decided to take the bait. 'Bobby, what are you talking about?'

Bobby pressed on, undeterred. 'Well if Shanks hadn't signed me, I was going to be a welder in the bridgeworks.'

We all just fell about laughing. He thought Mr Horne was the chairman of the League of Welders!

If Bobby had been intending to ask Rita out that night, he had certainly just blown his chances.

Gordon Wallace

Gordon was a player with wonderful ability. His career was sadly cut short by a succession of injuries. Shankly once said he was the closest thing he had ever seen to the great Tom Finney. I'm certain that in Shanks's eyes at least, there was no higher praise. Tom was an England international inside-left, with 76 caps for his country. He played 433 times for Preston North End between 1946 and 1960, scoring 187 times.

For Gordon to be compared to such a great player was a great honour. Carole and I have been lifelong friends with Gordon, his wife Susan and their family. We still play golf together regularly to this day.

Gordon made his Liverpool debut in the October of the 1962/63 season at the tender age of just 17. Liverpool's opponents that day were West Bromwich Albion and the game was played at The Hawthorns. Sadly, the Reds went down to a 1-0 defeat, a miserable result compounded by the fact that Jimmy Melia missed a penalty. Despite all that, though, Gordon had a wonderful debut. I recall he played on the left wing and gave Don Howe, a full international for England back then, an absolutely torrid time.

Back at my digs, I can remember thumbing through the *Football Echo* that evening and reading the headline 'Wallace has dream debut'.

Gordon's other proud distinctions included scoring the Reds' first-ever goal in the European Cup, in Iceland, and bagging a brace against Arsenal during what became the first-ever game to be shown on BBC's *Match of the Day,* at Anfield in 1964. He should have gone on to become a big star for Liverpool.

A footballer's life, as I know only too well, is a precarious one. The margins between success and failure are so fine, and sometimes a player's whole career can be decided by the whim of the gods. Such was the case with Gordon. A succession of injuries would rob Liverpool of a truly great player. Still, he gave the Kop many happy memories and me so many great stories.

I remember one day, Bill and Bob were coming up the passage towards the treatment room when they saw Gordon hobbling with a crutch under his arm. Shankly turned to Paisley, and said, 'Christ Bob! Wallace has been injured so bloody often his walking stick has had two operations.'

That about summed up Gordon's misfortune. For all of that, though, he would play 22 times for Shankly's first team and scored six priceless goals. There's many a young lad in cities all over the globe, who would give anything to say that.

After leaving Liverpool, Gordon went on to make just over 100 appearances in five years at Fourth Division Crewe, scoring 22 goals. He was being closely monitored by a number of big clubs when yet another serious injury sadly ended his playing career.

I feel I need to pause here and acknowledge my own feelings in relation to not making the breakthrough, while my best friend did. I have obviously reflected on this for many years, and what strikes me is that, six decades later, those feelings of disappointment still burn as brightly now as they did back then.

I can confidently say that I was, and still am, delighted and thrilled for Gordon and Bobby. They absolutely deserved their big breaks. I just feel I did too, and I now feel relaxed in saying that. It's not bitterness; rather I see it as a belief in my own ability and a recognition that sometimes, no matter how hard you work or how good you are, destiny has other ideas.

When I look back at my five years at Anfield, there is not a doubt in my mind that I deserved to at least be given a first-team debut. It's that nagging feeling of what might have been that still gnaws away at me. If I had been given just one chance, I'm sure I would have taken it with both hands (and feet).

From the day I made my debut for the reserves, in the Central League side in August 1962, until the last game I played in in April 1965, I made more appearances (107) and scored more goals (34) than any other player, with the exception of Alf Arrowsmith. I had also played 76 times in the junior teams, which included 14 appearances in the FA Youth Cup. In those games, I amassed a further 37 goals.

So, that meant I had represented Liverpool teams 183 times, scoring 71 goals and always putting my heart and soul into every appearance. Sadly, with no substitutes allowed in English football, it was never going to be enough for me to displace those 11 legends in the first team.

Sometimes I look longingly at the old programmes I have collected, stare at my records, realising that my reserve-team appearances and goals scored surpassed those of Bobby, Gordon, and Phil Chisnall – all of whom were brilliant players – I realise how fine the margins are between success and failure. They are wafer thin.

In such a high-stakes environment you must grasp whatever opportunity comes your way. My fellow Shankly Boys grasped theirs with both hands, and they deserved all their success. However, there is a sadness I feel when reflecting on those days that will always linger in my mind, at how I just missed out on achieving my breakthrough.

If only I'd had the confidence and maturity then, that I have now. Perhaps, like Tommy Smith, I could have fought my corner and persuaded the boss to put me in at least once. But Tommy was a giant of a man with a strong personality, and I was only five feet six inches tall and ten and a half stone.

Football is a very competitive business at all levels, and you can be the best of mates and still be the strongest of rivals. That's why players, in their hearts, never shed any tears if their rival for a position pulled a muscle or tweaked a hamstring. I'm sure it's no different today. You never want a fellow professional to suffer any serious injury, but a slight injury opening the door to opportunity was usually greeted with expressions of sympathy on the outside, but it felt like a gift on the inside.

When it comes down to it, I know that if things had turned out differently for me at Anfield, my future may have been very different. My life would almost certainly have followed a different path, and perhaps the wonderful family and business life I have enjoyed might never have happened. I'm sure I would have regretted that more.

Now, let's get back to the first Shankly Boys. There are many more to discuss.

Alex Totten

I'm sure this is an unfamiliar name to most Liverpool fans. Alex was a Scottish Schoolboy international who was a great character, full of humour. He always kept us entertained in our digs at 258 Anfield Road. Every day was a laugh with Alex.

However, he was also a very talented full-back. Sadly, as was the case with many of the youngsters at Anfield, his first-team chances were severely limited by supremely talented men.

In Alex's case his route to stardom was blocked by both Ronnie Moran and Gerry Byrne. The emergence, in due course, of the wonderful Chris Lawler at right-back would put paid to any chance he had of making the grade in Shankly's rearguard.

He was eventually released by Shankly and would return to Scotland, where he would play for Dunfermline. There he shared the same dressing room as Alex Ferguson. After his playing career came to an end, Totten became one of Scotland's most successful football managers. His incredible CV includes managing eight Scottish League clubs, including a spell as assistant manager to Jock Wallace at Rangers, before Graeme Souness took over.

He also won the manager of the year award on two occasions and has written a wonderful book called *From the Kop to the Kelpies*. He is not finished yet either. At the age of 74, Alex continues his life in football as commercial manager for Falkirk FC, a club he has managed twice before. Falkirk have even dedicated a lounge to Alex, Totty's Bar, and we remain the best of friends 60 years on.

Grant McCullough and John Bennett

Both were highly promising local lads, who joined us back in 1960. Grant, a very talented winger, had played for England Schoolboys against West Germany, at Wembley Stadium. John was a very promising and hard-working wing-half.

Grant had the amazing ability to take a long throw. He could hurl it to the far side of the opponent's penalty box. However, sadly for him, a player even more supremely skilled would emerge from the streets of Liverpool. Ian Callaghan broke into the first team around the same time and would be impossible to budge. Cally played 857 times for the Reds. There is certainly no shame in losing out to a player of such consistency and quality. I feel the same way about my career and Roger Hunt.

John Bennett was, and still is, a lovely man. In fact, he became the best man at my wedding in 1966. He wasn't only a tidy player but an extremely tidy individual. Everything about John was immaculate. When he eventually passed his driving test, his was always the cleanest car in the car park. And his sense of dress and style were unmatched by any other player.

One day, Bill Shankly walked into the Boot Room and his gaze immediately fell upon a pair of black Adidas boots on top of one of the benches. The boss picked them up and examined them. Curious, he turned to Joe Fagan, who was the reserve team trainer at the time, and asked, 'Whose boots are these Joe?'

Joe looked at them and casually replied, 'That's easy Boss. They are John Bennett's.'

Shanks wasn't one for the fancy things in life and the boots clearly offended his austere sensibilities. His reply was sharp and to the point.

'I don't know what they are doing here Joe, they should be on his bloody mantelpiece at home. They are shining brighter than a pair of brass candlesticks.'

John eventually left Liverpool earlier than I thought he would. However, he enjoyed a wonderful career in the lower leagues, with Chester FC and Macclesfield FC. He would captain the latter to an FA Non-League Trophy at Wembley. We remain good friends.

Phil Tinney

As I have mentioned, I shared my Anfield home with Phil for several years. He was another very gifted player who sadly never fulfilled his potential at Anfield. Phil could play in virtually any position on the pitch, and he had wonderful ability on the ball coupled with a cultured left foot.

I first met Phil when we were each representing the North of Tay against South of Tay in the Scottish Schools International Trials, at Claypotts Park, Dundee, in early 1959. Phil was a very talented player with a typical Scots dry sense of humour, something that wasn't always appreciated by the boss.

I recall one classic moment during a Liverpool Echo Schools Trophy Final, which was being played at Anfield. A game such as this was very important to Bill Shankly. He would always insist that the apprentices should attend. There was always something for us to learn as far as he was concerned.

We all used to watch the game from the old Band Box next to the trainer's dugout. Shankly would sit in the directors' box, where he would count the heads of us apprentices to make sure we were all there.

That day he was fizzing with rage because the first team had lost their previous game on the Saturday. So, when he noticed there was one head missing from his count, his anger would reach fever pitch.

The following day, a meeting was called in the snooker room for all playing staff. We were herded in by Bob, Joe and Reuben to face Shankly's wrath. None of us had any idea what was going on, until we heard the words:

'Where is young Tinney?'

They were directed at Reuben Bennett, but Joe Fagan interjected and explained that Phil was cleaning out the bath in the home dressing room.

Shankly wasn't impressed. 'Get him in here,' he shouted. Joe immediately sped off in search of the young lad, returning some moments later. Phil stood there, in front of us all, like some prisoner of war instead of the 16-year-old kid he was. Shankly roared:

'Where were you last night, son? I could see you weren't with the lads in the Band Box.'

Phil fidgeted and looked terribly nervous.

'I took my girlfriend Linda to the cinema at the Walton Astoria, Boss,' he explained. All eyes were on him now and not one of them was envious.

Shankly's face turned crimson. He looked at Phil as if he were a bank robber.

'You missed a match at Anfield to take your girlfriend to the Walton Astoria?' Shanks was incredulous. He continued, 'You should be in Walton jail, son. No wonder we are losing matches. You'll be doing extra training tomorrow afternoon. See to it Reuben.'

With that, a defeat for the first team in the previous game had been pinned firmly on the nocturnal habits of an apprentice, one Phil Tinney. More than a few of us had to cover our faces to hide our laughter.

I can remember seeing Phil score one of the best individual goals I have ever witnessed. He was playing for a Lancashire Select team against Shropshire, when he dribbled past at least seven players before despatching the ball high into the net.

Phil, like Alex Totten, was released by the club in 1963. He was sold to Bill Shankly's brother Bob's Dundee team. For Phil, it was a chance to return to his hometown club. There, he enjoyed a spell in the first team before playing in the Netherlands.

From the Netherlands, his life's adventure took him to the American Professional League, which had been created by the former West Ham United player, Phil Woosnam. He was an early trailblazer, and later on in the 1970s players like Pelé would make the same journey.

After his retirement, Phil spent his working life on Merseyside in social services, helping young people turn their lives around. I'm proud to still call him a friend.

James (Hamish) McKenzie

Hamish was a full-back from Glasgow. He played for the junior side Woodburn Athletic. Always a bit of a jack-the-lad and a stickler for appearance, he fancied himself as a bit of a ladies' man. I always felt he had the ability, but he never really gave as much effort as his talent deserved. He was a staunch Rangers fan. In fact, that's all he talked about. He seemed more concerned about the fortunes of his boyhood club than he ever did about Liverpool. Of course, his whole family were steeped in the Rangers Protestant tradition.

I can remember staying with them one time in Glasgow, when I was on my way home for the summer holidays. I couldn't for the life of me understand why there were all these pictures of King William of Orange, sat atop a white horse, hanging in their lounge. There seemed to be Orange Lodge certificates everywhere. However, his mum and dad were very kind to me. So kind, in fact, that I didn't think it wise to mention that the rest of my family was devoutly Catholic.

Hamish had the ability to make it. But his position was occupied by the likes of Byrne, Moran and Lawler. That was a considerable barrier to overcome. He would eventually be transferred to Scottish side Dunfermline Athletic. There, he would make few, if any, first-team appearances. Hamish ended his football career at Brentford, managing just 20 games for them.

He is the only member of the Shankly Boys I lost touch with. I was very saddened to hear that he had passed away a few years ago. We had some good laughs during the few years we spent together on Anfield Road.

Tommy Leishman

Shankly brought Leishman down from St Mirren in December 1959. He was as tough as nails and a very talented left-half. Liverpool paid £10,000 for him. He would play 118 times for the Reds, scoring seven goals, before making way for Billy Stevenson. He was an ebullient character and an experienced and successful professional having played for St Mirren.

He was in the side that beat my first love, Aberdeen FC, in the 1959 Scottish Cup Final at Hampden Park. He had played in front of more than 108,000 fans. I never tired of telling him how he broke my young heart by beating the Dons that day. Tommy showed me no sympathy, but the one thing he did show me in due course was his medal.

He made his debut for Liverpool in a 2-0 home victory over Charlton Athletic on 28 December 1959. His last appearance came in the 1962/63 season, a 1-0 defeat to West

Bromwich Albion on 22 October 1962. Two men would make their Liverpool debuts in that match, Tommy Lawrence and Gordon Wallace.

Of course, the Shankly glory years started with the club clinching promotion to the First Division by beating Southampton 2-0 in April 1962. Tommy played in that game. In the pouring rain and wading through mud, he was one of the men who helped drag the club out of the Second Division.

Those with an eye for history will know that Liverpool's goals that day were scored by Kevin Lewis, who I would play alongside in South Africa in 1966/67. But few will know that Tommy Leishman had been virtually an ever-present in that promotion-winning side. He made 46 appearances that season.

He was a really good professional with a very cultured left foot, but unfortunately Bill Shankly had other ideas. He found someone that he felt was more suited to the First Division to replace Tommy. That man was the brilliant Billy Stevenson from Glasgow Rangers. This was a player with an even more cultured left foot, and who had brilliant passing ability. Sadly, like so many others in football's ruthless world, Tommy's Anfield days were numbered the moment Stevenson signed for the club. He was sold to Hibernian in 1963.

Sammy Reid

Finally, another young pioneer at that time was Sammy Reid. Sammy was the very first player Shankly signed. Bill took him from Motherwell in 1960. Small in stature, he made up for his diminutive frame with bundles of energy. He was a fine dribbler of the ball and it's a great shame he didn't break through at Anfield.

Sammy would return to Scotland, where he would play for Falkirk and Clyde before going on to achieve legendary status at Berwick Rangers.

Berwick shocked the whole of Scottish football by beating Glasgow Rangers in the First Round of the Scottish Cup in 1967. Sammy scored the winning goal. I wonder what Hamish McKenzie and his family made of that.

The other Scots who joined Liverpool with me in 1960 were delighted to have Sammy in the squad, as Bill Shankly's first full-time professional signing. We were excited that another Scottish player was to join the club, and Sammy had a good reputation in Scotland. Tommy Smith wasn't so impressed though. I remember Tommy, a proud Englishman, though only a boy at the time, remarking, 'Does the boss think he is signing players for the Highland Games?'

When he arrived, the thing that stood out most about Sammy was his small stature. Up until he joined the club, I had been the smallest player on the books, at 5 feet 6 inches, another of my greatest regrets. I have joked with friends and associates many times over the years, telling them, 'If I had been four inches taller, I would have had 50 caps.' Meanwhile, Sammy, at 5 feet 4 inches, made me feel like a giant.

The only other player I can recall being at the club who was smaller than me was Willie Carlin. He later went on to have fantastic success at Derby County, with Brian Clough.

Sammy Reid was a wonderful player, but I think his lack of inches may have been a drawback for him. Players can be cruel, and I remember a few of the old professionals, many of whom Shankly would move on at the end of his first season, giving him a tough time about his height.

To his credit, Sammy took it all in his stride and, although he never made the first team at Anfield, he built a good career back in Scotland. Sadly, he passed away in November 2014 at the age of 75.

To the legions of Liverpool supporters across the globe, the names of these men will doubtless be unfamiliar. They may not resonate in the way that Chris Lawler, Tommy Smith and others do. However, they are part of the fabric of this great club. They were the first foot soldiers of that Shankly revolution, and I'm proud to count myself as one of them.

Chapter Four

The Men of Anfield

DURING MY time at Anfield I was blessed to have met, trained with and rubbed shoulders with some truly wonderful football people.

These are men who weren't only Liverpool legends, they were also some of football's greatest characters. Again, some of them you will know very well. Others you may never have heard of.

There were those I met and came to know, who formed the old guard – an unbroken chain that stretched back to the earliest days of the club. And then, there were those who stood ready to take it to even greater heights.

You will find their stories carved into the archives, their contributions documented in the history books and official records. However, to me they were more than statistics. Much more. They were people I was honoured to have known and who lit up my career and life.

Let me tell you all about them, from my perspective.

Frederick Albert Shelley
1899–1971

Bert, as we knew him, would have been 60 years old when I arrived at the club. He ran the Boot Room operation in those days, as the kit and stores man. However, he had an incredible footballing pedigree, having played a record 410 times for Southampton, winning the Third Division South championship in 1922.

After hanging up his boots, he had worked as a trainer alongside manager George Kay in 1935, and he brought him to Liverpool a year later when Kay took the Anfield hot seat. Shelley remained at the club as first-team trainer until 1956, and after that worked tirelessly behind the scenes until his death in 1971

Albert always used to wear a khaki coat, and I remember him as a real character, who gave us many pearls of wisdom. The one I remember most is, 'If you don't want the pick and shovel son, save your money.'

It's a strange expression, but what he meant was that football was a short career, and if you didn't want to end up digging up roads for a living at the end of your career, you should make sure you saved your money.

Ephraim Longworth
1887–1968

Ephraim had been a member of the coaching staff at Liverpool but continued to help at the club after his retirement. He would have been in his late 70s when I met him. He was also in the early stages of Parkinson's disease – something he used to his advantage when challenging us young lads to a game of snooker or pool. More about that in a moment. Ephraim remains a Liverpool legend to this day, having played 370 times for them and being capped five times for his country.

He had an astonishing career in the game, making his first-team debut in 1910 – a 2-0 defeat to Sheffield United at Bramall Lane – and hanging up his boots 18 years later, in 1928, with a 2-0 defeat to Birmingham City. However, in between those games he would form part of the incredible 'Untouchables' Liverpool team of the 1920s. Between 1921 and 1923, the Reds won back-to-back titles.

He had also played in Liverpool's first FA Cup Final, in 1914, suffering a narrow 1-0 defeat to Burnley. The game took place in front of King George V, at Crystal Palace. But for the war years, between 1914-18, he would have surely achieved even greater success. Ephraim was 40 years old when he finished his playing career, which is astonishing.

Longworth's other great distinction was that he became the first Liverpool player to captain England, in 1920. Of course, he wasted no time in pointing out to us Scots that the game was against Scotland, and England had fought back from 4-2 down to eventually win the game 5-4 at Hillsborough.

Bill Shankly revered Ephraim. He would often describe him to us as a 'living piece of Liverpool history', and we had tremendous respect for him.

He would often challenge us to a game of snooker and pool. His left hand would always be shaking as he tempted one of us to enter into a bet with him. He knew exactly what he was doing of course. No sooner had the wager been agreed and the snooker cue was in his hand, the tremor miraculously stopped. He would proceed to clean up and pocket our money.

We adored him and, of course, we loved his stories. Ephraim died at the age of 81 in 1968. He will be forever a Liverpool legend. In 2006 he was voted in at 72nd place in a survey of Liverpool supporters entitled '100 Players Who Shook the Kop'. I feel blessed to have known the man.

Billy Liddell
1922–2001

Billy is, perhaps, the greatest player to ever wear the red shirt. He remains a legend and an icon of Liverpool Football Club. A debate will rage, probably for as long as the club exists, as to who is Anfield's greatest. Younger supporters will understandably talk of Steven Gerrard. Their parents may say Kenny Dalglish. Their grandparents would undoubtedly say Billy Liddell. I prefer to argue that we are blessed to have had all three of them, and it's the honour of my life to have rubbed shoulders with Liddell, a man who played 534 times for Liverpool and scored 228 goals.

Billy was a legend in the game. He broke the record for the most Liverpool appearances that had been set by the immortal Elisha Scott. And, he was a league title winner, having helped to end the club's 24-year wait for the championship in 1947.

When I arrived at Anfield, Billy was coming to the end of his career. He was 38 years of age. However, he was loved by everyone at the club and his reputation in the football world put him right up there with the greatest players who have ever played the game in these islands.

Billy was Liverpool's leading goalscorer in eight out of nine seasons at the club and he had also played in an FA Cup Final in 1950. Sadly, he had been on the losing side that day, but it did nothing to dull his lustre.

He also loved representing his country, having been capped 29 times for Scotland. He had even been selected to represent Great Britain against the Rest of the World twice, in 1947 and again in 1955. Those honours put him alongside the great Stanley Matthews as the only two men to be selected twice for a Great Britain XI.

Most Liverpool fans have now heard about how Billy was so influential that supporters dubbed the club Liddellpool. It was Shankly who told us apprentices this when we arrived, and we were in awe of him. I have dined out for many years on the story of how Liddell once turned up at Melwood to watch us playing a match for the A team, in 1961.

We were warming up before the game and someone had managed to kick one of the practice balls off the pitch and towards the old pavilion. Billy couldn't resist it and even though he had his suit and raincoat on, he trotted over to it and launched it in my direction. I had been standing in the goalmouth and as I saw it coming towards me, I couldn't help myself. Instinctively, I leapt to meet it and crashed it into the empty net. I wasn't yet 17 but I had scored a goal from a cross by Billy Liddell. How many generations of Liverpool supporters would love to be able to say that?

I remember when Billy got injured and Shankly replaced him in a game against Bristol Rovers with a young 17-year-old, Ian Callaghan. Cally had a wonderful debut and in an amazing quirk of fate, he would go on to break Billy's all-time appearance record for the club. More about Ian later.

Billy realised his time to leave the stage was approaching and the club granted him a testimonial in the September of 1960. The game pitted Liverpool's first team against an International XI. Over 38,000 people attended. I was honoured to be at the game and saw first-hand the wonderful way the Kop and the whole of Anfield paid tribute to this wonderful servant.

My abiding memory of the game was to watch the great Tom Finney, who was well into his 50s, run Liverpool's left-back, the great Ronnie Moran, ragged before going off at half-time. Ronnie must have been thinking 'thank God I wasn't playing him in his prime'.

Billy was an educated man as well as a great footballer, and after retiring from football became a Justice of the Peace and finally Bursar of Liverpool University. In this way he continued to give wonderful service to the people of Liverpool over the years.

Johnny Wheeler
1928–2019

Alas Johnny left us on 16 November 2019. Although Johnny was coming to the end of his playing career when I arrived at Anfield, he was still playing regularly in the first team. His passing ability was peerless and, combined with his exceptional reading of the game, marked him out as a special player. I feel he would have done well, even during the Premier League era.

Johnny had started his career at Tranmere Rovers in 1946 and spent five years there. He made just over 100 appearances before being transferred to Bolton Wanderers in 1951. There, he enjoyed a wonderful time, even featuring in the famous 1953 Stan Matthews FA Cup Final. This was the game that saw the great Stan Matthews, at the ripe age of 38, finally win a cherished FA Cup medal.

Johnny would regale us kids with his stories of that game and how Matthews was simply unplayable. And, with tongue in cheek, Johnny told us that Ralph Banks (Bolton's left-back) didn't get a good night's sleep for the rest of his life due to the recurring nightmares he suffered about the game.

Stan Mortenson, the famous Blackpool centre-forward, scored a hat-trick in the final, but even that achievement was eclipsed and overshadowed by the sheer brilliance of Matthews's performance. Johnny, though, soon recovered from the devasting blow of losing the final. He won his first and only England cap soon after, in a game against Northern Ireland at Dalymount Park. The Three Lions won the game 2-0, with goals from Johnny Haynes and Don Revie.

For almost his entire career, the maximum wage for a footballer was £20 per week. Johnny would be worth millions today and would surely be earning a king's ransom. We all played for the love of the game back then, though, and money wasn't the main motivator.

It was a different era.

If only Johnny had started his career under the great Bill Shankly. Who knows what he would have achieved? Still, Johnny made 177 appearances for Liverpool Football Club and scored 23 goals. I remember him as a wonderful man and a great footballer.

Gerry Byrne
1938–2015

Liverpool supporters have been blessed to have watched some of the greatest players in the game. Professionals possessed with sublime flair and skill. But, to perform at the very highest level of the game, a player needs more than these qualities. To play for Liverpool, you needed sheer courage, loyalty, integrity and honesty. Those were the qualities that Bill Shankly loved.

When I was at Liverpool, there was one player who had all those qualities in abundance. That player was Gerry Byrne.

To the supporters, he was one of the hardest players to ever play for the club. Off the field he was a different person. He wasn't the only senior player to do this of course, but Gerry went out of his way to look after me and the other youngsters at the club.

As I gained experience and eventually made the reserve team, I became involved in full-scale practice matches at Anfield. We would be pitted against the first team. This was our chance to impress and maybe usurp one of the first XI. For them, it was about keeping the young upstarts in their place and holding on to their own position in the team. It was a recipe that kept us all super-competitive, and in those matches no quarter was sought and none was given.

I had always eagerly awaited the boss's announcement of the team line-ups. And, I would be quietly pleased if I was playing on the opposite side of the pitch to Gerry. Nevertheless, I knew only too well that I would be in for one of the toughest games of my life.

I'm sure, if asked, most Liverpool supporters would rate Tommy Smith as the hardest man at Anfield in the 1960s.

Tommy was a tough character for sure, but Gerry Byrne was his equal in that department. I have never been able to shake the memory of an amazing encounter between the two men in one of the many five-a-side matches we played at Melwood.

Tommy would have been just 16, but he was a supremely confident lad for his age. During the game, he had the temerity to nutmeg Gerry and scored a goal, which he celebrated quite too loudly for Byrne's liking. From that moment, young Tommy's cards were marked.

Later in the same game, the ball dropped between Tommy and Gerry. Smith went to head it, but Byrne got in first with no thought for his own safety. His head crashed into Tommy's and the youngster went down with a gashed eye. And, as he lay on the turf holding his face, blood pouring from the cut, Shankly strolled across from the touchline, looked down at Tommy and simply said, 'Lesson number one son. Never nutmeg Gerry Byrne and think you can get away with it.'

Gerry was a typical Scouser, full of confidence and always willing to argue the toss if he thought he was right. When he won a place in the England team, he felt he was worth considerably more than the new contract he was offered. However, the way Shanks saw it, Gerry was paid for what he did for Liverpool. The fact that he had made the England team had nothing to do with what he was paid at Anfield.

Gerry argued that international status was proof he had become a better player with his club. He was so convinced of his case that he even went toe to toe with the boss on the matter. That was a battle very few people, if any, could ever hope to win.

Exasperated that Shanks wouldn't yield to his argument, Gerry blurted out, 'Well, I may be wrong on the other points, Boss, but I'm right on this one, aren't I?'

Shankly bristled and barked back, 'So what if you are son?' By now the air was thick and sparks were flying. Shanks delivered the killer blow: 'Even a broken clock is right twice in a day, lad.'

Another classic Byrne story that stands out in my mind involves a game against Anderlecht. Liverpool were facing them in the European Cup at Anfield on November 1964. They were a side that featured eight full Belgian internationals, including the famous Joseph Jurion.

Jurion was a wonderful player and the only player in European football to have been authorised to wear lightweight glasses. Before the game, Bill Shankly pulled Gerry to one side and, with a tongue planted firmly in his cheek, told him, 'Their winger wears glasses Gerry son; your first job is to get the glasses and throw them in the Kop. The boys won't throw them back.'

Gerry thought he was being serious, and I have absolutely no doubt that he would have done it. Before the players left the dressing room, Gerry approached Bob Paisley, and quietly asked him how long he should wait before grabbing the glasses. Bob could barely believe his ears and had to tell him that the boss was joking.

Liverpool won the game 3-0 and Gerry never gave Jurion a kick (well not of the ball anyway). He had simply implemented the same instructions Shankly would issue every game, to the letter: 'Let the winger know you are there, Gerry son.'

Byrne was as big a legend as any who have worn the famous red shirt, and Shanks adored him, saying: 'I've had many skilful men in my team. And, the likes of Peter Thompson, Ian St John, Kevin Keegan and Steve Heighway were the ones who caught the eye. But the best professional of the lot was Gerry Byrne. He wasn't flashy and he wouldn't score you goals. But he was hard and skilful and gave you everything he had.

'More than that, he was totally honest, which is the greatest quality of all. He was a true Liverpudlian who couldn't look his fellow Scousers in the face after a game, unless he'd given everything he had for 90 minutes.'

Of course, the greatest and most iconic story of Gerry's grit and determination is one that justifies Shankly's remarks perfectly. And, it came in the 1965 FA Cup Final, against Leeds United. Gerry sustained a fractured collarbone early in the game but elected to play on. I was on the sidelines that day and still can't believe that he not only played on with that injury but saw out extra time and even laid on the opening goal for Roger Hunt.

When lying injured and being treated by Bob, Gerry was in terrible pain but didn't want to come off. Bob got him on his feet and told him that his collarbone had suffered a serious injury and it was doubtful that he could justify leaving him on the pitch.

Gerry was determined to stay on, so he was given the instruction to go on the left wing and make a nuisance of himself. It's a measure of Gerry's courage that the Leeds players remained unaware that Gerry had received such a serious injury and the rest is history. I'm still not so sure that Bob had made Shankly fully aware of the serious nature of Gerry's injury when he returned to the bench, but in any case,

Bob knew that they would have had to tie Gerry with chains to a stretcher if they tried to get him to come off.

I'm sure the publicity surrounding this incident contributed to the introduction of substitutes for injured players in 1966. In turn, that led to the development of the squad system we see today. It came too late for me, but benefits the game and young players greatly.

I lost touch with Gerry after I left the club. However, in 2010 I was invited to a former players' Christmas dinner at the Marriot Hotel in Liverpool, where we were reunited. I hadn't seen him for 45 years, but he went out of his way to come over to me. We shared a drink together and had a brilliant chat about the old days.

Of course, I told him of my lingering disappointment about not breaking into the first team. His response was typical of the guy. He told me that he thought I was very unlucky not to have been given my chance.

'You were the most consistent player in the reserves George. But it was a time when there were no substitutes and no vacancies.'

I knew that, of course, but to hear it from a fellow professional meant so much. His parting words meant more, though. He said we were all lucky to have been there in those days.

'Never look back with regrets at what you missed, George. Take pride in what you have achieved in life.'

We shook hands and I never saw Gerry again. Sadly, he passed away on 28 November 2015.

Both club and supporters alike are lucky to have had such a dedicated servant.

Roger Hunt and Tommy Lawrence

As a young reserve player with an eye for goals, the one player I aspired to be like was the great 'Sir' Roger Hunt. Sadly, I hadn't been blessed with his physique and I had never really thought of myself as a pure striker. My talent lay in my hard work and aggressive style in midfield, and it would often see me bursting through the middle and finding the back of the net.

Roger was banging goals in every week for the first team. He would soon set new records in that department. It's a measure of the man that although I had my eye on his place in the team, he has never forgotten me and has always been very generous to me. Anytime our paths have crossed, he always greets me with the same smile.

In the summer of 2015 Roger invited Gordon Wallace and myself to play with him and Tommy Lawrence at Leigh Golf Club in Lancashire. Roger is a long-standing member there. Our competitive nature meant that it didn't take us long to organise a First Team versus Reserve Team match.

It was just like the old days, when we pitted our wits against each other in five-a-side football games, only now we were on the golf course. Of course, it wouldn't be a game between ex-pros unless there was a wager at stake and we settled on a nominal £1 stake on the winner after 18 holes, as Tommy suggested. As you would imagine the game was very competitive, and soon Gordon began to harbour a few suspicions about the handicaps, especially Tommy's. He had told us that he needed a few extra shots as he hadn't played a round of golf for over six months.

Gordon and I eventually ran out winners by a narrow margin, and we all retired to the clubhouse. We shared drinks and stories of the old times. Then, before long, it was time to go our separate ways. As I got up, I asked Roger if he had forgotten something.

He looked at me, perplexed. 'What?' he said.

I smiled. 'What about the £1 you owe us?'

Roger laughed and told us we were 'typical Scotsmen'. Then with a twinkle in his eye, he pointed at Gordon and said, 'Even though he has a Welsh accent.' Both he and Tommy paid up and as we parted company, I shouted to him, 'It's not every day you get to take a quid from a World Cup winner.' I still have that pound coin in my trophy cabinet at home; it's only worth £1 but it will always be worth much more than that to me.

Tommy was a great goalkeeper and a lovely man. He played 306 times for Liverpool and was capped once for Scotland. He was also a pioneer of his trade, becoming the first genuine sweeper keeper. His runs from goal to take out opposition strikers saved his team-mates many times. He also helped bring through his own successor, Ray Clemence.

Who can forget that wonderful moment when Tommy was shopping in Liverpool and a local television journalist, who had no idea who this old fellow was, stopped him in the street, put a microphone in his face and asked him if he could remember the 1967 Liverpool vs Everton FA Cup match at Goodison. That was a historic game for more than one reason, as a huge screen was erected at Anfield and the game was screened via CCTV to a capacity crowd across Stanley Park. Around 100,000 people watched the match, which Everton won 1-0, live.

Tommy's reply was priceless and delivered with incredible comic timing. He simply said, 'Remember it? I played in it.'

'Sorry, who are you then?' the bemused reporter said.

With a twinkle in his eye, Tommy proudly declared, 'Tommy Lawrence. I was the Liverpool goalkeeper; Alan Ball scored the winner.'

The reporter's face was a picture of embarrassment and the video of the incident went viral, seen by millions of people all over the world.

Tommy joined Gordon Wallace and me at a legends evening, hosted by the Shankly Hotel in Liverpool, just a year before this classic moment. Radio City's Rick Houghton, partner of Emma Parry (Bill Shankly's granddaughter) was compering the evening. Liverpool were playing Norwich City away, and the game was being shown on the big screen in the Bastion Restaurant. The room was packed full of Liverpool fans.

The plan was we would get up and deliver our talk and take questions after the game was over. The only problem was that the Reds had thrown away a 4-3 lead with only seconds to go. The thought of delivering our speeches in front of a gloomy audience, rocked by a chastening defeat, didn't appeal. Tommy leaned over to me, with time ebbing away, and whispered to me, 'I'm not looking forward to this, George.' He looked genuinely worried.

Within minutes we were both smiling, but barely able to believe what we had just witnessed. Liverpool had dealt a hammer blow to Norwich's hopes of securing a valuable point. I'll never forget the noise and the scenes in that room when Adam Lallana scored a wonderful winner deep into injury time, before running over to the side of the pitch and leaping into Jürgen Klopp's arms. Tommy's face just lit up.

He turned to Gordon and me and said, 'Just look at the joy this club brings to so many people. I don't think we will have any difficult questions to answer now.' I remember thinking, I wonder if you realise how much joy over the years you have brought to these supporters, Tommy. From that moment on, he was in his element. It was a great night, and one that Gordon and I will always remember.

Tommy wasn't only a fantastic goalkeeper and amazing servant to Liverpool, he was also a lovely unassuming man. Tommy passed away on 10 January 2018, leaving behind a wonderful family who are all a credit to him. He was a genuinely modest and lovely man, who is sadly missed by everyone who knew him.

Ian Callaghan

Ian Callaghan was a 17-year-old lad when I arrived at Anfield. He had only played four games in the reserve team, and then his opportunity arrived, when he was chosen to replace the great Billy Liddell. Billy, who was coming to the end of his career and was well established as a legend of the club, had recommended Ian to Bill Shankly, suggesting that Cally was a ready-made replacement. He would enthuse about the youngster, saying, 'He's a talented boy who won't let you down, Bill.'

That might be both the greatest compliment and understatement of all time. Ian would make his debut against Bristol Rovers at Anfield. The game would end 4-0 to Liverpool, but it was more significant in that it was the first of 857 appearances for Cally, a record that will surely never be beaten.

Ian had a dream debut. He played brilliantly and was applauded from the pitch by the Kop and the whole of Anfield at the end of the game. A star was born and he would shine for many more years to come.

Graham Fisher, wrote in the *Daily Express*: 'For Liverpool, right-winger Ian Callaghan, a veteran of four Central League games, he just ended the most accomplished League debut I've had the pleasure to witness.'

Perhaps fearful of placing too much pressure on a young player's shoulders, Shankly brought in an old friend of mine, Kevin Lewis. He was a wonderful player who many underestimated. He would score 22 goals in 36 games, and his addition to the squad would mean Ian had to bide his time a little longer. Liverpool gained promotion in 1961/62, with Kevin scoring the two goals which clinched the Second Division Championship against Southampton at Anfield. I remember it poured down with rain that day, but it was glorious, nonetheless. Ian would finally get his chance and he would prove impossible to shift for the next 15 years.

Ian's story also provided Shanks with the perfect riposte to every player who ever moaned or sulked about being left out of the team. His stock reply to our entreaties would always be, 'Ask Ian Callaghan, and then ask yourself, why is Ian never out of the team?'

We all knew the answer, and it was no use arguing. Ian had bided his time, waited for his opportunity, trusted in his talent and when it finally came, he grabbed it with both hands and gave 100 per cent in every game.

I have two great memories of Ian in his prime. The first will never leave my mind's eye. If I close my eyes, I can see it now. I'm at Wembley, sitting on the sidelines. Wembley is majestic and the pitch is wet with the gentle rain falling. The stands all around me are packed and the air is full of anticipation and expectation. The hopes and dreams of two cities hang in the balance.

It's 1965, and with game locked at 1-1 and into extra time, I see Ian Callaghan crossing the ball into the penalty area. Time stands still; it's as if the crowd has gone silent as each and every one of us draws breath at exactly the same time. Then, whoosh, an eruption of ecstasy as Ian St John meets the ball and guides it into the net. Then we're on our feet. Everyone is on their feet and the FA Cup is ours at last.

My other abiding memory is tinged with sadness. It's the wonderful free kick at Anfield against the great Inter Milan. Ian was the recipient of the final pass of a well-planned free kick, which beat the Milan defensive wall. With supreme skill and calmness, he placed the ball beautifully into the far corner of the net, at the Anfield Road end. The atmosphere at that game was one of the best I have ever experienced. We owe much of that to the genius move by Shankly, which saw his players parade the FA Cup in front of the supporters before the game.

However, the memories are bittersweet, as this would be the last time that I would watch a match at Anfield as a player of the club. Within weeks, I would be on my way home to Aberdeen, but more of that later.

Shankly would say of Callaghan, '[He] is everything good that a man can be. No praise is too high for him. He is a model professional, and a model human being. If there were 11 Callaghan's at Anfield there would never be any need to put up a team sheet. You could stake your life on Ian. Words cannot do justice to the amount he has contributed to the game. Ian Callaghan will go down as one of the game's truly great players.'

Ian boasts without a doubt one of the most remarkable careers of any player in Europe, past or present. He was the epitome of the professional footballer and is a gentleman off the field. In addition to his appearance record, he was also the first Liverpool player to be voted Footballer of the Year, in 1974.

In addition, he played one game for England in the 1966 World Cup finals. However, he would wait 43 years before being presented with a winner's medal at a special ceremony in London. He will be remembered most fondly, though, for his record as a Liverpool player.

He was, of course, part of the team that clinched Liverpool's first European Cup, in 1977. This gave him the incredible distinction of being the only player in that game who had also played in Liverpool's first-ever European game, 13 years earlier – a testament to his amazing longevity.

Charles Lambert, writing in the *Liverpool Echo*, described Ian as being 'as great a Liverpool institution as the Mersey Ferries'. I can think of no more appropriate words to describe the man.

Ian Ross
1947–2019

Ian Ross, or Rossy as he was affectionately known (they called me Scotty), came down from Scotland in 1963. That meant we had quite the colony of Scottish lads at the club and I have to say all of us got on really well.

My granddad, Bill

My mum and dad's wedding, 1944

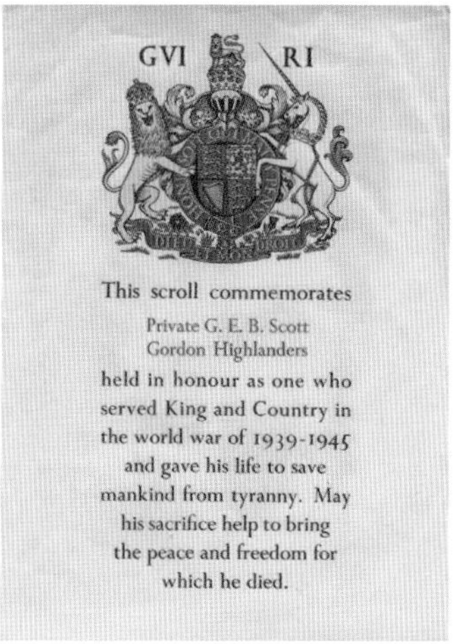

GVI RI

DIEU ET MON DROIT

This scroll commemorates
Private G. E. B. Scott
Gordon Highlanders
held in honour as one who
served King and Country in
the world war of 1939-1945
and gave his life to save
mankind from tyranny. May
his sacrifice help to bring
the peace and freedom for
which he died.

My father made the ultimate sacrifice

The squad Bill Shankly inherited in 1960. Soon, most would be gone

Our first lodgings at 258 Anfield Road (the white house)

With Gordon Wallace and Bobby Graham at Melwood, 1960

Bill Shankly's first full squad. Melwood, 1961

Attacking the Kop end with Bobby Graham in the FA Youth Cup semi-final, 1963

Ronnie Moran, myself, Tommy Lawrence, Tommy Smith, Gerry Byrne and Bobby Graham in San Remo, Italy, 1963

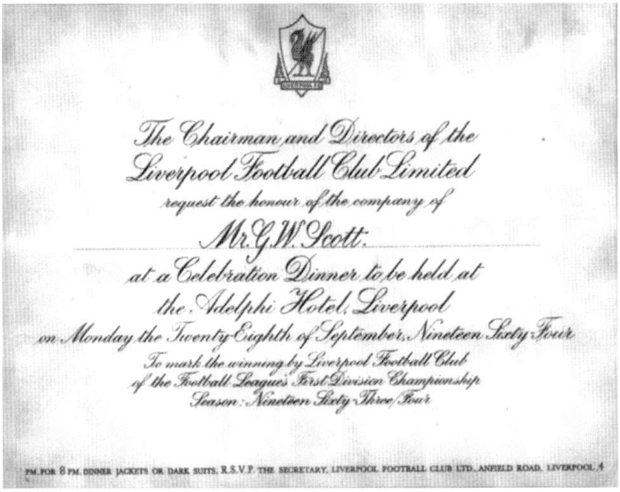

The Chairman and Directors of the
Liverpool Football Club Limited
request the honour of the company of
Mr G.W. Scott.
at a Celebration Dinner to be held at
the Adelphi Hotel, Liverpool
on Monday the Twenty-Eighth of September, Nineteen Sixty-Four
To mark the winning by Liverpool Football Club
of the Football League's First Division Championship
Season: Nineteen Sixty-Three/Four

PM. FOR 8 PM. DINNER JACKETS OR DARK SUITS. R.S.V.P. THE SECRETARY, LIVERPOOL FOOTBALL CLUB LTD., ANFIELD ROAD, LIVERPOOL 4

My invitation to the championship celebration dinner of 1964

Champions of 1964. I am in the centre of the middle row

Liverpool FC league championship squad, 1964

Being coached by the boss at Melwood

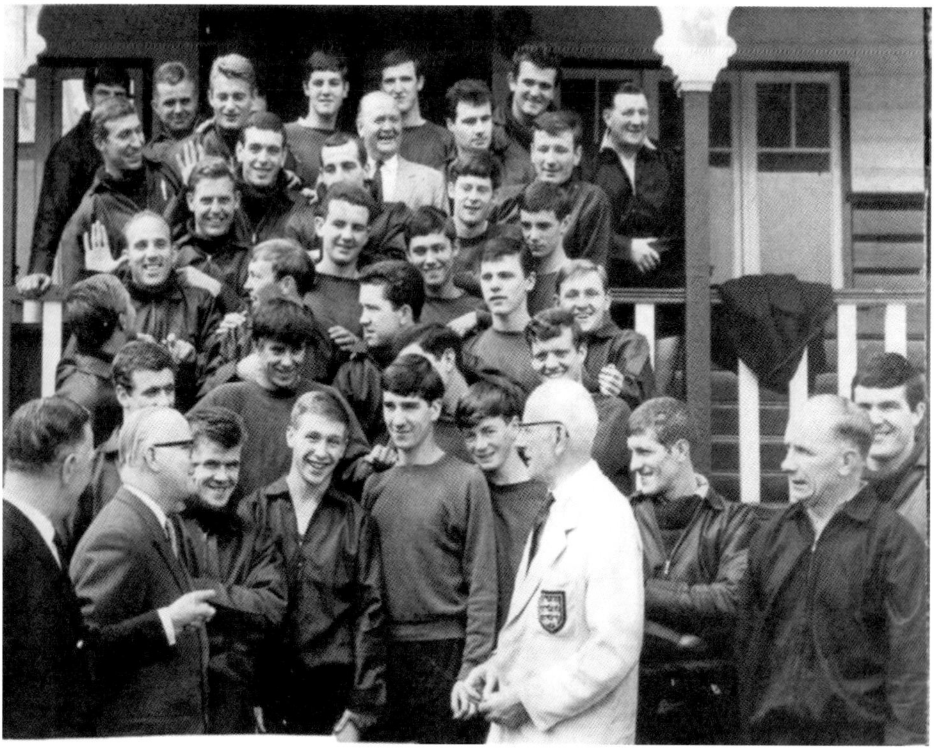

Welcomed by chairman TV Williams for pre-season training at Melwood

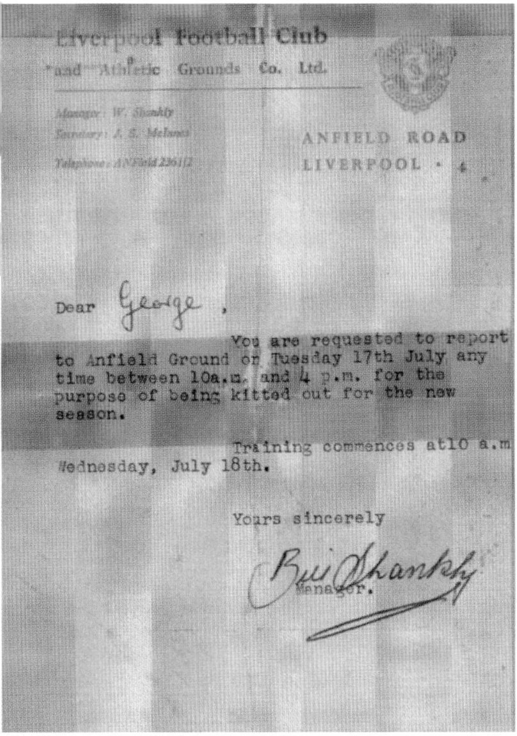

Liverpool Football Club
and Athletic Grounds Co. Ltd.

Manager: W. Shankly
Secretary: J. S. McInnes
Telephone: ANField 2361/2

ANFIELD ROAD
LIVERPOOL · 4

Dear George,

You are requested to report to Anfield Ground on Tuesday 17th July any time between 10a.m. and 4 p.m. for the purpose of being kitted out for the new season.

Training commences at10 a.m Wednesday, July 18th.

Yours sincerely

Bill Shankly
Manager.

The dreaded return-to-training letter from the boss

Wearing my American tour suit but sadly I missed the tour

Scoring a diving header at the Kop end with Tommy Smith looking on

Liverpool reserves v Manchester United reserves

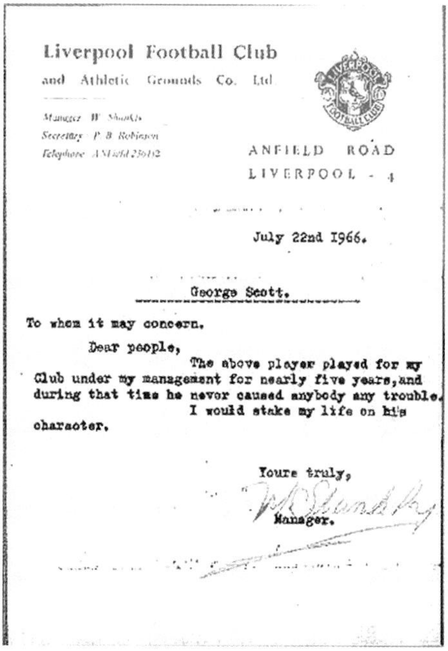

Liverpool Football Club
and Athletic Grounds Co. Ltd

Manager W. Shankly
Secretary P. B. Robinson
Telephone ANfield 2361/2

ANFIELD ROAD
LIVERPOOL - 4

July 22nd 1966.

George Scott.

To whom it may concern.

Dear people,
The above player played for my Club under my management for nearly five years, and during that time he never caused anybody any trouble.
I would stake my life on his character.

Youre truly,
W. Shankly
Manager.

My reference from Bill Shankly

OFFICERS

Directors :

S. C. REAKES, J.P. (Chairman).
H. Cartwright, (Vice-Chairman).
T. V. WILLIAMS (President).
Messrs. R. L. Martindale, M.B.E., J.P.,
G. A. Richards, J.P., C. J. Hill,
H. K. Latham, E. A. F. Sawyer.
T. Parker,

Manager : W. Shankly.
Secretary : J. S. McInnes.
Coach : R. Bennett.
Trainer : R. Paisley.
Asst. Trainer : J. Fagan.

Colours :

Red Jersey, White Shorts.
Red and White Stockings.

Ground : Anfield Road, Liverpool.

PLAYER'S TRAINING RULES AND INSTRUCTIONS.

1.—All players shall attend at the Ground for training at 9-45 a.m. daily (Match days excepted) and shall be under the orders of the Trainers for the rest of the day. Players must not leave the ground before 12-30 p.m.

2.—At the commencement of each season, every player must undergo a Medical examination and carry out the instructions prescribed by the Medical Officer of the Club. In cases of illness or accident, players must notify the Trainer or Manager, or arrange that he is notified immediately. Medical Officer of the Club—Dr. Reid, 111 Priory Road, Anfield, Liverpool, 4. (Telephone : ANF. 3724. Doctor's hours : Morning 9—10-30; Evening, 6—8.

LIVERPOOL FOOTBALL CLUB

Players' Rules and Fixtures

Season 1964—65

Bill Shankly's little red book of rules

3.—Players must not bring friends into the Dressing Room or Billiard Room without permission.

4.—Smoking in the Dressing Room during training hours is strictly forbidden.

5.—On match days all players must be at the ground 45 minutes before the advertised time of kick-off and at the station 15 minutes before the train starts.

6.—Players are entirely responsible for ascertaining the particulars on the Team Notices which are fixed in the Dressing Room each week.

7.—All players not selected to play in any team must be at the ground on match days and report to the Trainer in time to strip and play should any emergency arise. Players not taking part in Saturday matches must report at 9-45 a.m. on the following Monday for training.

8.—During the playing seaso players desiring to go Home a Week-ends must obtain the conser of the Manager.

9.—Players shall do everythin necessary to get and keep themselve in the best possible condition durin and after training hours so as t render the most efficient service t the Club. No player shall take pa in Dancing after Wednesday of eac week.

Players must not frequent Clul where gambling takes place intoxicants served.

10.—The Club will not responsible for the paying Players' wages for any period incapacity due to accidents wh motoring.

11.—No player shall write artic for the press or interview the pr without first obtaining permission the Manager.

12.—When on the field of play all players are under the orders of the Captain of the team.

13.—Any player wilfully disobeying the order of any instructions embodied in these rules will be dealt with at the discretion of the Directors.

14.—Players are responsible for the studding of their own boots. The Trainer will attend to them as desired.

W. SHANKLY,
Manager.

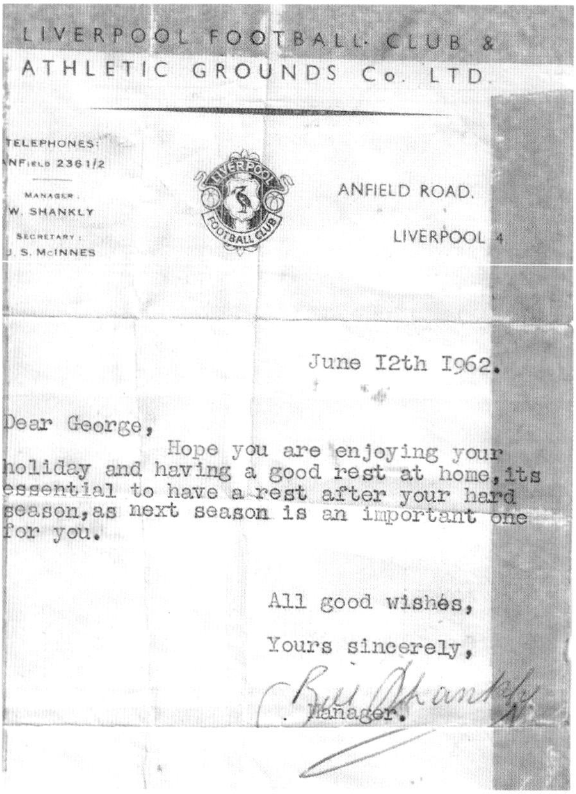

LIVERPOOL FOOTBALL CLUB & ATHLETIC GROUNDS Co. LTD.

TELEPHONES: ANFIELD 2361/2

MANAGER: W. SHANKLY

SECRETARY: J. S. McINNES

LIVERPOOL FOOTBALL CLUB

ANFIELD ROAD.

LIVERPOOL 4

June I2th I962.

Dear George,

Hope you are enjoying your holiday and having a good rest at home, its essential to have a rest after your hard season, as next season is an important one for you.

All good wishes,

Yours sincerely,

Bill Shankly

Manager.

Bill Shankly's letter telling me that next season will be an important one for me

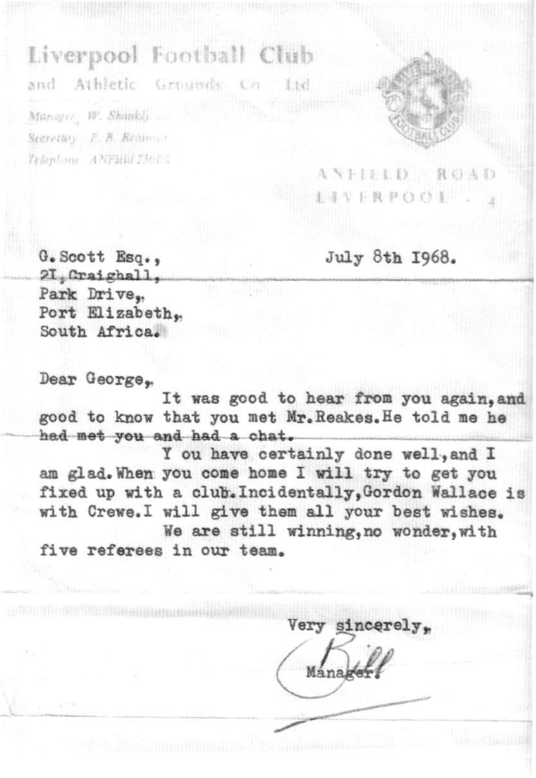

Liverpool Football Club

and Athletic Grounds Co Ltd

Manager W. Shankly

Secretary P. B. Robinson

Telephone ANField 2361/2

LIVERPOOL FOOTBALL CLUB

ANFIELD ROAD

LIVERPOOL 4

G. Scott Esq.,
2I, Craighall,
Park Drive,
Port Elizabeth,
South Africa.

July 8th I968.

Dear George,

It was good to hear from you again, and good to know that you met Mr. Reakes. He told me he had met you and had a chat.

Y ou have certainly done well, and I am glad. When you come home I will try to get you fixed up with a club. Incidentally, Gordon Wallace is with Crewe. I will give them all your best wishes.

We are still winning, no wonder, with five referees in our team.

Very sincerely,

Bill

Manager.

The letter Bill Shankly sent me in South Africa offering his help

Ian turned professional in 1965 and went on to play 69 times for Liverpool, scoring four goals. I became good friends with him at Anfield, although we didn't see much of each other for many years after I left the club. We did, however, get back together during his final years, at charity events and on the golf course. I'll always be grateful for that.

The last time I saw Ian was at one of these events. I remember the day vividly; it took place at West Derby Golf Club in the autumn of 2018. Gordon Wallace and I played a few rounds with Ian that day and we were both devastated to hear of his passing in February 2019. He left behind a wonderful family and many friends, and he is very sadly missed by everyone who knew him.

I remember, while we were having dinner, that Ian had the whole table in fits of laughter as he recalled what he described as the 'game of his life'. It had been against the great Bayern Munich. Shankly had surprised Ian and everybody else by selecting him for the quarter-final second leg of the European Fairs Cup in 1971, at the Sechzger Stadion in Germany. However, his delight was tempered by the fact that the boss had tasked him with the job of man-marking one of the greatest players in world football, Franz Beckenbauer. He recalled Shankly's words: 'Son, your job is to mark Beckenbauer. Don't give him a kick of the ball. If he goes to the toilet at half-time, you go with him.'

During the game, Ian stuck to Beckenbauer like glue and the German superstar grew increasingly frustrated. At half-time the game was goalless, which meant the Reds had maintained their 3-0 lead from the first leg at Anfield. As you can imagine, Ian was feeling really pleased with himself and he would have been brimming with pride when Shanks approached him in the dressing room and said, 'Well done son, you've got Beckenbauer in your pocket.'

In the second half, Ian got a bit more adventurous and in one move almost scored, but put his shot over the bar. His disappointment at not getting his first goal in European competition almost convinced him to stick to his defensive duties. However, with just 15 minutes of the game remaining, he spotted another opportunity to get forward. Suddenly he found himself in the Bayern box and on the end of a cutback from Peter Thompson. Ian smashed the ball high into the roof of the net and in that instant he was on top of the world.

Ian was ecstatic. Not only had he scored his first European goal, he had also marked one of the world's best players out of the game. Or so he thought.

Two minutes later, Beckenbauer escaped his shackles and delivered a great pass to his centre-forward, Schneider, who levelled for Bayern on the night. The Reds saw out the remainder of the game and ran out 4-1 winners on aggregate. They had reached the semi-final.

Ian had been in full-on party mood, jumping around the dressing room and high-fiving everyone. His grin was as wide as the Mersey, when Shanks approached him and wiped the smile off his face. He had expected to receive the great man's heartfelt congratulations but would be sorely disappointed. Shanks simply told him he should have scored two and reminded him that he lost Beckenbauer for the equaliser.

In future years Ian's career took something of a similar path to that of his contemporary at the club, Roy Evans, and he would eventually move into management. However, first there would be a spell at Aston Villa, who paid £60,000 for his services in 1972. There, he captained the side to promotion to the First Division and helped them to win the Football League Cup.

Loan spells at Notts County and Northampton Town followed, before he joined Peterborough United in December 1976. It was here that he took on a coaching role after making 100 appearances during two and a half seasons. After a spell as coach and caretaker manager at Wolves and then Hereford, Ian moved to Iceland in 1984 to manage Valur. There he would lead the team to the Icelandic championship in 1985 and 1987.

On 30 September 1987, he signed a two-year contract with Reykjavík Football Club but stayed until 1991. After a return to the UK and managerial roles at Huddersfield Town, Ian returned to Iceland in 1993 to manage Keflavík. By this time, Ian had become something of a legend, and a much-loved figure in Icelandic football.

He ended his football career, fittingly, in his native Scotland, managing Berwick Rangers in 1996. Ian was just like his great mentor Bill Shankly, a football man to the core. He gave great service as a player and in management. He loved the game so much and is missed by everyone who had the good fortune to know him.

Ronnie Yeats

I first met Ronnie Yeats long before he joined Liverpool – in Aberdeen Lads Club in around 1957. I would have been just 12 years old and Ronnie had just signed for Dundee United. He was attending an event where he would present prizes to the young players. Even then he was a giant, especially compared to me, a scrawny primary school pupil.

Ronnie was serving an apprenticeship as a slaughterman at the Aberdeen Cattle Mart, and the man responsible for looking after him was the father of my good friend, George Stables. The slaughterhouse was on Hutcheon Street, which was only a few streets up from where my family and I lived in Spring Garden. I still vividly remember the awful smell and the wailing of the farm animals being prepared for slaughter.

Such an inauspicious start for a Liverpool legend. It still amazes me to think he may have spent all his working days in that job, had it not been for his immense footballing talent. He had been initially noticed by the Scottish Highland League club, Elgin City. He had an unsuccessful trial with them, but was picked up by Scottish Division Two part-timers Dundee United. Ronnie played a huge part in getting the Tannadice team promoted in his first season there and he would help them maintain their position the year after.

All the while, Ronnie's progress was being monitored by Shankly, and Liverpool would eventually sign him for £20,000. That was a substantial fee for the Liverpool board to approve and they would soon top that by paying £30,000 to Motherwell for Ian St John.

Ronnie and St John would become the first two pieces in Shankly's jigsaw. Ronnie was instantly installed as captain, a role he carried out with distinction. He was, for me, one of the greatest captains in the club's history.

Who could forget that glorious day in May, when his mud-covered hand shook the gloved hand of the Queen of England, who was appropriately dressed in red that day, as she handed the FA Cup to him? Ronnie had become the first Liverpool captain in the history of the club to hold that old trophy aloft.

Ronnie was the Virgil van Dijk of his day. He dominated every game he played in. For a big man, his distribution of the ball was excellent, and he always seemed in control of any situation. Very few forwards could master Ronnie in the air, where his height and wonderful physique gave him such a big advantage when challenging for the ball, just as it did when he was making vital tackles.

Off the field he was a gentle giant and was always willing to give advice and support to the younger players. We all had the greatest respect for him as a man and as a wonderful captain of the club.

I often tell the story of how Ronnie once struggled to cope with close season boredom. It reached such a point that he started putting the word about that he would be willing to take up some sort of part-time job. The lads got wind of this and started to make suggestions as to what he could turn his hand to. One of the directors, I think it was Syd Reakes who later became chairman, was at Melwood and heard this banter going around. He decided to join in the fun and shouted to us, 'I tell you what would suit you in the summer Ronnie, a lifeguard job on Formby Beach.'

Tommy Smith shouted, 'That's no good, Mr Reakes, Ronnie is not a good enough swimmer.'

Bill Shankly had been standing at Tommy's shoulder, and immediately quipped, 'That would be no problem, Tommy. Look at him, he could wade out for two miles.'

Ronnie was unfortunately one of the high-profile older players who became victims of the ruthless cull Shankly implemented in 1970. Shanks knew he had to rebuild the team, who were fading after the glory of the mid to late 60s.

After 454 games, Ronnie left Liverpool in 1971. He would take over as manager of Tranmere Rovers, and he stayed there until 1974. His continuing football journey would see him tour around non-league football before leaving for a short spell in the US. Liverpool casts a long shadow though. Many of us ex-players can't stay away for too long, and Ronnie would return to Anfield as chief scout, a role he carried out until his eventual retirement in 2006.

Ian St John

The signings of Ian St John and Ron Yeats were without doubt a turning point for Shankly and Liverpool. St John was already a Scottish international. A prouder Scotsman you could never wish to meet; it amazes me that Shanks could persuade him to play in the second tier of English football.

Without a doubt, St John and Yeats became the cornerstones of Shankly's Liverpool. They were also huge personalities both on and off the pitch. Having said that, neither saw themselves as too big to help the younger lads at the club. Shankly had created a family; first teamers, reserves and apprentices were all equally important.

Ian St John had everything you could wish for in a player. He had charisma, personality and skill on the ball. Plus, he had tremendous vision when picking out a pass. I always felt his very name oozed glamour. He scored a hat-trick on his debut, a dream start to his career as it came against Everton in the final of the Liverpool Senior Cup at Goodison Park.

You could say that St John was Anfield's first superstar of the 60s. He couldn't go anywhere on Merseyside without being recognised and mobbed by the fans. Many of Roger Hunt's goals were from wonderful passes from Ian. They were the 1960s equivalent of Dalglish and Rush. Think, Gerrard and Torres or Gerrard to Suarez and you will get the picture.

Ian wasn't just a pretty face either. He had a huge personality and wonderful sense of humour. I always remember his laugh, always so contagious. It's a quality he retains to this day.

That was the St John you would meet off the field though. On it, he could be a true hard man who took no nonsense from any opponent. I remember on one occasion he felled Mark Pearson, of Fulham, in a match at Craven Cottage, with a left hook that Muhammed Ali would have been proud of.

There is another story that has been retold many times and while some may feel it has been embellished, I can personally vouch for its accuracy. It concerns St Simon and St Jude's Church on Anfield Road, which was virtually opposite our lodgings. Bobby Graham, Gordon Wallace, Phil Tinney and I used to go to the church youth club occasionally. One Sunday morning we were walking along when we noticed the sign outside the building had a new message written on it. In coloured print it asked passers-by to reflect on:

'WHAT WOULD YOU DO IF JESUS RETURNED TODAY?'

Never ones to miss an opportunity, some Scouse wag had scrawled in bold ink, the words:

'MOVE ST JOHN TO THE RIGHT WING'.

Ian was and is a Liverpool legend. He always will be. The success he had in later life, working in the media was much deserved and enjoyed by so many people.

In recent years Ian hasn't been in the best of health. However, in a manner typical of his character, he has shown tremendous spirit in fighting his health problems. We still meet up occasionally and I so enjoy his company, and his humour. He still greets me as 'Wee Georgie', a name he gave me all those years ago.

I was talking to him on the phone recently and telling him how Carole and I were planning a visit to Edinburgh for the weekend. In a flash he replied, 'You going up there to visit your money Wee Georgie?' He followed it with that trademark laugh and we both cracked up. It's typical of the man's humour.

Chapter Five

The Boot Room Cabal

THE NAME of the Boot Room at Anfield is as revered in football as the ground itself. It was home to some of the greatest and most successful minds in the game. From that humble cupboard – a less illustrious space you could never wish to find – sprang forth a sporting dynasty that has never been rivalled in the history of the game.

The root of its success lay not in the vision, skill or brains of just one man. Instead it was a collective, in which each of its members worked seamlessly and with synergy. In short, the Boot Room was greater than the sum of its parts. This is the reason why, when Shankly moved on in 1974, the club were able to appoint Bob Paisley, and simply sit back and watch as he took them to new heights. And, in turn, they would later turn to Joe Fagan who delivered a treble in his first season.

The Boot Room operated in secrecy and demanded loyalty and hard work. There was no playing one off against the other, and when a decision emerged from within those walls, each and every member would stand by it. There must have been disagreements, but we never knew it.

Here are my personal recollections of the great men who formed part of that magical collaboration. Sadly, except for Roy Evans, they are all gone now. But their legacy is all around us.

Roy Evans

Roy Evans was a Shankly Boy who became one of the Men of Anfield. Because of that, I have agonised over which chapter to put him in. In the end, I have opted to include him alongside his Boot Room colleagues in this one. It was, after all, in this arena that Roy made his greatest contribution to the club.

He joined Liverpool in 1963 and was an apprentice for a couple of years before signing professional papers in 1965. I was playing in the reserve team while Roy was battling away trying to make a name for himself, and I was aware of his ability and of course that he was another young local prospect.

I have read in recent years that Roy, as a schoolboy, had the pick of several clubs including Manchester United, Chelsea, Everton and Wolves. However, the call of Liverpool proved just too strong to resist.

I still have a photograph of the squad at home, and Roy is sitting in the front row, along with Shankly. I have often shown people that old photograph and asked them to identify the Liverpool managers in it. Only a few of them point to Roy.

Roy, like me, had to be extremely patient. He didn't see a hint of first-team action until the 1969/70 season. Of course, I had long since left the club by then. As is so often the case, it would take an injury to a first-team player – in this instance Geoff Strong – to open the door for him.

Roy would play just 11 times for the club and, just as I had, he would try his luck on foreign shores, joining Philadelphia Atoms on loan in 1973.

However, his destiny was intricately entwined with the club he had grown up supporting, and when Bob took over from Bill, he offered Roy a place on the coaching staff, in 1975. He would have been just 27 and it was surely one of Bob's most inspired signings.

Roy learned his trade alongside some of the greatest football brains in the game. Little wonder he led the reserve side to nine Central League championships and eventually went on to manage the club. His one League Cup seems scant reward for such dedicated and loyal service over so many years. However, his contribution to Liverpool Football Club is measured in the players he developed and the exciting football his teams played in the 1990s.

I feel great whenever I bump into Roy. He always has time for a friendly word, and he has never changed, despite all he has achieved in the game. There aren't many men who can say they rose from the Boys' Pen in the Kop before becoming an apprentice footballer at the club they adored and ultimately its manager. What an achievement.

Reuben Bennett
1913–1989

Reuben was an amazing character. His stories would keep us entertained for hours. By the time I met him, he had already had a distinguished career in football. A talented goalkeeper, he had played for Hull City, Queen of the South and, after the war, Dundee.

One of his tales was about how he held the world record for the longest punch-out by a Scottish goalkeeper. When we looked at him incredulously, he proceeded to regale us with this story:

'Well boys, I was playing for Third Lanark against Raith Rovers at Starks Park in Kirkcaldy,' he began, 'when a cross came over and I came out with both knees up, hit the centre-forward in the back, and punched the ball so hard that it went out of the stadium and landed in a goods carriage. It ended up in Aberdeen.'

This story may have been true, because Starks Park is Raith Rovers's home stadium and is right next to the Edinburgh to Aberdeen railway line.

If you went down injured in the five-a-side games and stayed down for any length of time, he would remind us of how lucky we were that we weren't playing in the Aberdeen junior leagues, as he had.

'We played on cinder pitches,' he would say. 'If you stayed down in those days, the trainer ran on brandishing a wire brush to scrape the cinders off your leg. We would always be on our feet before he reached us. There were no bloody magic sponges in those days, son.'

Reuben is rightly recognised as one of the founding members of the Anfield Boot Room tradition. He was loyal and devoted and would implement whatever strategy was cooked up in that sacred space with vigour. He had tasted management with Ayr United between 1953 and 1955. However, he was clearly cut out to be a coach. He would be the only one of that original 'gang of four' Boot Room legends who didn't go on to manage the club.

However, his contribution over the years is immeasurable.

We all loved and respected Reuben; he was always known by us as Ben and without doubt he was the company sergeant major of the coaching staff, always cajoling and shouting instructions. He used to pride himself on his toughness and used to walk around in the winter in his short sleeves and if anyone of us asked him if he wasn't feeling the cold, he would shout, 'What do you mean cold son? Its's bloody tropical. I'm from Aberdeen.'

Reuben would challenge us youngsters to 100-yard sprints but would stipulate we had to give him 'yards for years'.

He was 44 and we were 16, so that meant he got a 28-yard start in a 100-yard sprint. Needless to say, he always won.

Being fellow Aberdonians, I felt Reuben always kept an eye on me. He had promised my parents as much when I signed. He was an amazing and inspirational man.

Ronnie Moran
1934–2017

Ronnie was an incredible servant of the club. When I arrived, he was still a player, of course. However, during his time at Anfield he must have undertaken every job at the club.

As a player Ronnie was a really good, strong full-back with legs like tree trunks and he must have been a fearsome sight for some of the wingers who played against him over the years. Along with Gerry Byrne on the other flank, they were a good partnership.

He had a great left foot and his strategy for taking a penalty seemed to be to just put his foot through the ball and woe betide the keeper facing him if he got in the ball's way.

He struck me as being a very good organiser of play from the back, always shouting and encouraging his team-mates and I'm sure that Shankly soon realised the qualities that Ronnie's experience, enthusiasm and tactical awareness would bring to the Anfield coaching staff as his career was coming to an end.

Ronnie once shouted to me, 'Slow down Scotty son, you are running so much you are damaging the grass.'

One of my first memories of him, though, involves a preseason trip to San Remo in the Italian Riviera in 1963. The club didn't have a preseason tour that year, so Shankly took Tommy Smith, Bobby Graham, Gordon Wallace and me, along with the rest of the first team as a reward for reaching the final of the FA Youth Cup. Tommy Smith had captained the side, but Gordon had unfortunately been ineligible for the FA Youth Cup competition, due to being just over the age limit for the competition by a few months. I thought this was a huge blow, because Gordon's ability would have been a huge help. We will discuss that competition later.

Ronnie and another first-teamer, former England international Alan A'Court, took it upon themselves to look after us and keep us on the straight and narrow. Ronnie's speech to us at the start of the trip will stay with me forever.

'Lads, listen up; never forget that you are always on duty when representing this club and there are standards to uphold. I know you are young and looking to have a good time, but there are standards to uphold so don't let yourselves or the club down.'

A few years later, when I was leaving Anfield and on my way out of the stadium for the last time as a player, I bumped into Ronnie and had my last conversation with him until many years later. I told him how gutted I was to be leaving the club. Shankly had been very sympathetic and had said some very kind words, which we will come on to later. I told Ronnie what the boss had said.

I half expected him to fall about laughing, but he didn't. I suppose his years of experience told him that I wasn't in a good place and could do without any mickey-taking. Instead, he said to me: 'You know the boss is the world's greatest exaggerator George, but I can tell you he would not say those words to just anyone. So, take it as a compliment.'

With that, he shook my hand and wished me the best of luck at my new club, Aberdeen. He also told me to remember all the lessons I had learned during the five years I had spent working under, as he put it, the greatest coaching team in the game.

His parting shot was, 'I think you have been unlucky not to have made the breakthrough son.' Then, he paused and said, 'Mind you George, I think Pelé would struggle to get into this team.'

I always had the highest respect for Ronnie. We all did. To me, it was obvious he would eventually move on to the coaching staff. He would maintain discipline within the ranks and stood no nonsense. But he had a big heart and if you always gave 100 per cent, you had nothing to fear from him. He did everything with a great sense of humour too and his love for Liverpool always shone through.

Ronnie was an inspiration to us youngsters. We admired his enthusiasm; his fantastic determination to win, even in the five-a-side games, set him apart. He never held back on a tackle. These were, of course, the very qualities that Shankly admired in him.

The word legend is easily applied in football, but Ronnie (Bugsy) Moran is genuinely deserving of that title. He was there before Shanks arrived and he was there at the start of the glory years. More than that, though, he helped shape the success that followed.

What a privilege it was to see first-hand what miracles they produced at Anfield in those early days and to have been even a small part of all that.

Joe Fagan
1921–2001

Joe Fagan was the coach of the Liverpool reserve team for the whole of the three years that I played in the Central League for the club. He was a brilliant coach and mentor too, always encouraging me throughout my time.

I'm certain that players like Alfie Arrowsmith, Bobby Graham, Gordon Wallace and myself had the ability to walk into the first team of many other clubs, even though we were very young. Doing so at Anfield, though, was a different matter altogether. The others did make their mark at Liverpool, but I had to make do with the occasional selection, travelling with the team as 12th man. I would carry the skip full of kits, though I knew I would never get on the pitch as there were no substitutes allowed in those days.

I remember one day when I was selected as 12th man for a game against Leicester City at Filbert Street in October 1962. It was two weeks before my 18th birthday and we stopped for a light meal. Roger Hunt was complaining of a stomach ache.

I dared to dream that I may just have got my opportunity as, if Roger was out, I would have been Shankly's only option. I recall feeling disappointed when Roger made a rapid recovery and my chance had gone. Such was the life of the reserve and Joe understood that, and would always know when it was the right time to put an arm around the shoulder.

Like Ronnie, Joe was also passionate about maintaining the very highest of standards at the club. When I first arrived at Anfield, Joe had delivered a stern warning about the many temptations the city had to offer. He was particularly vocal about Scotland Road, where there was famously a pub on every corner. We were left in no doubt as to what the consequences would be if we were ever seen in one of them.

Having hardly missed a game in three years playing for Joe in the reserve team and given my all, I was naturally disappointed to not make the breakthrough. It seemed that no matter how much effort I put in, no matter how many goals I scored, it was never enough. Anyone who has played the game at any level will understand how hard that can be.

Keeping yourself motivated through all of that can be a huge challenge. Occasionally, you lose heart. Whenever that happened to me, Joe was always able to lift me and keep me motivated. Towards the end of my time at Anfield, during the 1964 season, I did start to get very frustrated. I had scored eight goals in four games and felt I had earned my chance. I plucked up the courage and approached Joe.

I asked him, 'What more do I have to do?' I felt so frustrated and I'm sure he could see that in my eyes. His reply, though, was so matter of fact.

'George, you are one of the fittest lads in the club. You just need to maintain your enthusiasm and be ready when you get your chance. Keep going. Be the top scorer for the reserves again if you can. That's all you can do. Your chance will come, and you'll be ready.'

Of course, sadly in the end it didn't. But from the tone of his reply, I knew he was right. What choice did I have? Joe had no time for sulking or moaning. He continually stressed that I should never give up and keep giving myself personal targets. It was the only way. It was the Liverpool way.

I'll always remember my last meeting with Joe, after Bill Shankly had told me that my time was up at the club. Joe told me he knew I would be successful in my future football career. 'But,' he said, 'you'll do well in whatever you choose to do.'

I genuinely thought I could see in his face the same sadness that I felt. His job as reserve-team coach was to create players for the first team, and I think he was upset that he hadn't managed that for me. He went on:

'Don't ever think of yourself as failing son.' Then he shook my hand and said, 'Good luck and never lose your enthusiasm.'

I never saw Joe again, but like Bill Shankly, Bob Paisley and Reuben Bennett, he had a tremendous influence on my life. I was so thrilled when got the manager's job after Bob. He achieved something quite incredible in winning three huge trophies in his first season in charge. He had already decided to leave prior to the Heysel Stadium disaster, but the impact of that on this very special man was significant. I feel it almost broke his spirit. It was a terribly sad end to a wonderful career.

Bob Paisley
1919–1996

I only knew Bob as the first-team trainer during my five years at Anfield, and at the time I don't think I was alone in thinking that that perhaps that was as far as he would want to go at the club. Shanks was such a dynamic personality, the opposite of Bob in so many ways. Paisley was always so calm. It was almost as if he was operating under the radar.

Bob's main role, alongside Reuben and Joe, was to implement Shankly's instructions to the letter. But Bob was also master in the area of physiotherapy and the treatment of players' injuries. He could quickly diagnose injury problems and he used to spend lots of time in the treatment room, helping players recover as quickly as possible.

At Melwood, he was regarded as a brilliant tactician and a master at analysing the strengths and weaknesses of opponents. Bob and Shankly would have many meetings, preparing the training modules and discussing tactics with the first team. Often Reuben Bennett and Joe Fagan were involved too. Joe was the reserve-team trainer at the time.

When Shankly retired, there may have been some doubts amongst the senior players about whether Bob could fill Shankly's shoes, but I know, without exception, the players were delighted to see continuity maintained. He was a hugely popular figure with the players and he really did have a dry sense of humour.

Ronnie Whelan tells a wonderful true story of how he scored on his debut at Anfield, but his dad, who always watched Ronnie play throughout his career, had missed the game due to illness. The following day, Ronnie's father said he would be coming over from Ireland for the next game, and asked Ronnie to get him four tickets. Ronnie dutifully went to see Bob and asked for the tickets. Bob asked him why he wanted four, and Ronnie said that his dad and his three uncles were coming over from Dublin for the game.

'No problem,' said Bob. 'You can have five.'

'That's brilliant Boss. Thank you so much. I really appreciate it,' Ronnie said, surprised by his manager's apparent generosity. 'But why five?'

'Because you're not bloody playing son,' came the instant response.

Bob had all the qualities needed for the manager's job: brilliant tactical awareness and years of experience as a player and as a coach under Shankly. He knew the Liverpool system inside out and there was a tremendous amount of respect for him. However, he was a man who never craved the limelight. Bob was never comfortable in front of a microphone or with addressing members of the press. He just didn't possess Shankly's charisma and knew it. So, he played to his own considerable strengths, which lay in his ability to judge players and to weave them into his wonderful team structures.

We now know he had, on many occasions, persuaded Shankly not to retire. He tried to do so again in 1974, but the great man wasn't for turning. This is evidence that Bob would happily have continued to serve in the background, if necessary. However, he would eventually settle into the role of boss and he would do it well.

For all Bill's achievements, and they are many, it's fair to say that Bob matched and eventually exceeded them. Bob signed some incredible footballers and ensured that the team continued to evolve throughout his tenure, adding one or two players a season and delivering success on an unparalleled scale.

The lyrics of Frank Sinatra's great song 'My Way' sum up Paisley's managerial career for me. It was a career which, in the end, surpassed even the great Bill Shankly's by some way. Bob delivered 19 trophies in just nine years. However, his style was uniquely his own, and how successful it proved to be.

While I have been writing this book, the club have recognised Bob's contribution with a new statue on Paisley Square at Anfield. It was just wonderful to see the unveiling of that statue, which depicts the iconic moment when an injured Emlyn Hughes is carried from the field of play on Bob's back. Like the great Bill Shankly, Bob will never be forgotten. Liverpool Football Club owes them both so much.

Bill Shankly
1913–1981

As I look at what Liverpool Football Club have achieved since I first travelled down from Aberdeen in 1960, I'm in awe. That success of course has many fathers. However, there is no doubting that without Bill Shankly it's unlikely we would be where we are today. He was undoubtedly the catalyst for everything that followed.

There have been many column inches and books written about the great man, so many in fact that it's difficult for me to do him justice here. Nevertheless, I'll do my best. I feel the best way to sum up the man's impact on me and the club is to share anecdotes that illustrate his personality and power. These tales of his tremendous wit and intellect may feel like old friends to the devotees out there, but to those for whom they are new, I feel they will give you a glimpse into the mind of the man.

So many come to mind, I barely know where to start. However, let's begin with one that relates to a great Liverpool forward, Alf Arrowsmith. Alf had been injured in a clash of heads right in front of the players' tunnel. He lay crumpled on the ground in front of the bench, which contained Shankly and his back-room staff. Today, the club doctor would run on, quickly followed by paramedics and various technicians armed with neck braces and spinal boards. Not back then, though.

As Alf lay unconscious on the Anfield turf, on rushed Bob Paisley armed with a bottle of 'smelling salts'. He promptly wafted the potion under Arrowsmith's nose and the player dutifully came to. Shanks was getting increasingly agitated in the dugout. His concern was that with no substitutes allowed, his team would be reduced to 10 against 11, and there was another half of football to be played. So, with hand cupped at the side of his mouth as if to amplify the sound of his voice, he shouted to Bob:

'Is he okay, Bob?'

Bob, who was busy assessing Alf's mental capacity and clearly deeply worried, replied, 'No Boss. He doesn't know who he is.'

Without a second's hesitation, Shanks shouted back, 'Tell him he is Pelé.'

Bill Shankly had no time for injured players. If you weren't fit to play, you didn't exist. To him all that mattered was winning the game. It may seem harsh, even cruel, but it was the mentality that built a footballing empire.

However, his desire to rush players back to first-team action would see him go to extraordinary lengths and sometimes with comic effect. The following story is a classic to those used to the after-dinner circuit. It has grown legs over the years, and some may fear there has been a fair bit of embellishment. Perhaps, but this version of the tale is reproduced here, exactly as Bob Paisley told it to me. I'll leave you to judge.

The story involved Jimmy Melia, Bob Paisley, Bill Shankly and some experimental German medical equipment. Jimmy was an old inside-forward in the late 1950s and early 60s. He was a brilliant player, but he was coming to the end of his career and, as a result, he would often find himself in the treatment room with various ailments.

Shankly had seen an advert for a German-manufactured machine that promised to clear up muscle injuries within a very short time. It used electrical impulses, something like a modern TENS machine. It arrived by special delivery and the boss couldn't wait to try it out. He asked Bob Paisley who was in the treatment room. Realising he had a guinea pig in Jimmy Melia, he said, 'Perfect! Let's try it out on him.'

Bob and Bill stormed into the treatment room with the machine and Bill started boasting of the machine's benefits and German technological efficiency.

'You are the first player in Britain to benefit from it, Jimmy; it will have you back playing in a week son,' said Shanks. Jimmy wasn't convinced, as he was a sceptical old pro. Bill told Bob to place the electric pads on Jimmy's thigh. Jimmy was nervous about an electric current going through his leg and wasn't keen to proceed.

'There is nothing to worry about Jimmy son; you will feel no pain, just a steady rippling of the muscle. I guarantee it will have you back playing by next weekend.'

'Start it gently Bob. Just give him 30 per cent power,' Bill said. There was no response from Jimmy. Bill pressed on.

'Increase it to 50 per cent Bob.' There was still no response and Jimmy continued to read his paper.

'It must need time to warm up, Bob. Increase it to 100 per cent power.' Jimmy still felt nothing and began to laugh.

'It looks like you've been conned by the Germans boss,' he said. 'Send it back and you might get a refund from them.' Just then, Bob bent down and picked up a loose cord.

'Sorry Boss,' he said, looking a little embarrassed. 'It's not switched on at the wall.' With that he flipped the switch on. The player began convulsing. I would imagine it felt like being tasered. Poor Jimmy didn't have much hair, but what hair he did have stood up like a bad perm, as he bounced around on the table screaming in agony.

Bob immediately switched it off at the wall and Jimmy settled down, probably cursing the boss and his assistant. Shanks simply walked out casually, declaring as he left, 'Serves you right for getting injured Jimmy. At your age you need to train harder.'

Another story relates to Shankly's handling of the media. He would always have them eating out of the palm of his hand. His skill with words and sublimely comic timing were among the characteristics that marked him out as a tremendous leader. Bill's big footballing idol was Tom Finney. To Shanks, Finney had no equal.

Following a home game against Southampton, which had seen a young Mick Channon shine, a young reporter from the

Liverpool Echo collared Shanks in the tunnel. With a degree of bravery that must be admired, the journalist asked what the boss thought of the Saints player.

Bill was very polite and told the reporter that he thought Channon was a very good winger indeed. The young scribe then decided to press his luck.

'Would you say he's as good a player as Tom Finney?' he asked, pencil and notebook in hand and ready to scribble the reply. Perhaps he could see the headline, with his name under it, 'SHANKLY SAYS CHANNON IS AS GOOD AS FINNEY.'

He would be sorely disappointed.

'Oh, aye,' Shankly said earnestly. 'This boy Channon is as good a player as Tom Finney; he has all the qualities Tom has, and he is every bit as good as him.'

The young reporter was busy scribbling away when Shanks delivered the killer punchline:

'But of course, what you have to remember is that Tom is 62 years of age now.'

I often entertain myself with thoughts of how Shankly would handle today's press and I'm sure he would thrive. He didn't reserve his rapier wit for the print media though. He could be equally devastating with the opposition.

Denis Law once told me this story, so it must be true. Before a home game at Anfield against Manchester United, Shankly came out of the club's daily draw offices and shouted to Matt Busby, Denis Law and Bobby Charlton, as they were walking to the players' entrance from the United bus: 'Matt, I've just bought a ticket in the daily draw raffle giving the time of the visiting team's first goal.'

Busby smiled, ready for the inevitable punchline. Bill didn't disappoint. 'It says a fortnight,' he shouted, to great hilarity.

His quick wit and irreverence were more than just entertainment, though. They helped create an aura around the man. You wanted to be in his company, you were desperate to play for him and you believed every word he said. He was a truly inspirational leader.

Bill was a major influence on my life and I'm sure the lives of countless other players and supporters of Liverpool Football Club. His passion and enthusiasm lit up the game, and the standards he set have inspired me over the last 60 years, since I first met him. I owe him so much and I'm grateful and very lucky that I crossed his path. Even though I was within a whisker of the first team in 1964/65, I understand why he had to let me go.

Bill looked after me over the years and that shows the caring nature of the man and his commitment to anyone who showed enthusiasm and gave of their best at all times. It's no wonder he is so revered and he will never be forgotten. What a man he was and what an unforgettable character. In reading this book, I hope you will see what a profound impact he had and continues to have on my life, not just in terms of football but in how I have conducted myself through all of these years. There really was, and always will be, only one Bill Shankly. He was the founder and undisputed leader of the Boot Room cabal.

Chapter Six

The Culture Club and the Stress of Empire-Building

THOUGH MY Anfield journey ended in disappointment, I was privileged to have witnessed life behind the scenes during the emergence of one of the greatest sporting institutions on the planet. In the five years I spent at Liverpool, I was blessed to have worked with the very best football people around. The lessons I learned there served me throughout my football life, but also in my personal and business life.

I want to transport you through the years and take you behind the scenes of that world. In this chapter, I'll reveal what the atmosphere of the place was like, uncover the unique culture created by Shankly, his 'little red book' of rules and regulations, and the relationships I built up with the players who served him and the club. You will gain an insight into the day-to-day routine of a young apprentice making his way at Anfield and the training routines implemented by the Boot Room Boys.

And, you will learn that the demands for success were relentless and, for some, they became unbearable. The Anfield empire was built with blood, sweat and tears and though we are talking about the game of football, nobody should underestimate the seriousness of the business behind it.

Every season started in the same way, with a written summons from Bill Shankly himself to report for preseason training. On club headed paper, the letter would be addressed to each player in person and would be brief and to the point.

Dear George,
You are required to report to the Anfield Ground, Tuesday 17th July anytime between 10 and 4pm for the purpose of being kitted out for the new season. Training will commence at 10am on the 18th July.

Sincerely
Bill Shankly, Manager

Not many players looked forward to receiving that letter, especially those who may have gained weight in the off-season. Today's players maintain their fitness year-round, but in the 1960s that wasn't always the case. As soon as that letter landed on the doormat, life at 258 Anfield Road would settle into a familiar routine until the following May. Each morning we would be encouraged out of bed by Mrs Murphy, our landlady, and assembled in the kitchen for breakfast.

There was no muesli, nuts, pulses and the like back then. Instead we faced a standard breakfast of egg cooked in every way possible: boiled, scrambled or fried and sometimes accompanied by a bit of bacon and sausage. This would be washed down with a cup of strained tea. Coffee was off the menu in those days.

Bobby Graham and Gordon Wallace would make the brief journey from their digs further along Anfield Road in time for us to make the short walk to the stadium together, arriving on time at 9am.

On arrival, we would collect our training kit, which consisted of a red shirt, white shorts and a burgundy tracksuit top. If it was cold, we got the tracksuit bottoms too. Footwear depended on the state of the pitch at Melwood. We would wear either leather boots with studs in them or rubber-studded boots. On one occasion, during a particularly rough winter in 1963, we were issued with baseball boots. We would run around in them in the snow for a few months.

As apprentices, we were responsible for the care of our own kit and for cleaning the senior professionals' boots as well, but more of that later. As soon as we were sorted out with our training gear, the coach would arrive at Anfield at around 9:30am. The whole squad, playing staff, senior professionals and we humble apprentices, would pile on to the bus together and make the journey to the club's training base, Melwood.

I recall how every time we boarded that bus we would be greeted by a sarcastic shout of, 'Hang on boys, here come the bloody stars of the future,' from Jimmy Harrower. This was part and parcel of life as an apprentice in those days and we took the many barbed comments and mickey-taking on the chin.

Jimmy had been with the club since 1958. Phil Taylor had signed him from Hibernian in a deal worth £11,000. And, like many of the lads who preceded the arrival of Shanks, he would have been worried about his place in the team and whether the boss fancied him or not. So, although his comments would have been made with a tongue firmly planted in his cheek, there was an edge to what he said.

Jimmy and others were right to be worried. Shankly would oversee a huge clear-out, as he began to stamp his mark on the club. I'm not sure I would say he relished this aspect of the job, but he didn't for one second shirk from the task. Jimmy, a talented, if not slightly inconsistent attacking player, would leave at the end of his contract in 1961, along with many others.

Harrower was quite a character, though. I remember one time, when I had secured a couple of tickets for a game. I left them on a table in the snooker room to do something else and when I returned, they were gone. Of course, nobody would own up to taking them. I was furious, and on the day of the game, I made my way to seats that the tickets were for. There was a young red-headed woman with her friend. I politely asked where she had gotten the tickets; she replied proudly, 'I got them from Jimmy Harrower.'

When I confronted him about it later, he just looked at me with an expression that said he had no idea what my problem was, and with a twinkle in his eye he just said:

'Ah, son, I thought you'd have a better view in the Band Box.'

That was the end of it. There was no arguing with that. Not as an apprentice anyway.

The journey to training would see us leave Anfield and turn on to Utting Avenue and then Queens Drive. Of course, this route would one day become the scene of future victory parades. Then we would reach the Jolly Miller pub and Holly Lodge Girls' School. As we waited at the traffic lights, we would often see the children waving to us from the playground. Then, the bus would make a left turn and head towards Melwood Drive. For five years I made that journey on virtually every weekday and on every other Saturday. As apprentices our trajectory was clear; we started in the C-team before moving through the B-team and eventually into the A-team. That's when the tension really kicked in. With our 17th birthdays approaching, a fateful meeting with the boss would loom large on the horizon. This was truly make or break for every one of us and the stakes couldn't have been higher. To a football-mad youngster like me, who dreamed of becoming a professional, the idea that the dream could be snatched away from me in a single conversation with the boss was hard to bear. Failure meant starting all over again at another club, or even looking for work outside of the game.

But, back to training and our preseason routine; Shankly, Paisley, Fagan and Bennett were masters at orchestrating training. In those days, at least unofficially, they would be ably assisted by Ronnie Moran. The whole squad would train together before being split off into apprentices, reserves and first-teamers for shooting practice. Great wooden boards had been erected on the Melwood grass and it's not hard, in the quiet moments, to still hear the thuds echo around my head as the balls hit their target.

Their installation led to the most intense sessions. Players were measured against the clock, with Paisley and Fagan, like drill sergeants armed with whistles and stopwatches, shouting at them at the top of their voices. Woe betide anyone who complained or slackened. Each player had to strike the ball against the board then control the rebound, run with it for 20 yards and then do it all over again, against the second board. It wasn't unusual to see players being physically sick as the body adjusted to this rigorous programme. The creation of the famous shooting boards in the corner of Melwood was a real innovation and it was eventually copied worldwide.

The attacking players lined up, each taking their turn, Callaghan, Hunt, St John, Thompson and even Tommy Smith. Reuben would call their name out and then pass a ball in front of them. In front of those boards would be a keeper (Tommy Lawrence on one board and Jimmy Furnell on the other). Their life's mission was to make it impossible for the striker to hit the woodwork. As each player ran on to the ball, their choice was to either power the shot past the keeper or take it round him and finish coolly. They were even permitted to use any rebound to torment the goalie a second time.

Across the Melwood grass, another four boards would be arranged in a tight square. Here the task was to keep rebounding the ball around the square without stopping. The ground would be muddy, and it would be churning up as you laboured away. It always seemed an eternity before the whistle blew and they allowed you to move on. It was torture and it had to be.

Once the first team had completed their timed sessions, it would be the turn of the other full-time professionals, mainly the reserve team, to repeat the routines. Once they were finished, the apprentices were up next.

I used to enjoy watching the old pros going through their paces. In later years, I would study the strikers and look for tips. I always noticed a difference for example between St John and Hunt in terms of the way they approached the sessions. St John would use his skill and guile, often taking the ball round the keeper or drawing him on and dinking it over him.

Meanwhile, Roger would just blast it into the board. Both were equally effective, of course.

It wouldn't be over then, either. Once these shooting and defensive routines were finished, the groups were reorganised and an apprentice could easily find himself on the same team as a first-teamer. This was incredibly important to me. To be able to train with the pros meant an opportunity to pit your wits against the best and learn from them.

The only exception to this was if Shankly and his lieutenants wanted to organise tactical plays, such as corners, throw-ins or free kicks. In these instances, the reserve team always provided the opposition.

This felt like gruelling stuff, but it helped Shankly's teams achieve a level of fitness necessary to climb out of the Second Division and go even further. I don't remember seeing too many players shirking or not giving it their all, either. If anyone was deemed to be taking it easy, they would be told firmly and immediately. It was tough, but fair.

Another challenge involved some players being corralled into groups and tasked with a couple of full laps of Melwood. The first would be conducted at a leisurely pace. It would then crank up a notch for the second, though, as each player jostled the man next to him in order to make it to the front of the pile. Each player's goal here was to get noticed and impress the coaching staff. It could get very hectic, particularly for us youngsters.

Once we got this out of the way, we would then be divided into specific groups, tasked with tailored exercise programmes. Some would be working with weights, others would be doing press-ups or push-ups, while some players would be asked to throw themselves into sprints.

The whole process was like a great production, beautifully choreographed by the coaching staff and the metronome would be the time taken for the completion of the laps. Once a group had completed two laps the whistle blew, and we would move on to the next training module. There was no escape and no hiding place. This was where you proved you had what it took, or you were out of the door. It was intense and utterly ruthless stuff and we worked at the highest level for the first few weeks of preseason, before things levelled off. Then, the ball-work would be introduced along with the five-a-side games. These felt like a blessed relief and it would seem as though the cobwebs of the closed season were finally blown away and you felt your fitness levels starting to return.

In all, preseason would last about five weeks. Shankly's whole philosophy revolved round the now famed pass-and-move theory, working in small triangles. The mantra was always about retaining possession and then switching things, even playing a long ball if appropriate.

Much like Jürgen Klopp today, he believed in the high press. You would hear him shout:

'Retain possession of the ball. If you lose it, get back behind it and fight to get it back.'

Full-scale practice matches would begin after about four weeks. This would usher in extremely competitive games between the first team and the reserve players. While a couple of games would happen behind closed doors, most matches took place on the main pitch at Melwood. Shankly would boast that the turf on that pitch was as good as Wembley.

The reserve sides played the same system as the first team and it was a recipe for massive success. As I look at what

Liverpool are doing today, bringing the youth teams and first team together at Kirkby, it just reinforces my long-held belief that in so many ways Shankly and the men in the Boot Room were ahead of their time.

Some of the boss's ideas may have been a little wide of the mark though. For example, Shankly had this theory that it was important for the sweat glands to close after training, and this took time after training finished. So, that's why we always drove back to Anfield from Melwood, before having a bath together. Then we would all eat together, usually steak, which Shankly swore by.

Today, the focus would be on warming down and plunging tired and aching muscles into ice baths, filling up on energy drinks and supplements. Science and sport move on, of course. But, in terms of Shankly's understanding that conditioning, psychology and diet were important, he was spot on.

Occasionally, he would insist on the players running back to Anfield from Melwood at the end of training. I often think what a sight we must have been to the locals, running through the streets in our training gear. I recall one day when we had all finished a particularly tough session. Shanks obviously thought we needed more of a push. Maybe he thought we weren't working hard enough. Whatever it was, as we all prepared to get back on the bus, he suddenly announced, 'Never mind the bus today. We'll be running back.'

Nobody dared complain but I could tell by the expressions on some of the senior players' faces that some of them didn't fancy it. I was always eager to impress, so I jumped straight into the task and made it back to the stadium in what I thought was a decent time. However, when I arrived with the other apprentices we were met with a disapproving scowl from the boss. Ian St John, Willie Stevenson and Ronnie Yeats had all made it back before us.

'You should be ashamed of yourselves boys. You are young lads and yet these older boys have beaten you back.'

Bill would later overhear Tommy Smith telling someone that he had seen the trio jumping on the 17D bus, where they had spent their time signing autographs and fraternising with surprised and delighted passengers, while we did the hard yards on unforgiving pavement. I have no idea what punishment he meted out for that infraction, but it wouldn't have been pleasant, I'm sure. In any case, those post-training runs were always chaperoned by Reuben Bennett from that day on. As strict as the boss could be, the lads would often find ways around his rules, within reason. It was all part of the game really and those stories would help bond us all together.

Everything was planned to the last detail during preseason. The management were always keen to avoid injuries to the players. I have always believed these men were way ahead of their time.

Then, it was on to the schedule of preseason friendlies. These were usually between local teams and they would cement our match fitness before battle commenced. Melwood in 1960 was a pretty run-down piece of land. There were three football pitches overseen by a wooden building raised above the grass. It contained just two dressing rooms and two large communal baths. That was it. Shanks saw massive potential in this humble training ground, though, and began a process that would transform it beyond recognition.

In 2019, Gordon Wallace and I were invited by club CEO Peter Moore to give a tour of Melwood to a representative of the Swedish Supporters Association, the wonderful Andy Beyer and his son. It was as much an eye-opener for us as it was for them. The facilities we observed were fantastic and included a top-class restaurant, where only the most nutritious foods were available. We wandered past rooms replete with banks of computers, and men huddled around them working out strategy, tactics and the current fitness of each player. There was a huge indoor training area, swimming pool and plunge pool, and lovely modern offices, especially Jürgen Klopp's.

The walls were adorned with photographs of legendary players and games. Inspirational quotes from my old boss were everywhere, even on the wall of the current manager's office. It felt strange yet uplifting to think that these sayings had passed into folklore, and that I was there when they were first uttered.

The biggest surprise for me, upon entering the modern Melwood, was seeing a photograph hung in the foyer. My heart leapt and I felt butterflies in my stomach as I spotted myself and the lads, captured in monochrome and being lectured by Shankly in front of the perimeter wall that sealed Melwood off from the surrounding community, well almost. Sitting atop the wall was a host of young kids. What memories that brought back. I felt the ghosts of long-passed heroes, of great men and incredible sporting feats everywhere. I thought of all those kids, who had bunked off school, clambering on top of bins or scrambling up the concrete barrier, their tiny hands and boots searching out the cracks and nooks in the wall and rising ever higher, until, at last, they could perch at the summit and gaze upon their heaven, just as my friends and I had clambered up that embankment at Pittodrie all those years ago.

I only had to close my eyes to bring back those memories, of all of us as young players living out our days behind that wall and sharing the same dreams as those urchins. I do feel a pang of sadness that this historic piece of land, soaked with history and the scene of so many great stories, will soon be sold to developers and turned over to housing. I still feel it would have made a fantastic facility for the local community in West Derby. That would have been a tremendous legacy. In today's world, I suppose money speaks louder than tradition.

I can only hope that those residents who are eventually fortunate enough to make a home on that piece of hallowed ground appreciate all that went before, that the walls of their houses resonate to the voices of Bill, Bob, Joe and Reuben, barking their orders through eternity.

As I gazed upon that old photograph, a wonderful snapshot in time, I was struck by how I looked exhausted, leaning on my knee for support, while the great Ian St John looked like he had been out for a stroll in the park. I confess that I can't remember much of what Bill was saying to us, except that he told me to stand up straight and take deep breaths. But, for sure, I do remember that he told us to sign every single autograph book offered to us by those youngsters on the wall. Shankly would never refuse an autograph.

Back to my account of an apprentice's life – after training, bathing and lunch were over, the established stars at the club and the senior full-time professionals all went off to do whatever they wanted to do in the afternoon. For the apprentices, our day was just beginning.

There were numerous jobs to do around Anfield. We would clean the first team's boots, fork the Anfield pitch and paint the turnstiles. The worst job of all, which we undertook after every first-team match, was to sweep up the rubbish on the Spion Kop. I'll leave to your imagination the detritus we encountered on that terrace. I'll simply say that it was virtually impossible for anyone to get to the toilet during a game.

The crush of 28,000 fans would be so great that many supporters would use rolled up newspapers through which they would urinate on to the stone steps. Today's match-going fans would be repulsed by this, but it was normal and necessary back then.

After our chores were over, we may have managed to fit in a game or two of pool or snooker, before heading back to our digs, exhausted. Our evening entertainment consisted of playing cards or listening to the hits of the 60s on a contraption called a Dansette record player. This was a monophonic unit, with a lever in the centre which could hold six or seven vinyl discs in place at the same time.

We thought it was a quite advanced device, because it would automatically drop each disc on to the turntable when the previous disc had ended. The needle would then swing across the record and drop on to it at just the right place. Then, the music would begin. I suppose it was the 60s equivalent of a playlist on today's MP3 players.

In my view, what we lacked in terms of technology, we more than made up for with the quality of the music, particularly in Liverpool. It was great to be young then, and particularly great to be young on Merseyside.

By 1963 things had started to change for me at 258 Anfield Road. My three fellow lodgers had left the club. Phil Tinney had been transferred to Dundee along with Alex Totten, and Hamish McKenzie was also released by Shankly and moved on to Brentford, eventually settling in London.

In addition to this, my landlady Mrs Murphy wasn't in the best of health and neither was her husband. So, I found myself in need of alternative accommodation. Fortunately, I had developed a close friendship with Peter Thompson, and he suggested that there was a spare room at his digs. He was staying with a Mrs Thomas in Lilley Road, just a short distance from the stadium. I jumped at the opportunity. This simple decision would prove to be one of the most momentous of my life.

Peter was one of the greatest wingers ever to play the game. I would marvel at his ball skills during training. He had everything; skill, pace, balance and supreme confidence. His ability to run any full-back ragged is now the stuff of legend.

In 1963 Peter travelled with the England team to Brazil in South America for a tournament which was billed by the press as the 'little world cup'. He would come home with an Outstanding Player of the Tournament trophy. That was some accolade, given the likes of Pelé took part in the same competition. However, that wasn't the only trophy he secured. When England played Brazil, a game they lost 5-1, Peter swapped his England jersey with one of the Brazilian players and I had initially thought he was prouder of that than of his trophy.

Peter and I were preparing to cut our landlady's hedges for her, and half in jest I asked if I could don the Brazil shirt for the task. Amazingly, he said yes. So, there I was, armed with a pair of shears and wearing a shirt worn by a Brazilian international player, while clipping shrubbery in an Anfield street. After a short while a young kid approached us. We were so accessible back then and locals would often come over to us and ask for autographs. I could see this lad was armed with a notebook and pencil and he was making a beeline for Peter, who was clearly his hero. Then he spotted my shirt.

'Is that a real Brazilian jersey you are wearing?' he asked. Of course, replica shirts weren't the thing back then, so it's easy to see why it would have caught his eye. I decided to exaggerate the truth a little and have a little fun.

'Of course it is son. It belonged to Pelé, the best player in the world,' I said.

His jaw dropped. 'How did you get it?'

'Peter swapped it with him in Rio de Janeiro. It belongs to Peter now. He's just letting me wear it for a little bit.'

With typical Scouse wit, the young lad simply retorted, 'Well, if it belongs to Peter now, then it still belongs to the best player in the world.'

Given that Peter and not Pelé won the player of the tournament award in South America, maybe the young lad had a point.

The two years I stayed with Peter in Lilley Road were great days. Every Saturday, when the first team were playing at Anfield, I was playing away with the reserves, and vice versa. After the games, we would meet up in town with the other players. Saturday evening was the only time we could really relax with a few drinks. Shankly had forbidden weekday attendance at any premises where intoxicating liquor was served, or where there was dancing. He always had his spies on the lookout for player transgressions and woe betide anyone who fell foul of these rules.

Living next door to us in Lilley Road were a Mr and Mrs Huxley. They were a lovely couple, whose young daughter Linda would often chat to Peter and myself. One day I happened to look out of our front window and saw this attractive dark-haired girl walk up next door's path. I immediately turned to Peter and said something like, 'I think Linda has a friend I'd like to meet.'

I wasted little time in asking Linda who this girl was and found out her name was Carole Kelly, they had been classmates at Childwall Valley Grammar School and now this raven-haired beauty was working at Coastlines Shipping Office, in Water Street, Liverpool, as an accountant.

Before long we were introduced and a few weeks later Peter and I were invited to a party in the house next door, as Linda's parents were away on holiday. I was determined to get to know Carole better and that evening I monopolised all her time. I still remember her beautiful dark hair, matched perfectly by huge brown eyes.

We kissed each other goodnight in the doorway of that house on Lilley Road, and neither of us knew then that we had just begun a love affair that would last a lifetime and go on to produce two wonderful sons and four fantastic grandchildren. It's a love that burns as brightly today as it did 54 years ago.

Carole and I were married on 30 July 1966, the same day as England won the World Cup. Peter Thompson and his then wife Barbara were guests at our wedding. If Sir Alf Ramsey hadn't decided to dispense with natural wingers in 1966, I'm sure Peter, who was part of the initial squad, would have been otherwise engaged on that day.

My friendship with Peter would also see me rubbing shoulders with stars of Liverpool's Merseybeat culture. One of them was Gerry Marsden, who I met at a party in Jimmy Tarbuck's house. Peter was quite a character back then and would often rub shoulders with local celebrities. This meant that I could impress Carole by taking her along to this star-studded event. Not that she was easy to impress.

In fact, our initial courtship had experienced a few ups and downs, but it seemed that destiny would ensure we would survive those. One example of this happened one evening, when I was thirsty and fancied some cola. There was none in the fridge at our digs, so I told Peter I was heading off to the local shop to buy a bottle.

Carole and I had lost touch for a few weeks, and it had seemed as though the relationship had fizzled out. As I walked along Lilley Road and turned the corner on to Prescot Road, I bumped straight into Carole.

'Oh, hello Carole,' I said. 'Are you calling in to see Linda?'

Carole wasn't about to give me an easy time of it, and she simply breezed past me calling out over her shoulder, 'I might be.' Then she was off on her way, but I would seek her out once more and we have been together ever since. From that moment, I couldn't have been more hooked. I knew I couldn't let her slip away again. How lucky it was that I felt thirsty at the precise moment she was walking along Prescot Road. It wasn't the first time I felt the hand of destiny, and it wouldn't be the last.

So, there we were, thanks entirely to Peter, sitting together in Jimmy Tarbuck's party when up comes Gerry Marsden. He was carrying a record album; I remember the cover was yellow and he was making a beeline for Peter.

'Listen to this Pete,' he said, sliding the vinyl record from the sleeve and placing it on to the Dansette. I was loving this. Here was I, with my girlfriend, rubbing shoulders with musicians and artists in a city that was at the centre of the cultural universe.

'This is going to be our next single,' continued Gerry. 'It's from *Carousel* and it's called "You'll Never Walk Alone". Let me know what you think.'

None of us knew what *Carousel* was, but we listened intently anyway. Gerry then lifted the needle from the record and turned to Peter.

'What do you think Pete?'

I'll never forget Peter's reply.

'Don't take this the wrong way, Gerry. But it's a bit slow. I preferred your last single, "How Do You Do It". I don't think it's as good as your other number one hit, "I Like It", either. They were more upbeat.'

Gerry just smiled, but he didn't look offended in any way. 'You wait and see,' he said with a grin. 'It's going to be big.'

So, there you have it; Peter Thompson and I were probably the first people on Merseyside to hear the song which came to represent the heart and soul of Liverpool Football Club. Thankfully, Peter was a better footballer than he was a music critic.

No matter what we did in the evenings, we always knew that the next morning the real work would start all over again. We loved the work, though, and looked forward to it so much, despite the toil. We especially loved the five-a-side games against the coaching staff and the trips to play our counterparts in the Lancashire League.

For home matches, Bobby, Gordon, Phil, Hamish and I would be picked up in a huge taxi, driven by a man called Fred. We got to know him well; he had a business on Utting Avenue. He would drive us to Melwood with a trailer attached to the back of the vehicle containing our playing kit.

They were great days, but of course in the fullness of time for those of us who were fortunate enough to be signed as professionals on our 17th birthday, things changed. Becoming a professional meant someone else was cleaning your boots, we were closer to the first team and, of course, we got to compete in the wonderful Central League, for the reserve team. I used to love boarding the coach at Anfield for the away games and travelling to play in many of the greatest stadiums in the Midlands and the north of England. It was a major step up and it felt like it.

The highlight of every week was the Friday morning. We would report for training and go through our routines as usual. But our minds would always be firmly fixed on what came afterwards.

As soon as the session had ended, there would be an almighty stampede, as we raced to the home team dressing room. There, on the noticeboard, Shankly would post the names of the first team and reserve team starters. Your stomach would ache with anxiety and anticipation as you rushed to see whether you had retained your place from the previous game.

I can remember the reactions of those who made it and those who didn't, and there couldn't be a greater contrast. Some would punch the air with their fists, spitting out the word 'yes!' through gritted teeth. Others would walk away silently, cursing their luck and nursing their frustration. There was a sort of pecking order to the squad lists. Nobody wanted to be a reserve for the reserve team. That meant you weren't likely to feature, and you would wonder if you were in the boss's plans at all. However, if you were reserve to the first team, you regarded that as a pat on the back and even a promotion, even though you weren't likely to feature in a game.

I think I only missed a couple of reserve-team games in those three seasons in the Central League, but the nerves would never diminish as I raced towards that dressing room. It was a great life, however, and I loved every minute of it. Shankly had created a tight-knit group of players who lived and breathed the club and the culture that surrounded it. He was a disciplinarian, but he could motivate and inspire also. He had so many gifts. Then, he had his rules, written in his 'little red book'. I still have a copy of mine from the 1964/65 season at home.

It's an official looking document and we would be presented with a new one each season. On the cover, in black capitals, are the words:

LIVERPOOL
FOOTBALL CLUB

Players' Rules
And Fixtures
Season 1964-65

Inside would be the names of the club hierarchy and officials. We were left in no doubt that this was the club's code of conduct and none of us would have fancied our chances if we ever transgressed.

Some of these rules were unsurprising – the need for an annual medical, what time you had to attend training, etc. Others may seem funny to today's supporters, but we lived and died by them all. The following, which I have selected from a longer list, may raise a few eyebrows to devotees of the modern game:

3 – Players must not bring friends into the Dressing Room or Billiard Room without permission.

4 – Smoking in the Dressing Room during training hours is strictly forbidden.

8 – During the playing season, players desiring to go home at the weekend must gain consent of the manager.

9 – Players must not frequent clubs where gambling takes place or intoxicants are served.

10 – The club will not be responsible for the paying of players' wages for any period of incapacity due to accidents while motoring.

11 – No player shall write articles for the press or interview with the press without obtaining permission from the manager.

12 – When on the field of play, all players are under orders of the Captain of the team.

13 – Any player wilfully disobeying the order of any instructions embodied in these rules will be dealt with at the discretion of the Directors.

Then, last of all and reading as something of an afterthought, especially given the menacing tones of the penultimate rule, we had:

14 – Players are responsible for the studding of their own boots. The Trainer will attend to them as desired.

W. Shankly
Manager

The addition of Shankly's signature was totemic. It was his seal and none of us dared to break that and hope to come off better for it.

After years in the second tier of English football, seeming happy to drift along without any real ambition, Liverpool Football Club was turning into a machine with only one purpose. Shankly's desire to not only gain promotion to the First Division, but to win it and then go on and dominate Europe was carved into the psyche of everyone at Anfield.

Supporters' dreams of glory and their demands on the players to give their all were as real in 1960 as they are today. Shankly would lecture us all that we owed them a debt of gratitude and that the greatest crime we could commit was ruining their weekend.

'They work hard all week and look forward to the game,' he would tell us. 'Do not let them down.'

Shankly was from a mining family and knew that playing football was nothing compared to the labours endured by those who pay up at the gate every week. We played for them and the club, but for them first and foremost, in his eyes. That message would seep into every corner of the club, and as we grew and developed, the strain would be felt amongst the team whose job it was to administer our rise.

One of the saddest days I can ever remember came right at the end of my time at Anfield. It involved the tragic suicide of Jimmy McInnes. Jimmy was the club secretary and a former Scottish footballer, who signed for the Reds as a defender in the 1937/38 season for the sum of £5,500. He played 48 times for Liverpool, managing one goal. Sadly, the outbreak of war would put paid to his playing career. He would retire in 1946 and later moved into the back office, where he became an extremely competent secretary for the club.

McInnis wanted success as much as any member of the Boot Room, player or supporter. He took the responsibility for delivering that upon his own shoulders. We would later learn that on many occasions he had taken to sleeping in his office.

He was under enormous strain and one day, at the end of his tether, the poor man ended his own life just four days after the FA Cup Final, on 5 May 1965. I was told that a group of apprentices and groundsman Arthur Riley were tending to the Anfield turf when they saw Jimmy emerge from the players' tunnel and walk straight past them towards the Kop. About 20 minutes later, his assistant Bill Barlow ran on to the pitch asking if any of the lads had seen Jimmy. They pointed him in the direction of the old stand on Walton Breck Road. It was at the back of the Spion Kop that poor Jimmy had hung himself from a beam, near one of the old turnstiles. The news rocked the club. Jimmy was a lovely man and such a great secretary for the club.

None of us had any inkling of the pain and torment he must have been experiencing. We all demand the very best as supporters, coaching staff and players, but we very rarely consider the impact that drive has on people who, like us, are just flesh and blood. The club took steps to strengthen its commercial and secretarial departments following the tragedy, in an effort to reduce the load on its staff. However, the provision of mental health support in football was still a very long way off.

Shankly was creating a machine, his bastion of invincibility. He wanted success for the club and its people more than anything else. He despised losing and he wanted everyone at Anfield to feel the same way, but he was devastated by the loss of Jimmy, a man he had worked with for over five years. In his autobiography, he would write:

'Jimmy was honest, and he was also quick-tempered. Sometimes he could be rude to people – some of them needed it, and he was right – but he would be gentlemanly with people he respected.

'There were some of us at Anfield with whom he never had a harsh word. Others would find him difficult to deal with and hard to understand. I've heard him calling somebody on the telephone and suddenly, bang! The phone would go down. Jimmy loved a game of snooker, and he was a good player. It was a change from his chores as Secretary.

'When the club began to be transformed, Jimmy got the lash of the success. There were only a few seats in the stand in those days and when we won the Second Division Championship, reached the FA Cup semi-final, won the First Division Championship and then won the cup, Jimmy's work was doubled and everything began to pile up on top of him. He needed help.'

There is a pang of regret in those words. I suppose that would have been felt by everyone who worked with the man. Success so often comes at a terrible price. For all the glory associated with those formative years, I'll never forget that the building of Shankly's empire wasn't easy or without pain or struggle.

Chapter Seven

Scott of the Reserves and Watching the Reds Hit the Summit

TODAY'S YOUNG Liverpool players are split into many age groups at the Kirkby Academy and the system is just so different to the one I experienced in the 1960s. Then, the Central League consisted of the First Division reserve teams and covered the north of England and the Midlands. We played every week, at Anfield if the first team was away, or on the road when the first team were in residence. It was an amazing experience to play in the great stadiums in English football. Running out at places like Old Trafford, Maine Road, St James' Park, Villa Park, Goodison Park, Hillsborough, Bramall Lane and all the rest of them will linger in my memory for all my days.

For the most part, the teams competing in the Central League were made up of young, up-and-coming players, trying to make their way in the game. This meant that youngsters like me got to play against some of the greats of the age. I'm privileged to be able to say that I have played against the likes of Alan Ball, Howard Kendall and Colin Harvey, and many more.

I'm also so grateful to have had the opportunity to play at Anfield every other week. Today's youngsters have variously played at Prenton Park or on the pitches at the Academy and rarely, if ever, sample what it's like to play on that hallowed turf. I can't help thinking we had it better in that respect.

Joe Fagan was our trainer for the whole time I played for Liverpool Reserves. He was the perfect mentor and ensured that we lived up to Shankly's famous quip, 'On Merseyside we've always had two great teams: Liverpool and Liverpool Reserves.'

Occasionally, if the first team weren't playing or if we had a midweek game, the boss would come with us on the coach. His presence meant the games would have added spice and we would be desperate to impress the great man. It meant he got to see us first hand, rather than just relying on Joe's report.

I recall one such trip, when Shankly was travelling with us to Preston North End, when he forced the driver to make a detour and drive past a plumber's business which was owned by his all-time hero Tom Finney. At this point he became a tour guide, regaling us with tales and tall stories about Finney's exploits for Preston before and during the war. Then we were driven past Tom's house; it was like a Mecca to Shanks.

We had to stifle the laughter when he came out with things like, 'Tom Finney could have played in an overcoat and still run past any full-back in the league.' Then there was, 'when Tommy took a corner, he made sure the lace of the ball was facing away from the centre-forward, so he didn't cut his head.'

It was all nonsense of course, but told with such passion you could almost imagine it was true.

After each away game for the reserves, I would meet Peter Thompson and his business partner Bernard Bargh for our regular trips to the city centre for drinks. I would boast about scoring for the reserves, only for Peter to top all of my tales, outlining in detail how he had beaten two men, raced to the byeline, then cut the ball back for Roger Hunt to smash it into the net.

I don't begrudge him those experiences. I loved my time playing in the Central League and in the FA Youth Cup. However, after 60 years it's hard to recall all of the details, particularly as the reserve-team games aren't as well documented as those of the first team. In preparing this book, I'm very grateful to Jonny Stokkeland, Liverpool Football Club archivist, who has provided me with my full Central League record. For all my obvious disappointment at not making the cut at Anfield, I can take great comfort from my record during five years at Liverpool Football Club. I simply could have done no more and I'm proud of my achievements.

I played 107 games in the Central League over three years, scoring 34 goals. In the Lancashire Cup, I managed five games and scored once. I loved playing in the FA Youth Cup too and managed six goals in 14 games. When you add in the 55 games and 30 goals I scored as an apprentice across the A, B and C teams, it's not hard to see why I feel I had earned at least a chance in the first team.

My 71 goals from midfield during 182 appearances would eventually endear me to Shankly, but sadly it was never enough. I think Shanks knew this and, in the years ahead, he would do his best to look out for me and guide my career. I'll talk more about that later.

Perhaps the pinnacle of my youth-team career was reaching the final of the FA Youth Cup at the end of the 1962/63 season. Our opponents were West Ham United and Shankly was brimming with pride. The competition was founded in 1953 and had quickly grown into one of the most prestigious competitions in English football, with clubs seeing it as a test of their scouting and development programmes. This would be Liverpool's first-ever appearance in the final.

The youth teams were referred to as 'Colts' back then. So, it was a final between West Ham Colts and Liverpool Colts. The Hammers were a strong side and featured players like John Charles, a future FA Cup winner, John Sissons and a young Harry Redknapp. Redknapp played on the right and Sissons on the left, and Shanks had earmarked them both for special attention when West Ham arrived at Anfield for the first leg. In the pre-match team talk at Anfield, Shankly had issued instruction to Tommy Smith to keep Sissons in check.

'This lad Sissons is a flyer, son. So, I want him in the Band Box in the first 15 minutes.'

Tommy, ever the loyal servant, dutifully obliged. Within 20 minutes Sissons was hobbling off the pitch, battered and bruised and cursing Smith as he went. He could be heard declaring angrily, 'The number four is a bloody psycho.'

It meant the Hammers' attack was blunted and we took full advantage, running out 3-1 winners. Unfortunately, Sissons would be fully fit for the second leg.

During the home leg, I crashed a header off the underside of the bar at the Kop end, in the final seconds of the game. I cursed my luck that night, but not as much as I did on the way home from the second leg in London. Had that strike gone in, we would have taken a three-goal lead into the second leg. I'm certain that would have been enough.

We made the trip down south just 48 hours later, on Saturday, 25 May. I remember the turnout being a shadow of the crowd at Anfield, with just 13,000 attending the match. It was an incredible game, and the Hammers, who had played four games in eight days, emerged victorious. However, the manner of their victory was truly heartbreaking.

As soon as the whistle sounded, we got straight into them. We were buoyed by our two-goal advantage, and with Shanks's battle cry ringing in our ears, we knew how much it meant to him. However, perhaps our enthusiasm and adventurous play left us vulnerable, because within seven minutes our aggregate lead was halved.

Trevor Dawkins hit a shot from distance that sailed straight past Rodney Swindlehurst in our goal. We could see that Shankly was all fire and brimstone in the dugout and immediately got straight back at them from the kick-off. There was no quarter given and none asked for. It looked like we had done it too, when Phil Tinney hammered in an equaliser after the goalie had saved his initial shot. Then Bobby Graham made it 2-1 on the night. We were leading 5-2 on aggregate and seemingly had one hand on the cup, midway through the first half.

Then Martin Britt levelled the score on the night. There were just 35 minutes on the clock, West Ham clearly had their tails up and we did well to keep the score as it was by the interval. At half-time, Shankly told us that the game should have been out of sight. He thought we were by far the better side. We had proved that at Anfield.

As we left the dressing room, his words were ringing in our ears. 'Play with more freedom and confidence in the second half, boys, but make sure you keep it tight.' He was still concerned with their wingers, Sissons and Redknapp. He could see they were the only real danger we faced. Unfortunately, we couldn't execute his commands.

We went into the second half still believing we would be leaving with the trophy. I was convinced we had more than enough to see off this West Ham team, and when Bobby Graham hit the post with a curler from distance, I thought it was only a matter of time before we got another. However, our opponents seemed to take inspiration from the near miss and came back at us.

On the hour mark, our defence was all over the place as Bobby Howe rounded two of them to cross to Britt, who grabbed his second of the night. West Ham were now 3-2 up on the night and within a goal of levelling the tie. Britt would grab the all-important equaliser in controversial circumstances from a cross by Redknapp. To say we were furious that the goal was given was an understatement. It would be disallowed in today's game, but as Britt bundled Swindlehurst into the net, after the keeper had risen to claim the ball with both hands, the referee's whistle signalled that we had a huge battle on our hands.

There were 18 minutes left to play and we were rocking. It was now 4-2 on the night and 5-5 on aggregate. I thought we were heading for extra time, when disaster struck. If only we had heeded Bill's half-time instructions to get tight on Redknapp and Sissons.

In the 86th minute, Redknapp, racing down the wing, sent a teasing cross into the penalty area and Britt smashed in the winner with his head. It was his fourth in an inspired performance, but it broke my heart.

All we could do at full time was get off the pitch as quickly as possible. There was a pitch invasion as the Hammers' support couldn't believe that they had won the Youth Cup at the third time of asking, especially after being 3-1 down in the first leg. Neither could we.

Shankly was incandescent with rage. He just couldn't accept the circumstances of our defeat. I thought Tommy Smith was going to do something to referee Jack Taylor that he would later regret. Somehow, he kept himself in check though. Taylor would survive the night and go on to referee the World Cup Final in Munich, in 1974.

Shanks was furious after the game but not with us, with the referee. After things had settled down, he addressed us in that wonderful passionate manner of his. He was complimentary about the way we had played throughout the tournament. And, he told us that we had been robbed of becoming the first Reds team to win the trophy through a combination of bad luck and bad refereeing.

I remember him saying, 'I'm proud of every one of you boys. That was the biggest injustice in any cup final since Nat Lofthouse bundled Harry Gregg into the net to win the 1958 FA Cup for Bolton Wanderers, against Manchester United.'

A few weeks later, Shanks told us that Bobby Graham, Phil Tinney, Gordon Wallace and I would be joining the first team on a trip to San Remo in Italy. It was to be a reward for our efforts. It was a wonderful experience to be with the first team squad for a week. It really made us feel like we were finally on the way to breaking through.

The first team lads were all great with us and I recall it was a very relaxed trip. We spent most of the time lounging about on the beach. Of course, there was also the addition of the odd five-a-side-match. Shankly didn't accompany us on the trip though. I imagine he was beavering away back at Anfield and preparing for the challenges that lay ahead. Ronnie Moran and Alan A'Court kept a close eye on us during the week and there would be little opportunity to veer off the straight and narrow.

The Italian Riviera was so beautiful, as was the day trip we took to Monaco and Monte Carlo. I remember it was all so thrilling for a young lad like me, who had never until that point left the country.

Many years later, while working in the perfume industry, I travelled to Monaco and Grasse on the Riviera many times. It was part of my job to visit the factory where the ingredients for the cosmetics were produced. Each time I went there, those memories of my youthful adventure all those years ago would come flooding back.

However, despite Bill's warm words and the fine holiday in Italy, that FA Youth Cup Final remains one of the most disappointing experiences of my football career. We only had ourselves to blame though. Every time I look at the runners-up medal all these years later, I remember Bill Shankly's words:

'First is first and second is nowhere.'

For all our heartache in the FA Youth Cup, there was no doubting that Liverpool, under the guidance of Shankly and his Boot Room boys, were going places. Promotion to the

First Division had been secured a year earlier in 1962. What a remarkable season that was.

The signs that the 1961/62 season was going to be a momentous one were there from the beginning. The squad was the fittest and most focussed I had ever experienced in my life. Those gruelling hours on the training pitch, the relentless drills, and punishing runs from Melwood to Anfield, when all any of us wanted to do was collapse in a heap on the floor, were about to pay off in spectacular fashion.

All I could do was keep plugging away in the reserves. I was carving out a name for myself as a goal-scoring midfielder and I always gave everything I had. That was the minimum acceptable standard. You could have an off game, but you couldn't hide, ever.

As the season got underway, Liverpool looked head and shoulders above the rest. They outran, outfought and outthought every opponent, racing to the top of the league from the start. They wouldn't be moved. The Reds went on a run of 11 straight wins, scoring 33 goals and conceding just four. One victory in particular gave Shanks immense pleasure; a 5-0 mauling of Leeds United.

What a game that was. Roger Hunt smashed a hat-trick and you could feel, all around the club, that this was going to be a special season. The boss would later claim that the league was won during this period of the season, and who could argue with that?

The championship and promotion were secured on an awful day in April 1962. The heavens opened and, as I watched the match against Southampton from the old Band Box next to the dugout at the bottom of the Main Stand, I felt so sorry for the supporters who were caught in the most dreadful downpour. The wind blew the rain into the stands and puddles would gather on the turf before the game was up. I wasn't immune to the deluge either.

It seemed such a shame that a momentous occasion such as this one should take place in such miserable conditions. Still, you could sense something magical was in the air. Liverpool, after eight long years in the second tier, were on the brink and the crowd knew it, all 40,000 of them.

It was a 42-game season and Liverpool had played 36 going into the game against the Saints. We had a game in hand over our nearest rivals, Leyton Orient, who were five points behind. Our game against Swansea Town the previous week had been postponed due to an outbreak of smallpox in South Wales. However, we knew that a win would render the remaining five matches meaningless. Everybody knew it and as the game got underway the noise from the crowd was deafening.

The Reds were without St John for this game, who was suspended. It felt like a handicap – goals from the Saint (22) and Hunt (42) had obviously played a huge part in our title charge. The job of filling Ian's boots fell to Kevin Lewis, who would score a very creditable ten goals in 21 appearances that season. Two of those goals turned out to be the most important of his career though. They would be the strikes that took the club back into the big league and restored pride to half a city.

As a footballer, you live every day just hoping to catch the eye of the manager, to win a place in the first XI. It's an all-consuming obsession and it can take over your every waking moment. It even leaks into your dreams, so much so that you can miss the big moments in a career. You only really become aware of them after your playing days are over, when you have time to look back and reflect.

This is the case for me. For all my disappointment at not making the cut at Anfield, I can also look back fondly on those days, and feel pride at being there for the genesis and the great moments in the club's history, to have known the men involved and to have earned their respect, if not a place in the team.

What must it be like for Kevin? To have scored the goals that set in motion a period of unparalleled success, to be such an important part of the history of a football club and a city. At the end of a career, all we have are those moments to look back on. I'm privileged to have shared in so many.

Kevin got both his goals in a tempestuous first half, during which Liverpool slogged it out in the mud and the rain. I don't remember much of the second half, just that the conditions were dreadful, and I remember the players coming off at full time absolutely covered in mud. I fully expected them to embark on a lap of honour, instead they headed straight down the tunnel. The dressing room was raucous, and the players jumped straight into the hot bath that had been prepared for full time. Shanks and his team were grinning from ear to ear.

What they hadn't realised was that more than 25,000 people had refused to leave after the final whistle. Shouts of 'We want the Reds' could be heard echoing around Anfield. Who could blame them? They'd waited so long for this moment. They wanted their chance to honour their heroes properly.

First, T. V. Williams, the club chairman, went on the public announcement system to thank the supporters and players for their efforts. He told the waiting crowd that winning the

Second Division was the hardest thing in football. Then it was Shanks's turn, but their voices were drowned out by the insistent pleas of the throng. 'We want the Reds; we want the Reds.' There was nothing else they could do; the crowd wouldn't be leaving until the team reappeared.

So, a message was delivered to the team, still celebrating in the bath, that they needed to get out, get dressed and get back on the pitch. It was, of course, something they were only too glad to do. However, they would have no idea what was going to hit them. As soon as they ran from the tunnel, they were hit by yet another deluge, this time a vast swathe of humanity, as supporters poured from the stands and swamped the players. I remember seeing fans placing hats on the lads' heads and scarves around their necks. Then, they disappeared amongst the masses.

I think Shanks and the chairman got a little worried at one point, because T. V. almost got knocked down some steps as he tried to rescue Ronnie Yeats from the clutches of his adoring fans. It was raucous, a little scary at times, but it was all good-natured and these people just wanted to show their appreciation for the men who had made their dreams a reality.

Shankly's achievement can never be overstated. The club had been sleepwalking for years. His arrival in 1959 simply electrified the place. Everything changed: the infrastructure, the training, the squad and the mentality. It was genuinely a revolution. Now a place at the top table was secured, there was no way the boss was going to rest on his laurels or dine out on the win. A seat at the table was never going to be enough for Bill. He wanted to be at the head of it, and he had his eyes on two other goals. He wanted the FA Cup and the European Cup, in that order. He thought it was a 'bloody disgrace' that Liverpool had never won the FA Cup and he knew how much it meant to the fans. However, he wanted to conquer Europe too; he knew that would make his Liverpool the greatest.

The 1962/63 season would be a tough test for the boys. They finished eighth and more than held their own. They also reached the semi-final of the FA Cup, losing 1-0 to Leicester at Hillsborough. It was such a one-sided affair and none of us could believe we were out after such a great performance. The Foxes scored with what must have been their only meaningful attack. Liverpool couldn't muster a response. There was even a penalty appeal, as Leicester seemed to handle in the box. Everything went against Liverpool, it seemed.

It was heartbreaking, but Shanks had seen what it took to compete at the top level, and he would use those insights to good effect the following season.

One new arrival in 1963, who deserves special mention, is Alfie Arrowsmith. When he joined the club from a Derbyshire team called Tintwistle Villa, for a fee of just £1,500, nobody considered him a major signing, and few of us could understand what the boss saw in him.

Alfie was a larger-than-life character, with a great sense of humour and a broad Lancashire accent. However, he looked a very awkward player and I remember in one or two of the early preseason training sessions, he seemed like he was always about to trip over his own feet.

He suffered his share of early mickey-taking, but Alfie could more than hold his own and always gave as good as he got. That certainly endeared him to the rest of the squad.

Scoring on my debut for Aberdeen FC, August 1965

Aberdeen FC 1965/66

China Cottage overlooking Aberdeen Harbour

Port Elizabeth City – Champions of South Africa in 1967

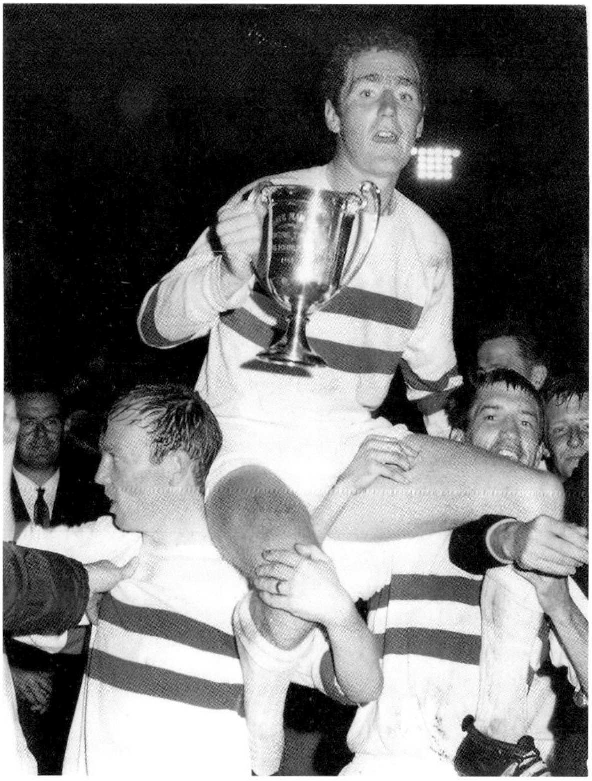

Champions of South Africa, 1967

Rand Stadium Johannesburg v Highlands Park FC – the game that clinched the title

Scoring with a diving header at New Kingsmead, Durban

Scoring for Tranmere in the FA Cup v Port Vale, 1969

Tranmere Rovers FC, 1969/70

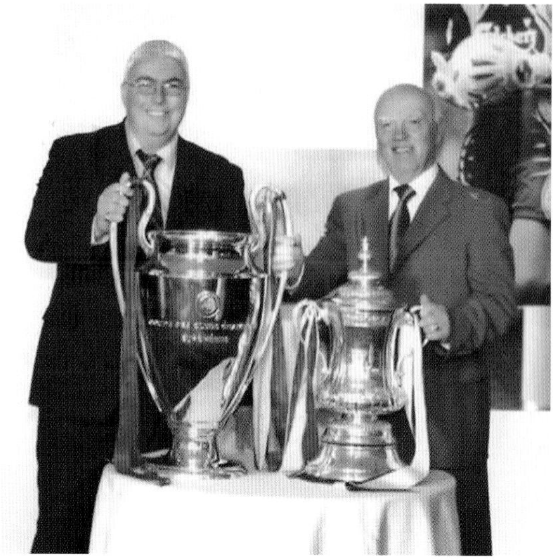

With Liz Taylor in the Ritz Hotel Paris, 1988

My son Gavin and I with the 2005 European Cup and the 2006 FA Cup

In 2009 I was appointed captain of Bromborough Golf Club. Here I am with Carole, my sons Gavin and Craig, and my daughters-in-law Diane and Joanne

At the 2017 Masters in Augusta with Craig

Carole and I – both still smiling after 54 years!

With the great Gerry Byrne

With 'Sir' Roger Hunt

After a round of golf with Roger Hunt, Tommy Lawrence and Gordon Wallace

With my son Craig at the home of golf

Pointing to my young self in the Bill Shankly Suite at Anfield

With Chris Lawler and Ian St John – 'The silent knight and the saint'

With fellow Aberdonian Big Ronnie Yeats

Back in the Anfield dressing room

Back at Anfield with the boss: 'He made the people happy'

We won it six times

Gordon Wallace and I have been friends for 60 years

With the amazing Ian Callaghan

At the Shankly Hotel with the typewriter Shankly typed my reference on

With Bill Shankly's grandson Chris Carline and Gordon Wallace

The boss is still looking over my shoulder

With the great Peter Thompson, my fellow housemate

On the glorious Turnberry links with Craig

With my two brothers Ian and Alan – three proud Scots!

The Glory of Istanbul with my son Gavin. Simply unforgettable!

Gavin's favourite photograph – us with our first European Cup

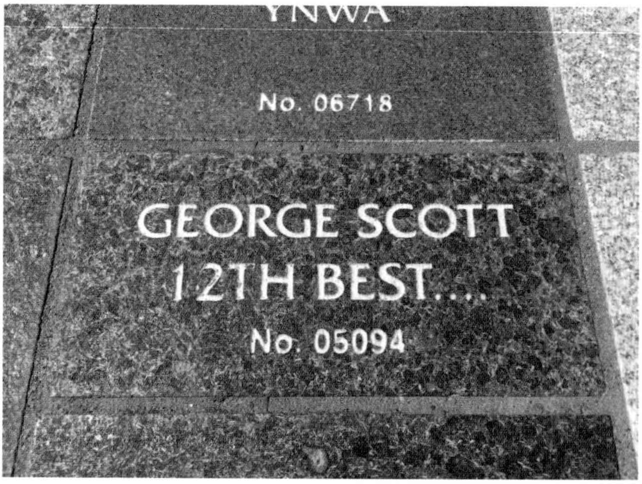

My stone at Anfield arranged by my family with a familiar message

Of course, the jokes would soon stop once the real games came around.

He played with me in the Central League during the 1962/63 season and scored an incredible 31 goals in 35 games. Shankly had indeed unearthed a diamond, and his breakthrough into the first team came in the latter part of that 1963/64 championship-winning season. Alfie made a massive contribution, bagging an astonishing 19 goals in 24 games.

Hunt, St John and Arrowsmith between them contributed a massive 67 league goals that season. Their goals undoubtedly powered the club to its first league title in 17 years. Alfie was a brilliant lad and great team-mate, and his future looked bright. Then tragedy struck. Sadly, he injured his left knee badly in the 1964 Charity Shield, and as a result, he missed most of the season.

Over the next three seasons, he made just 19 appearances, six of them as a substitute (substitutes were eventually introduced during the 1965/66 season). I recall sitting with Alfie in the treatment room at Anfield during his prolonged spell on the sidelines. He was showing me how much muscle strength he had lost in his thigh. It was just such a tragedy. Shankly was correct in his assessment of the player, Arrowsmith was a natural-born goalscorer.

I was desperately sad to hear of his passing in 2005. I remain in contact with his children and am well aware of how proud they are of his achievements.

The Reds would win the league with a spectacular 5-0 win against Arsenal at Anfield, on 18 April 1964. The game was a spectacle and, of course, has now passed into folklore, as much for the incredible supporters on the Kop, who were filmed by the BBC for their documentary series, *Panorama*, as for the exploits on the pitch.

I remember former Reds keeper, Jimmy Furnell was in goal for the Gunners, and he saved a penalty from Ian Callaghan. But Liverpool came out firmly on top and, again, the crowd were jubilant, but this time they were celebrating winning the big league for the first time in 17 years. The Kop that day would have been a mixture of the old guard, who had watched George Kay's Liverpool win the title in 1947, and the callow mop-topped youths who had never seen such glory. The generations were united in verse and they sang the songs of Liverpool in the 60s, with the older men joining in with as much vigour as their youthful counterparts. We'd won the league, we'd won the league, ee aye addio, we'd won the league, at last.

The year 1964 was also a milestone for me. I had again made the most appearances in the Central League team that season and I was also top scorer in the reserves over the two previous seasons by some distance. Before the end of the campaign, I had been chatting to Peter Thompson. He encouraged me to ask for a wage rise. I didn't want to. It wasn't in my nature back then. I wasn't as confident as I'm now.

I'm sure you can imagine how nervous I was, when I went along to the manager's office to plead my case. My heart was pounding, and my mouth went completely dry as I knocked on the door. It seemed like an eternity before he answered, and my stomach was doing cartwheels.

'Come in,' came the voice from behind the door with an air of Jimmy Cagney mixed with the gravelly sound of a Glenbuck miner. I swallowed hard and turned the handle.

'George. Come in son. Sit down.' The boss was in a genial mood and my optimism began to grow.

I told him I had been working hard all season and pointed out that I had been an ever-present in the reserve team. I had always given my all, even though I hadn't yet had my chance in the first team. I had never moaned or sulked. I had scored the most goals. It all just poured out of me. I was 19 years of age now, I said, and after four years at the club, I felt I deserved a raise for my efforts.

Shanks just nodded as I spoke, but I thought I saw a twinkle in his eye and a smile at the corner of his lips. Maybe I was getting through, I thought. I finished my plea and waited for his response. The boss leaned forward and fixed me in his stare.

'Well, son. It's not normal practice to award pay rises while the season is still in play. Of course, you understand.'

I nodded. What else could I do?

'However, you're a good lad. Son, in your case, I'm prepared to make an exception.' My heart soared, as I watched him open his desk drawer and pull out an envelope.

'Take this, son. Don't open it until you get home. You understand?'

I thanked him and got out of there before he changed his mind and raced back to my digs to open the package. Clambering up the stairs to my room, I couldn't wait to see what was in it. As I pulled out the paper inside my heart sank as I realised that he had given me a £15 voucher, which entitled me to a mohair suit from a men's outfitters in London Road.

The next day I showed the voucher to Joe Fagan and asked him what it was all about. I was expecting some sympathy. Joe had a very dry wit, and his response makes me chuckle today, but at the time I didn't know whether to laugh or cry.

'I heard you'd been to see the boss, George. Very brave of you that. Bill told me he wants you to look as smart as the first team when you're at the celebration dinner in the Adelphi Hotel next month.'

That was that. No raise, but I got a lovely mohair suit, and we had a great night celebrating the championship win at the special dinner.

Season 1964/65 was going to be make or break for me and I could sense that if I didn't make the breakthrough soon, it would never come. Hope sprang eternal though, and when I was included in the first-team squad for a tour of North America during the summer of 64, I began to dream that I would finally get my chance.

My excitement built as I was given a club suit, bag and all the equipment needed for the trip. I was riding high after scoring in a 7-1 victory over Huddersfield Reserves and following that up with a fine display in a 1-1 draw against Bolton's second string. Then I got what I can only describe as a hammer blow, practically on the eve of the tour. Liverpool signed a player called Phil Chisnall from Manchester United for £25,000.

I was told Phil would be travelling instead of me. I was heartbroken to be missing out on the tour, but also because this undoubtedly meant my route to the first team had just got even trickier. Bill simply told me not to worry. 'You can keep the suit, George. It'll be a collector's item one day. You go home and have a good rest son. Next season will be an important one for you.'

It didn't feel that way and I left his office feeling so disappointed. However, despite the setback, I resolved to knuckle down and work even harder to prove the boss wrong. It was what I always did, I knew no other way. In any case, I had a contract for another year, and I decided this was going to be a big one.

I must also add that Phil and I never let our rivalry get in the way of our friendship. He was a fine player and an even better person. I feel lucky to have played alongside him many times in the Central League. And, though I was crushed at not making it at Anfield, I could bear him no ill will.

My pain at being the only player left out of that trip was made worse when I learned how the team had toured places like San Francisco, winning 14-0. I'm sure I would have bagged a few in that one. They had even crowned the tour with an appearance on the *Ed Sullivan Show* in New York.

It was hard to pick myself up after all of that. But I did. As for the suit, just before I left to play football in South Africa in 1966, I gave it to my mother for safe keeping. Unfortunately, she gave it to the Salvation Army by mistake, along with a bundle of old clothes. That felt like the perfect metaphor for my Anfield career. No matter how hard I toiled, other people seemed to reap the rewards.

The season 1964/65 would prove to be one of the biggest in the history of Liverpool Football Club. For me, however, it would be the final act of my Anfield adventure. My onward journey would take me home for a brief spell with my first love, Aberdeen FC, before I would eventually taste personal glory on foreign shores. Let's not get ahead of ourselves though; there is an FA Cup to win and an emotional chat with Bill Shankly to talk about first.

Chapter Eight

The Twelfth-Best Player in the World

IT WAS one of the most dramatic and unforgettable days in the history of Liverpool Football Club. Yes, 1 May 1965 was the day that they finally brought the FA Cup home to Anfield for the first time in their history.

The following day, in the early evening, I stood in the hallway of my digs at Lilley Road in Anfield. I had just returned from the biggest victory parade in the history of the city, maybe even in the history of football. In my hand I clutched an envelope bearing the crest of the club I had served for five years. I trembled as I contemplated opening it.

Behind me, Peter Thompson was urging me to leave it alone and come out on the town with him and the other players. I could open it tomorrow, he argued. I told him this could be the letter I had been waiting for since I arrived; it could represent, at long last, my breakthrough into the first team.

'Peter,' I said 'you've had the glory. You've played in the final. I need to know if I'm ever going to sample what you've had. I need to see the letter before I do anything else. It will eat me up if I don't.'

This was the culmination of one of the greatest two-year periods in the club's history. Having won the First Divison the season before, 1964/5 was a campaign that cemented Shankly as the unquestioned leader of Liverpool Football Club and almost deified him in the eyes of the supporters.

Even though we kicked off that season as First Division champions, by the time the FA Cup came around in January, we were well off the pace in the league, sitting in tenth place and 13 points behind the leaders, Leeds United. The cup had become something of a Holy Grail to Liverpool. The club had never won it before, something that the Blue half of the city never tired of pointing out. Shanks had made it his personal crusade to win it for the club, but also as he would put it, 'For the people'.

We were drawn against West Bromwich Albion in the third round of the cup and the game was played on 9 January. I was having a great season in the reserves. I had become an ever-present, and would go on to play 38 games, scoring 16 times. Of course, I harboured dreams of somehow making it into the first team for any game, but to get into the team for a cup game would have been magical.

Today, the FA Cup is nowhere near as revered as it was back then. It was the pinnacle, and some will have put it above the European Cup, even the league title. The final at Wembley was such a national occasion and every young player dreamed of walking out on that pitch, in front of the Royal Box and tens of thousands of supporters, in May.

When Shankly cut me from the preseason tour of the United States in the summer of 1964, he had told me to go home and stay fit, as the following season was going to be a big one for me. I took him at his word and threw myself into training every day and I gave it my all in each reserve outing.

After winning the title, the whole club felt like it had gone up a level. The players seemed taller, more confident and you just sensed we were at a huge club with a great future. Couple that with the re-emergence of the city on the world stage, and it was difficult not to think all of your birthdays and Christmases had come at once. We all started to believe something special was happening and we were desperate to be a part of it, from the apprentices to the reserves and, of course, the first team.

Not that any of us would have been allowed to get big-headed of course; Shankly, Joe and Reuben would never have stood for that. But they wanted us to believe we were the best, and then prove it in training and any game we played in, at any level. Their demands were no less than excellence, all the time.

The first-team lads threw themselves into the tie against West Brom, as if their lives depended upon it. The cups had become their only hope of silverware and maintaining that buzz we had all felt the season before. They would take the same approach in the European games too. For virtually the entire game, the West Brom team couldn't live with Liverpool and the lads took a two-goal lead in the 63rd minute. Roger Hunt had put them in front just on the stroke of half-time and the Saint doubled the lead in the second half. The Baggies battled away but we never seemed in danger, until about 15 minutes from the end.

Jeff Astle was having a right good go at Ronnie Yeats, looking for any chance to get under his skin. Yeats was handling him, but one tackle was a clear foul. Ronnie got up and inexplicably picked up the ball in the penalty area. The referee immediately blew his whistle and pointed to the spot. Ronnie was beside himself and appealed to the ref that he had heard a whistle and was convinced a foul had been awarded. We later found out that the linesman had also heard a whistle and so had Tommy Lawrence, but the referee insisted he hadn't blown. It can only have come from the crowd.

Robert Cram stepped up to take the spot kick. It seemed a certain goal. He had a record of five out of five that season. However, miraculously, he missed. Maybe the delay and the arguments and protests had put him off, maybe he felt a sense of injustice himself, or maybe his touch just deserted him that day.

West Brom did pull one back a few minutes later, through Astle, but the lads hung on and booked their place in the fourth round. That brought up a tie against Stockport County at Anfield. Shankly was in confident mood, and with the club also facing a trip to Germany ten days later to face Cologne in the second round of the European Cup, he opted to miss the game and embark on a scouting mission instead. He would leave Bob Paisley in charge.

Liverpool drew 1-1 with Stockport and Bill wasn't best pleased, to say the least. The Reds won the replay at Edgeley Park comfortably, with two goals from Roger Hunt. The game against Cologne went to a play-off match, after a couple of goalless draws. Amazingly the second replay was settled in our favour by the toss of a coin, after it had ended 2-2.

According to Ronnie Yeats who was captain on the night, he had jumped in quickly and shouted 'tails' before his German counterpart could say a word. As the coin fell, it landed in the mud, edge on. It looked like it was leaning towards heads, but Ronnie again seized the initiative and argued that the ref should toss it again. He did, and this time it landed on tails. The Reds were through and the joy behind the scenes was incredible. Imagine the tension of your fate being decided on the toss of a coin.

Next up for Liverpool in the FA Cup was an away trip to Bolton in the fifth round. The game had been a slog and looked to be heading for a replay, when in the 85th minute, Ian Callaghan smashed in the winner in front of the Liverpool fans in the away end. As the ball hit the net there was a surge behind the goal among the jubilant supporters, which caused a barrier to collapse. People spilled on to the touchline and police and St John Ambulance crews rushed to their aid. Cally later told me of his disbelief that the referee didn't stop the game. Instead he just carried on.

The sixth round brought up a trip to Leicester, at Filbert Street. That was a tense game and it ended goalless, but the Reds would book their place in the semi-final, thanks to a 72nd-minute strike from Roger Hunt in the replay at Anfield. Now, standing in the way of their first FA Cup Final in 15 years and hopefully their first-ever triumph, was Chelsea.

The semi-final would take place three days after the epic tie against Cologne had finally been settled, and it was played at Villa Park. Everybody at the club could sense destiny calling, and the mood in the camp was one of determination. This was our moment and we weren't going to let it pass without a fight. We were yet to play Chelsea that season; both league games against them would come during the run-in. However, the lads would have known all about them from the previous season, when they had beaten them twice.

With Liverpool out of the running in the league, the season felt like it was building to an almighty crescendo. The Reds faced Chelsea in the FA Cup semi-final just a fortnight before lining up against Inter Milan in the semi-final of the European Cup. The sense of history around Anfield was palpable. I remember sitting there one day, having lunch after training and looking around at the boys and just drinking it all in. I recalled arriving at Lime Street five years earlier, as a 15-year-old apprentice, with a suitcase in my hand and £20 in my pocket. I had dreamed of glory. What young kid didn't? I had never have imagined that the club I was joining – a club and a city my grandmother hadn't even heard of – could rise so quickly and so successfully. Though I still felt part of it all, thanks to Shanks, Bob, Joe and Reuben, there was an ache in my belly and a yearning for more.

I believed wholeheartedly, that if I could just get one chance, if I could start just one game for the first team, I could add something to the team. I believed then and I still do, that I was good enough and I could have helped the boys. Still ringing in my ears were the words of the boss, as he cut me from the preseason tour, 'Next season is a big one for you, George.'

I always believed Shanks. He was an honest man, a manager of great passion and integrity. If he said it was a pivotal season for me, then who was I to argue. Though it was April, and the 64/65 season was reaching its conclusion, I refused to let hope slip away. I kept my head down and waited for my chance.

It was a glorious day at Villa Park and the crowd reached around 69,000. Liverpool supporters were of course conspicuous, and their colour and noise were incredible. Perhaps they too could sense destiny was knocking at their door at last. It wouldn't be long before they would be able to hold their heads up and have the perfect answer to Evertonian taunts. 'You said come back when we've won the FA Cup,' they would say. 'Well, now we're back.'

Shanks and all the lads knew how much it meant to the city and to Liverpool supporters in particular. We all felt like we were ambassadors for the city of Liverpool and the sense, even if you weren't playing, that you were carrying the hopes and dreams of the people with you was palpable. If it felt like that for me, goodness knows what it felt like for Ronnie, Saint and the others.

Liverpool went 1-0 up in the game, in the second half. It was around the hour mark. And, it would be my mate, Peter Thompson, who got the goal. I was genuinely jubilant for him, though I would have given everything to have been alongside him on the pitch. All we had to do was hang on and we would be at Wembley. I knew this team was good enough to win the final. Every one of these boys deserved their place at Wembley. They had put in a magnificent effort. I knew also that with no substitutes the best I could hope for was that one of them might pick up a knock in the run-up to the final, and that I would get the call. It was a terrible thought, but that was the life of a reserve.

The lads did more than hang on though, and as the game was heading towards the last ten minutes, we won a penalty. It had already been decided that Gordon Milne would take the penalties, if any were awarded. However, he would later tell us all that in that moment, as he looked at the goalkeeper, he just didn't fancy it. By sheer fluke, Billy Stevenson just happened to be standing next to Gordon, and he simply agreed to take it. Everyone was surprised as Billy wasn't known for his spot-kick prowess. I'm not sure if he had ever taken one before, while at Anfield. However, I do know he was a player who had supreme confidence in his own abilities. I can recall playing alongside him in those old five-a-side games at Melwood. He would yell out, 'Pass It to me George, don't waste it.' It was as if passing to anyone but him would be a waste. I love that self-belief and enthusiasm. Every player needs it.

So, Gordon didn't waste that spot kick. He passed it to Billy. It looked like a good penalty too, but the way Billy tells it, he slipped at the vital moment and, for a second, thought the ball was going to balloon over the bar. Instead it hit the roof of the net. And, with that, he had all but guaranteed the Reds' place in the final.

Like all of us at the club I was excited about going to Wembley with the squad. By then, I knew I had no chance of playing in the game, but just to be near the first team and part of the occasion was special. The team would have picked itself, but for the fact that Gordon Milne had been injured and was replaced by Geoff Strong. The run-up to the match seemed to fly by in a blur of publicity and the media interest in the club reached fever pitch. Of course, Shanks was always ready with a quote and I know he was revelling in it.

Then, the day was upon us and we all set off for Wembley together. The whole squad, first team and reserves travelled together. As we neared the stadium, we were left in no doubt what this meant to the people. London had been invaded and hordes of Liverpool fans ran alongside the buses, waving to us and cheering as we passed them. There were flags and rosettes everywhere. Then we were through the barriers and inside the greatest and most famous stadium in world football. Inside the dressing room. the atmosphere was composed, but you could sense the nerves in the players as they took in the enormity of the occasion.

I couldn't believe it when, a few hours before kick-off, Reuben Bennett approached me to say that three of his relatives from Aberdeen couldn't make it and their three tickets were up for grabs. He asked me to go outside the ground and see if I could find a group of Liverpool fans who didn't have a ticket. So, off I went. Amazingly, amidst the vast throng of supporters, I spotted three lads I recognised. They frequently appeared at the players' entrance and at Melwood too. I walked over to them but realised I didn't even know their names. They recognised me too but seemed shocked to see me and asked why I wasn't inside with the team. They had all travelled without tickets and had been wandering around the stadium all morning in desperate search for anyone who had a spare. They had no idea I was about to make them the luckiest supporters on the planet.

I have never experienced such a reaction of pure joy as the one I saw from the boys that day and I don't suppose I ever will again. As I handed over the tickets, I realised a crowd had started to form around us. I think some people may have thought I was a tout, so I shook their hands and beat a hasty retreat. However, that was when my problems really started. I now had the not insignificant problem of getting back into the stadium. As I approached the barrier at the players' entrance, I realised that the police officer who had supervised me leaving the stadium had been replaced. The new guy didn't know who I was and wouldn't believe that I was a Liverpool player. His primary concern was that the Queen was due to arrive in the next 15 minutes, and his job was to vet everybody coming in and out of the ground. I was getting desperate and, in the end, I pleaded with him to send someone inside to verify that I was with the Liverpool party. To my relief, he relented. A few minutes later a rather annoyed Bill Shankly came to the door and gave the policeman a short sharp rebuke before vouching for who I was. It all gave the lads a good laugh at my expense. I think the boss was happy that three fans who didn't have tickets were going to dine out on their good fortune forever.

Back inside Wembley Stadium, my thoughts journeyed back to my childhood. I had watched so many finals on the television or on old newsreels at the cinema. They included the famous 'Matthews' final in 1953. As a schoolboy I could recite a list of all the teams who had featured in those games, going back years. Now, all those dramatic moments were flashing before my eyes. It was a surreal experience, thinking of those historic games. Now here I was, in the middle of an event that would be talked about for as long as Liverpool Football Club exists.

I recall the dressing room was a flurry of activity and chatter, with kit being unloaded and the players changing into their cup final suits. The time seemed to race by and there was barely enough of it to get nervous. Before we knew it, it was 90 minutes before kick-off and we were walking down the tunnel towards the sunlight and the magnificent turf beyond. Then I was on that hallowed turf, walking side by side with my good friend Peter Thompson, and we were just a few steps behind

Bill Shankly and Bob Paisley. We were all walking towards the Liverpool fans behind the goal and the rain began to drizzle, spattering our suits and shoes.

I had reached the age of twenty and this was the first time I had ever been to Wembley. I remember the playing surface was like a bowling green. Bill and Bob were deep in conversation and I quickened my pace to get closer, so that I could hear what they were saying. Bill was looking over at the vast ranks of Liverpool supporters who had gathered on the terrace. The sight of them all there together sent a shiver down my spine and filled my stomach with butterflies. What Shanks said to Bob gave me goosebumps.

'Look at them Bob. Look at them. We just can't lose for these fans. It is not an option.' I still shiver thinking about it today. Being so close to the men I had shared the last five years of my life with, and who were about to become immortal, was something of a spiritual experience.

I remember looking at Tommy Lawrence and thinking to myself how big the pressure must have seemed for him. It was raining and I hoped that every cross into his penalty box would stay firmly in his gloves.

Our opponents, Leeds United, were a fantastic team. They had the likes of Billy Bremner, Jack Charlton, Bobby Collins, Paul Reaney, Johnny Giles and goalkeeper Gary Sprake. Two years later, at Anfield, Gary would inadvertently throw the ball into his own net. The Kop would instantly launch into a rendition of the Des O'Connor hit 'Careless Hands'.

I couldn't really enjoy watching the final. The pressure and expectation made it such a tense affair. I remember feeling that our lads simply wore Leeds down. When the match entered extra time, we were the team that wanted it more, plain and simple. Billy Bremner's 25-yard thunderbolt equaliser, after Roger Hunt had put us ahead, could easily have broken our spirit. Instead, somehow, we found the extra energy to keep going and I'll never forget the huge roar when Ian St John headed in the winner.

The Queen was appropriately wearing a red coat that day, and when she presented the FA Cup to big Ronnie, he took great care to wipe his hands on his shorts to clean the dirt off before shaking her hand.

They were all heroes that day, but one man deserves more credit than most. Gerry Byrne, surely the bravest to ever wear the shirt. We all now know that he played virtually the whole of the game with a broken collarbone. Shankly just loved him for that. He had often said that 'for a player to play for me, he has to be willing to run through a brick wall and come out fighting on the other side'. Gerry was the living embodiment of that.

I'll never forget the fantastic winners' reception that evening, at the Grosvenor House Hotel in London. The alcohol flowed freely all night. There would be a few sore heads on the train ride home the following day, but we all still found room for champagne, especially after it had been poured into the FA Cup.

All of us knew that we could expect a hero's welcome back home. We knew also that the whole city would turn out, Reds and Blues. It was a matter of civic as well as sporting pride. However, I don't think any of us could have foreseen in our wildest imaginations the absolute outpouring of emotion, nor the tide of humanity that filled the streets of the city centre that day.

The first indications that this was going to be a day to remember came as we passed through Crewe, some 47 miles from Liverpool. You couldn't see the buildings for flags and bunting. By the time we arrived at Lime Street station, there must have been over half a million people on the streets. They seemed to fill every inch of pavement, as we made our way to the town hall for the official reception. We travelled from the station to the town hall with the first team parading the cup from an open-top bus at the head of the convoy, and the rest of us reserves and the wives following behind on another bus. However, at the town hall, we all mingled together as we climbed the steps, covered with a red carpet, until we reached a reception room leading out on to the balcony overlooking Water Street and Castle Street. There were people as far as the eye could see. Tens of thousands of them all the way down Dale Street in one direction, and as far as the Pier Head in the other.

I stood behind Shankly, who emerged from glass doors and stepped out on to the balcony to thunderous cheers. He was waving to his adoring admirers, like an emperor. The feelings it invoked, and the atmosphere, were electric. I have never witnessed anything like it since. I doubt I ever will.

I felt on top of the world, at the threshold of greatness. I had given my all for the club at reserve level and felt certain that the boss knew I hadn't wasted my opportunity. He had told me it was a big year for me, and I hadn't let him down. Now here I was amongst it all and I was confident that I could make the step up. I wanted more than anything to be part of this magic forever.

It took hours, but eventually the crowds subsided, and the festivities ended. It was time to return to normality and my digs back at Anfield. So, Peter Thompson and I made the journey back together. We were both exhausted and a little hungover. The plan was to freshen up and then head into town with the rest of the squad and continue the celebrations into the night. As we were on our way out of the door, I noticed a letter addressed to me on the stand in the hall. On the envelope was the official crest of Liverpool Football Club.

My first thought was that this would be confirmation of my new contract and promotion to the first team. In the previous 24 hours I had been given no reason to believe that I wouldn't be starting my sixth season at the club after the summer was over. At my shoulder was Peter, urging me to toss the envelope aside and come out on the town with him. It was never going to happen, and I think he knew that I wouldn't have been able to enjoy myself, knowing that the letter was waiting for me, unopened on the hall stand. So, with a huge lump in my throat and a stomach in knots, I opened it.

As I tore it open and pulled out the sheet of paper inside, I felt the tension threaten to overwhelm me. My eyes raced across the page, digesting every word, and as the reality soaked in, my heart sank. The letter was to inform me that the club had received an offer of £12,500 from Aberdeen Football Club for my transfer. It finished by telling me to contact the manager at my earliest convenience to discuss the matter in more detail.

It completely shattered me and, for a brief moment, I thought my knees would give way. I felt sick to my stomach and told Peter that I couldn't join him and the other lads in town. I would need to try to deal with this alone. Perhaps I should have expected this, but I just wasn't prepared for it at all.

Liverpool were playing Inter Milan the following Tuesday in the first leg of the European Cup semi-final. Shankly played a masterstroke and sent Gerry Byrne and Gordon Milne out before kick-off to parade the FA Cup in front of a delirious crowd. It ramped up the atmosphere and the Reds saw off Milan 3-1. As I sat in the crowd, I realised that this would be the last time I would watch the team as a player of the club.

In my heart I was dreading the trip to Shankly's office. I wanted to know if he was going to accept the offer, though I felt certain he would. I was desperate to speak to him, but at the same time I knew that as soon as I did, my dream would be over. At the end of that week, I finally plucked up the courage to see the boss. From the moment I walked in, he could see I was upset. For his part, I was surprised to see that he was uncomfortable too. He had always been a tough character, demanding and utterly driven. I hadn't seen this side of him before.

Then he spoke. His voice was full of compassion and empathy and it took me a little by surprise. It may have been easier if he had been rude to me, at least that way I could have been angry with him. Instead, he proceeded to deliver what must have been the kindest sacking ever implemented.

As I struggled to hold back the tears, he sat back in his chair and said, 'George, son, there are five good reasons why you should leave Anfield now.'

I looked at him, my eyes barely able to contain the tears. My face must have been an expression of sheer bewilderment. What were these five reasons?

'What are they Boss?'

He paused, leaned forward and in a quiet voice he simply said, 'Callaghan, Hunt, St John, Smith and Thompson.' I knew what he meant. He continued. 'The first-team forward line, they are all internationals, George, and they are going nowhere anytime soon.'

By this stage my tears were in full flow. Shankly looked visibly moved by my display of raw emotion. He got out of his seat, walked around it and perched himself on the edge of the desk in front of me, placing his hand on my shoulder. I'll never forget the words he said in that moment.

'Always remember, that at this moment in history you are the twelth-best player in the world, George.' I was incredulous at this and asked him what he was talking about.

'The first team here at Anfield, son, they're the greatest team in the world – they have won the league and the cup in the last two seasons – and you are the leading goalscorer in the reserves. I have sold you to Aberdeen because I know you will be in their first team. You'll also be back staying with your family. Go back home and prove me right.'

As I was leaving his office, still very upset, he rose and shook my hand. His final words meant the world to me.

'Son remember this; you were one of the first players to come here and sign for me. So I want you to think of yourself like the foundation stone of the Liverpool Cathedral. Nobody ever sees it, but it has to be there otherwise the cathedral doesn't get built.'

I have often wondered how a man who came from such humble beginnings, from a mining community in Glenbuck in south-west Scotland, could speak in such poetic and profound terms.

I wonder also whether he truly understood the value and power of his words to me. I hope he did.

Although I left his office in tears that day, I also felt inspired. I still had hope that this might not be the end of my dreams. Instead, I was beginning to believe that this could in fact turn out to be the beginning of a new phase in my life. That's of course what Shanks wanted me to feel. And, as it happened, that's exactly what transpired.

Chapter Nine

Back Home with the Heavenly Dancers

MY PAIN at having to leave Anfield and Liverpool – a place I now regarded as home – was tempered by the fact that I would be returning to the city of my birth and to my first football love, Aberdeen FC. I had received a good first-team contract at the Dons, or the 'Heavenly Dancers', as I had always known them.

The phrase the 'Heavenly Dancers' in reference to Aberdeen comes from an old song, which I now know was written by an English woman called Mary Webb. She had never set foot in Aberdeen but wrote the song for a homesick native of the city who she worked with in a hospital kitchen.

The song, which is called 'Northern Lights of Old Aberdeen', was sometimes sung in the pubs of the city and certainly a favourite amongst Aberdonians. It was also a party piece of mine and I would often sing it at family gatherings. It goes like this:

When I was a lad, a tiny wee lad
My mother said to me
Come see the Northern Lights my boy
They're bright as they can be

She called them the heavenly dancers
Merry dancers in the sky
I'll never forget, that wonderful sight
They made the heavens bright

The Northern Lights of old Aberdeen
Mean home sweet home to me
The Northern Lights of old Aberdeen
Are what I long to see

I've been a wanderer all of my life
And many a sight I've seen
God speed the day when I'm on my way
To my home in Aberdeen

There is third verse to the song. But, in all honesty, I don't recall ever singing it at any family gatherings or hearing anyone else singing it.

However, in honour of the lady who penned the tune, I have included it below.

I've wandered in many far-off lands
And travelled many a mile
I've missed the folk I cherished most
The joy of a friendly smile

It warms up the heart of a wanderer
The clasp of a welcoming hand
To greet me when I return
Home to my native land

Today, the former players' association at Aberdeen FC produce a newsletter, which is entitled *The Heavenly Dancers*. I was once invited to write a piece for the publication and was very proud to see it published. Some weeks later I received a letter from Duncan Davidson, chairman of the Former Aberdeen Players' Association and enclosed was a letter from Alex Ferguson, on Manchester United headed paper, which read:

Dear Duncan
Thank you for continually sending me a copy of *the Heavenly Dances* [sic].

To be honest, I normally scan through the pages looking for the interesting bits, you get a bit lazy at my age! However, I had some time on my hands today and read the whole number 2 issue and what a good read it was, well done.

I was particularly taken by the article on George Scott who played at Liverpool as a youngster and later came back to the Dons. What amazed me was his recall of events of 50 years ago, very impressive.

I thought I should drop you a line on an excellent read and wish you and your committee continued loyalty to a fantastic Football Club and City.

Yours Sincerely
Sir Alex Ferguson CBE
Manager

Somehow, I think his reference to a fantastic city and football club was referring to Aberdeen, not Liverpool. The thought of United's manager reading through my recollections of life at Anfield in the 60s did amuse me greatly, though. However, for all the rivalry between the clubs and Ferguson's undoubted desire to usurp Liverpool as the most successful club in English football history, he was and still is, a decent football man and would have been interested in and appreciated the methods of a fellow Scot like Shankly.

I do have a deep recall of my early football career, and my memories of Anfield in particular are strong and vivid. My desire to document it all while I can stems from a need in me to leave something of those days behind. To record my thoughts and feelings at key moments of my life. A literary image of those times, if you like.

My move to Aberdeen, back in 1965, brought me a signing-on fee of £1,200. Given the fact that you could pick up a semi-detached property for £3,500, at the time that fee was hugely welcome. However, as I had just passed my driving test, I opted to splash the cash on a brand-new shiny white Mini, which set me back £535. I remember my pride as I drove it straight out of the showroom of Aberdeen Motors.

I spent the summer in Liverpool with Carole and her family, who lived in the Kensington area of the city. I wrestled with my disappointment in the weeks that followed. The pain of not making the grade at Anfield weighed heavy on me at times, but at the back of my mind I couldn't get rid of the sense that Shanks had looked after me in the best way he could.

Football was a ruthless business, even then. And Bill could be unwavering in his desire to drive Liverpool to the very top of English and European football. You only had to look at his attitude towards injured players to see that he could be unsympathetic and even harsh with those he deemed were no good to him.

The fact that he had shown me such compassion in his office, taking the time to explain his decision to me and even attempting to comfort me, told me that he did value me and rate me as a player. Eventually those thoughts won out and I slowly began to look forward. I even managed to feel a degree of happiness at the prospect of returning to Aberdeen. It may seem strange for a player who has been let go by a manager to feel gratitude towards the man who sacked him, but that's how I would eventually feel, and how I still feel today. I can only put that down to the incredible character of the man and his ability to find the right words for the right moment.

I have spoken to many ex-players and coaches. Not everyone felt this way about Shanks. I read that Roy Evans always felt that Shankly communicated in facts and statements and that there was little dialogue. Bob Paisley always said that Shankly didn't give advice, he gave instructions. There is an element of truth in all of that. But I can only speak as I found, and with me Bill Shankly showed a real human side to his character, a genuine concern for my wellbeing. Sure, his mind was made up and he wasn't going back on the decision to let me go. But I took comfort in his attempts to lessen the blow and allow me to have hope.

I would benefit from his support again, in the latter part of my career. Throughout my life, whenever I have been faced with big decisions, I have often asked myself, 'What would Shanks do? How would he deal with this situation?' I'll talk more about this later, but for now we will return to Aberdeen and a fresh start in Scottish football.

I approached my new adventure with great positivity and hope. After all, as Bill had told me, I was the twelth-best player in the world, and who was I to argue with him? My family were so delighted to see me back home, especially my mother. They had all moved into a two-bedroomed house while I had been away, and my moving back meant my two brothers shared a room, while I had my own. It may surprise some to hear that my brothers had no issue with this. I think that's because they were both strong Aberdeen FC supporters and were just happy that I was back home and playing for the Dons. I think the whole family had missed me while I was away at Liverpool, and although all my focus had been on making it there, I had missed them too. Over the years, both Alan and Ian became huge Liverpool FC supporters and still are to this day.

I was something of a returning hero, given my exploits in England and association with Liverpool FC, who were the FA Cup winners. Shankly was obviously a huge figure in Scottish football, so I'm sure that helped too. In addition, Aberdeen had paid a decent sum of money for me; this was a significant signing for the club.

The local press gave me some great coverage, and everything seemed set fair for me to move my career forward. I would be plying my trade in the first team at last, and if I could see this as the opportunity it was, who knew where it may lead.

I remember lying on my bed and thinking back to the days, all those years earlier, when I used to lie on top of the old pie hut with my school friend, George Stables, watching my heroes playing Hearts in the Scottish Cup. In every sense this felt like coming home and I was ready to embrace it. Liverpool was now behind me, literally and in the emotional sense. And, although I knew I would always have a soft spot for the place and the club, I knew it was time to move on.

In Scotland, back then, the season would always commence with the early rounds of the Scottish League Cup, which would see clubs drawn into groups. The winners of each group went through to the quarter-final stage. That year Aberdeen found themselves in Group Two, a very tough section, along with Rangers, Heart of Midlothian and Clyde.

The manager at Aberdeen FC was the former Hibernian legend Eddie Turnbull. He was a strict disciplinarian, having been a Royal Navy man during the Second World War, and had only just taken over the role of manager at Pittodrie. One day, after training, he told me that Shankly had made him aware of my ability and had convinced him to pay such a big transfer fee for me.

'I have high hopes for you, George,' he said. 'You're going to be an important player for this club.' My confidence soared and I was ready to give it my all.

Eddie was a huge character in Scottish football. He had previously led the line for Hibs, as part of their 'famous five' strikers, which also included Gordon Smith, Bobby Johnstone, Lawrie Reilly and Willie Ormond. These men have become so legendary that in 1995 the club renamed the north stand at Hibernian's Easter Road in honour of their achievements. All of them have, quite rightly, been inducted into the Scottish Football Hall of Fame.

Eddie played 349 times for Hibs, scoring an astonishing 150 goals. His seal of approval meant a lot to me. He eventually managed the club for six years, from 1965–1971, winning the Scottish Cup in 1970 and leading Aberdeen to a second-place finish in the Scottish First Division. Of course, I would be playing football elsewhere by then.

My debut came against Clyde in the Scottish League Cup, at the Shawfield Stadium in Glasgow. I had a terrific game and bagged the fastest goal of the day, with a strike after only 13 minutes. We went on to win the game 2-1 and I couldn't have been happier. I couldn't wait to see the papers when I returned home to Aberdeen after the game and was delighted to read the headline:

'Dons win at Shawfield. New boys Scott and White the heroes.'

In my childhood days, all I ever dreamed about was playing for Aberdeen. That I had finally achieved my childhood ambition felt beautifully bittersweet. In a curious coincidence our next game would be a home fixture against Hearts, the same opponents I had watched as a kid from the roof of that pie hut. The game drew a big crowd of 18,000 and ended 1-1. Tommy White scored again. Tommy was a big, powerful centre-forward whose brother, John White, was a legendary star of the Tottenham Hotspur team of the early 1960s, which included Dave Mackay, Jimmy Greaves, Bobby Smith and Alan Gilzean.

John was sadly struck by lightning and died whilst playing golf and sheltering under a tree. This was a great tragedy for Tottenham and a great loss to Scottish football and football in general.

Tommy and I had made our debuts together on that first day of the 1965/66 season at Shawfield against Clyde, alongside another Eddie Turnbull signing, Jimmy Wilson. Jimmy was a very talented left-winger who joined Aberdeen from Morton. He was only 5 feet 4 inches tall but fast as lightning. He was a wonderfully talented player who spent three years at the club, making 75 appearances and scoring 24 goals. He would eventually become player-manager at Elgin City in 1976, after spells at Motherwell, Dundee and Falkirk.

The win against Clyde was a great moment for a young Aberdonian like me, but things were to get even better on the Wednesday evening of the following week when we played our next group game against the famous Glasgow Rangers at Pittodrie Stadium. I'll never forget that day for as long as I live. At last, I would be playing at the very top level, and for my hometown team against one of the most famous football clubs in the game.

The Rangers team we faced that day could count amongst their ranks ten full internationals. I was lining up against the likes of the famous wingers Willie Johnston and Willie Henderson, the captain of Scotland, John Greig, full-back Dave Provan and centre-half Ronnie McKinnon. This was a team of superstars.

The official crowd for the fixture is recorded as 24,000. Even if I acknowledge that my memory may be somewhat clouded by the mists of time, I can't accept that. It was at least 30,000. And amongst the throng were all my uncles, including my Uncle Pat who had been first to notice my ability. The same man who, years earlier, had warned me of the perils of not eating the crust on my bread. Luckily, I had heeded his advice and here I was playing in the biggest game of my life.

My stepfather Johnny and my two brothers were also there and many of my old school friends had turned out too. I still get butterflies, and the hairs on my arms stand up, when I remember sitting in that dressing room before the game and listening to the manager's team talk, which went by in a blur. Before I knew it, we were heading out the door and running out on to the pitch. The noise was deafening. I looked over to the section of the terrace near the corner flag at the Beach End. It was packed tight and full of Rangers supporters. The track in front of them was littered with empty beer cans.

I had been selected to play on the right wing and wore the number seven shirt. This wasn't my natural position, but Turnbull's instructions were to play as a winger when we attacked and a wing-back when we lost the ball. He wanted me to dig in and help our full-back to contain Scotland's left winger Willie Johnston. Johnston was a wonderful player who a few years later was sadly involved in an alleged doping scandal, which resulted in him being sent home from the World Cup. On the other wing for Rangers, Henderson was also one of the greatest wingers in the Scottish game.

Although I enjoyed the first half, it was very hard fought and I remember we were happy to go in at half-time with the scores level at 0-0. Try as I might, I was struggling to get the better of Scotland's international left-back Dave Provan. I was a little concerned that I wasn't showing my best, playing out of position. At half-time, Turnbull made a major change to the system, moving me from the right wing to midfield. This was my natural position and I immediately felt relieved.

As we emerged for the second half, I remember the sun had gone behind the clouds and the rain started to come down. The weather had gone from bright to dull but my performance and that of the team went the other way. Now comfortable and in my preferred position, I started to find my feet and spray the ball about in good style. I even nutmegged the Scottish captain John Greig at one point. I often recall with amusement how, as he passed me on the pitch just moments later, he growled at me and enquired which hospital I would like to wake up in the following day. This was, of course, the sort of thing that goes on in football matches all the time. Meanwhile, I was happy that we seemed to have them rattled.

The longer the half went on, the more our game started to come together. I found myself with the ball at my feet and noticed our forward, Billy Little, had got in behind their defenders. Conscious that I was about to be clattered, I slipped a pass to Billy, who placed the ball beyond the keeper. Pittodrie went wild as our supporters showed their utter joy. However, in that corner at the Beach End full of Rangers supporters, the mood was anything but joyous.

There was more to come though, and I was about to cap one of the finest performances of my young career. There was just ten minutes left on the clock and most people were expecting a Rangers onslaught. We had other ideas though. I raced out wide to collect the ball and whipped in a cross from the right. It was a perfect ball and was met sublimely by the head of our Danish centre-forward Jørgen Ravn. He buried it in fine style. I was delirious, but as I ran back to our half, after celebrating somewhat exuberantly in front of the away end, I was met by a hail of bottles from our visitors. Fortunately, they missed their mark.

I'll always cherish the memory of that game. The fact that all my family and friends were there to see me fulfil my childhood dream was so special. That my girlfriend and future wife Carole from Liverpool was there to witness my exploits was the icing on the cake. We would marry the following year.

That evening Carole and I were invited to a celebration at a venue in Aberdeen, which went by the name the Gay Gordons Hotel. It still exists and is called, simply, the Gordon Hotel. The whole place was bouncing and full of Aberdeen supporters. I was being given the hero's treatment, like something of a messiah. It was a great atmosphere, with fans coming up to shake my hand, and at that moment in my life I couldn't have felt happier to be back home at Aberdeen. To be with my family and Carole, and to have played such a big part in defeating the famous Glasgow Rangers at Pittodrie Stadium – well, the feeling is hard to describe.

Life couldn't have been better, but I couldn't have known then that destiny was about to play its cruel hand once more. The difference between glory and despair is often wafer thin in football, as I was about to find out once again.

Our next game in the league was a match against Stirling Albion. We won that one, thanks to an excellent goal from Jimmy Wilson. Then it was back to Shawfield and another clash with Clyde. We won this game 2-0 and I managed to get on the scoresheet again, grabbing our second.

I was playing well, cementing my place in the team and really starting to feel like I belonged. I had the faith of the manager and was starting to imagine a long spell in Scottish football. My confidence grew further when I received rave reviews in the local press following a 2-0 defeat to Hearts at Tyncastle. It was a really tough match and, of course, I would have preferred to have won, but I had given everything for the cause and to read that my performance had been noticed by the press did cushion the blow of the defeat a little.

I remember the Hearts player, Roy Barry, scoring their second goal with a thunderbolt of a shot from 30 yards out. It sailed past our goalkeeper John (Tubby) Ogston. He had no chance with it. Sometimes it's just not your day. The following season John Ogston was signed by Bill Shankly at Anfield but was never able to displace the incredible Tommy Lawrence.

We moved on as quickly as we could from that defeat and started to prepare ourselves for the next big test, which was the return League Cup game against Rangers at Ibrox. Eddie had arranged for us to train all that week on the sand down at Aberdeen beach and was putting us through our paces with endurance training sessions. It was tough stuff and designed to make us fully equipped for the rigours of Scottish football. I was no stranger to the hard yards, having been put through my paces time and again under Bill Shankly. As usual, I threw myself into it with gusto. I knew that moaning and complaining was the surest way to find yourself out of the game.

So, every morning in the run-up to the game, I reported for duty down at the shore. It was during that week that I sustained a terrible injury to my knee. During a five-a-side match I was tackled from behind by fellow new boy, Tommy White. My knee was very badly twisted, and the injury was later diagnosed as a serious ligament injury. I was out for most of the remainder of the season, and worse still my whole career was in jeopardy.

I was beside myself. At times like this it's easy to start to feel sorry for yourself, to imagine that the world has got it in for you, but I couldn't think like that. Instead, I worked hard to recover and to rebuild the muscle strength in my leg. We didn't have sports scientists or psychologists in those days. All you could do was rest up and receive regular heat and massage treatment until the pain eased and, when you could manage to train, you just did the hard yards alone.

However, even though I eventually made it back to almost full fitness, I got the distinct feeling that Eddie Turnbull had already moved on and that he had given up on me. Years later, Jimmy Wilson told me that Eddie hadn't been too keen on the way I would often tell the lads Shankly stories. With the benefit of experience and hindsight, I can totally understand how he felt.

I would have the lads in stitches with my impressions of Shankly and they would be enthralled at my tales of Anfield. Within a few months of arriving at the club my nickname had become Shanks. I'm still called by that name whenever I get together with any of my old team-mates from Aberdeen. Little did I know it all those years ago, but I had probably done myself no favours and it was a valuable lesson to learn.

I still have great respect for Eddie, however, and he was quite complimentary of me in his book, *Having a Ball*. Sadly, Eddie passed away several years ago. He remains, without a doubt, a legend of Scottish football.

As the 1965/66 season ended, I was released from my contract. I was 21 years old and facing the end of my football career. I knew nothing else; I had no skills and no trade to fall back on. I was out of work and had little savings to fall back on. It felt for all the world like the dream was finally over and this was a real low point in my life.

I could see no other option but to return to Merseyside, where I would stay with Carole's mum and dad, Marjorie and Jack, in their terraced house in Toft Street, Kensington. They were both the salt of the earth types and didn't hesitate in taking me in, not for a second. I was made to feel just like one of the family. My own family never forgot their kindness, and a close bond was formed on either side of the border. It was a bond that would last our whole lives.

The worst thing I could do was wallow in my poor fortune, though. Carole's mum knew that, and there was no way I would be allowed to rest on my laurels. One day, she declared that she was going to find me work and I was marched off down to the local biscuit factory, Crawford's, in Binns Road near the Edge Lane area of the city. I was given temporary work, which involved throwing ropes around pallets of biscuits then pulling them on to the trains, which would transport them across the country. I stuck at it, realising that I had a duty to pay my way, though the work was mundane and a far cry from my life as a footballer.

So, I clocked on every morning without fail. I got to work with some brilliant characters and began to realise how they stuck together and fought for each other. This was a strongly unionised factory and I immediately identified with that ethos.

I was only there just over a month and all I can remember was that there were quite a few Jack-the-lad Scousers, always trying to outsmart the management by clocking on for each other. The culture became very handy for lads who were arriving late with hangovers, for example. The feel of the place, at least as far as I could tell, was very much 'them and us' when it came to the management.

Naturally, this being Liverpool, everybody was football mad and the workforce was split down the middle. I'm sure you can imagine the banter with Reds and Blues working side by side on the shop floor. It didn't take long for the news to spread around the place that I had played for Liverpool reserves under Bill Shankly. That meant I was treated as something of a minor celebrity by the Liverpudlians. To be fair, even the Blues used to love to hear my stories. It made the job bearable, even enjoyable. But there were still dark moments when I would lose hope and worry about how I was going to build any sort of future for Carole and me. Could this really be what destiny had in store for me?

Whenever things got rough, I always fell back on the words of my grandfather: 'Never worry George. Your destiny is all mapped out for you.' I knew I couldn't lie down, and that destiny would eventually deal me another hand. And so it did, in July 1966.

Chapter Ten

Glory in South Africa and a Brush with Death

I WAS 21 years of age in 1966. I knew that if I didn't get back into professional football soon, my chances of ever having a career would vanish altogether. I was desperate, but also. I wanted to play at a decent level. I felt if I was given just one more chance, I could prove myself.

Unfortunately for me, though, the only offers on the table were from Derry City in the Irish League and Ellesmere Port Town, who plied their trade in the Northern Premier League. I mean no disrespect to either side, but neither felt like attractive options to me. I could only bide my time at the biscuit factory and hope something came up.

One afternoon in June, I was reading the paper in my mother-in-law's house, when the phone rang. It was a man called Dave Watson. Turned out he was in the UK recruiting players for a team in South Africa, Port Elizabeth City FC. Dave explained that Bill Shankly had recommended me via Cliff Lloyd, the secretary of the Professional Footballers'

Association (PFA). Port Elizabeth were very keen to sign me, he said.

I know a lot more about the history of South Africa and the impact of apartheid on its citizens now than I did back then. My experiences in the country, which I'll describe in this chapter, certainly left me with a sense of how unjust and inhumane the system was. I know now also that there was a cultural boycott of South Africa, largely by actors, musicians and artists. In all honesty though, none of this was on my radar.

I was advised that going there would be a 'politically sensitive move'. In all honesty, I just wasn't aware enough of politics back then and it didn't really register with me the way that it should have. I lived for football and being a professional was my overriding concern. That, and being able to build a life with Carole.

It's easy for me to trot out the 'if I knew then what I know now' line. I won't do that. Truth is I don't know what I would have done, even if I had have researched it. I know I desperately wanted to play professional football more than anything in the world. Perhaps if I had investigated it more deeply, I might have waited a bit longer to see if any other offers came in. But, if they hadn't, I may still have travelled. For a young lad like me, in 1966, it would take witnessing apartheid first-hand to fully appreciate its terrible injustices. That saddens me, but it's the truth. Even without the political issues though, this was a big decision to make. It meant moving thousands of miles away, a journey into the unknown. And for my in-laws, it meant me taking their daughter with me.

The money was good, very good by English standards. I would be paid roughly £30 per week. Port Elizabeth would also pay me a £1,500 signing-on fee and provide an apartment for the duration of the contract, which was to be for two years. To put that into perspective, a house in England might have cost around £4,000 at that time. Along with the brilliant weather, it was all a very attractive proposition to Carole and me.

Prior to putting pen to paper, I went to speak to Cliff Lloyd at the PFA. Cliff's advice was to get a written agreement that would allow me to move back to England after two seasons. This was just in case I proved successful and an asset and Port Elizabeth City became reluctant to let me leave. This seemed to be a trend amongst South African teams at the time. So, I spoke to the manager of Port Elizabeth, Matt Crowe, and convinced him to sign a letter on their official headed paper agreeing that I could return to England after two seasons if I wished. I knew Matt, who had played for Norwich City before emigrating. This would prove to be a very shrewd move for me, and I'm grateful to Cliff for his advice.

By far the most difficult aspect to all of this for me was having to speak to Carole's mum and dad, and her sister Eileen. Carole and I were getting married on 30 July 1966, which coincidentally was the day that England played West Germany in the final of the World Cup. It seemed timing wasn't one of my strong points. However, having to explain that we would then be leaving for a two-year stay in South Africa just one week after our happy day was a very tough conversation.

I must give them huge credit and I owe them my deepest thanks for the way they responded. Although they were obviously rather shocked and emotional, they were completely supportive in every way. I told Carole's mum and dad never to worry as I would always look after their beloved daughter. I like to think that was a promise I have never broken, and it's one I'm keeping to this day.

Our wedding was therefore tinged with a little sadness for them, I'm sure. It was still a wonderful day for all of us. There was one moment in particular that stands out and perhaps symbolises beautifully the rivalry between the Scottish and English contingents in attendance. Just as Carole said the words 'I do', a huge roar went up at the back of the church. I smiled to myself and thought, 'How nice is that.' However, my mistake became obvious in seconds. It turned out that the roar had come from one of my Scottish uncles, who was sitting at the back of the church and listening to the World Cup Final on a transistor radio, with the volume just high enough to hear without disturbing everybody else. Germany had just scored their last-minute equaliser to take the game into extra time, and it seemed he could no longer contain himself.

With the wedding celebrations out of the way, all that remained was for us to pack our bags and say our farewells. However, I couldn't resist one more trip to Anfield and Bill Shankly, the man who had made my imminent adventure possible. I found him in good form, and he welcomed me into his office. We chatted for some time, until I felt it was time to say goodbye. I was grateful that he had found time to see me but I didn't want to outstay my welcome. Just as I stood up to leave, he gestured to me to sit back down, saying:

'Wait there, George. Let me type this out for you, son.' He then proceeded to tap away at that old Olivetti typewriter of his as I sat waiting. Then he pulled out the paper and handed it to me. I confess that as I looked down at the sheet of headed paper in my hand, I was overcome with emotion to see what he had written. It said:

To whom it may concern
Dear People

George Scott played for my club for five years and during that time he caused no trouble to nobody[sic].

I would stake my life on his character.

W Shankly
Manager

That wonderful reference has served me so well over the years. As I'll discuss later, it has even helped me find work in the years after football. I have always felt that it was my duty to do justice to those words.

And, with that, my young wife and I were on our way to South Africa via Frankfurt and Nairobi before arriving in Johannesburg. I had been billed as a big signing and a former Liverpool player to boot. This meant that when Carole and I stepped off the plane, we were greeted by a huge reception. It all felt so strange.

On our first night we were taken to the Algoa Hotel in Port Elizabeth by the owner of the hotel, a chap called Snowy White. He was a very wealthy supporter of Port Elizabeth City Football Club and a hugely influential figure in the town. The Algoa Hotel overlooked the city and Algoa Bay from the top of a famous landmark called the Elizabeth Donkin Memorial Park. From the rooms on the top floor of the hotel, you could see all the way down to the harbour and Kings Beach.

However, we would have to wait before we could sample the splendour on offer. Once we had checked in, we were told that our room for the night was in the basement. We were led down some stairs and with each step, our unease increased. Eventually we reached a less than salubrious doorway in a dark, dingy corridor. I flung the door open and immediately my heart sank to the floor. However, my reaction paled by comparison with Carole's.

What lay before us resembled something of a cell, a box with no window. There was no bath or shower, just two single beds in the corner of the space. In the centre of the room was a table, on which sat a ceramic basin. In it was a jug full of water. It appeared that was it for drinking and washing. I was immediately despatched by a tearful Carole to remonstrate with the management. I did so, and mustering as much bluster as I could, told them that Port Elizabeth City's latest signing wouldn't be staying with them, unless my wife and I were immediately moved to more suitable accommodation. I was quite humbled to find out that the room we had been mistakenly allocated was used by two local maids, who worked hard looking after the guests and cleaning their rooms.

Later that evening, we were moved to a room at the top of the hotel. We would awake the following morning to a most breathtaking view. As Carole pulled back the curtains, we were treated to our first real glimpse of Port Elizabeth and the beautiful Algoa Bay, shimmering in the early morning below. It was a far cry from the living arrangements enjoyed by the housemaids.

I was so impressed with the set-up at Port Elizabeth. My first glimpse of St George's Park Stadium came just two weeks later, when I was selected for my first game and it almost blew me away. It towered over the skyline and with its floodlights blazing it looked incredible. The drive up to the ground took us past scores of parked cars and the sight of people marching towards the stadium, which the locals called the Crusader Ground, put me in mind of Anfield. That wasn't the only similarity either; St George's was also something of a fortress.

The game was against Durban United, who were one of South Africa's biggest clubs at the time and huge rivals of Port Elizabeth City. The atmosphere was incredible. What followed was a lively game, with players getting stuck into each other at every opportunity. I remember thinking this was my kind of football. Both teams were fairly evenly matched and as the game wore on, I knew that one goal could settle it. Deep into the second half, I saw a cross coming into the box and dived to head it. It flew into the net and the home fans who were massed behind the goal erupted in delight. It would prove the only goal of the game and we ran out 1-0 winners.

I had once again scored on my debut and it had proved to be the winning goal. It was a terrific start to my two years in South Africa and it endeared me to the club's massive local support. I would go on to feature in all 12 of the club's remaining fixtures and managed to score nine goals. I couldn't have asked for more.

My success on the pitch was in sharp contrast to life off it. Initially, the squad were retained on part-time contracts. That meant we were training just three evenings per week. That might sound great, given it freed up my daytime to sit on the beach, enjoy barbecues and lapping up the sunshine. The problem was part-time football meant part-time wages. I needed to earn more money and went looking for a job.

Firstly, I pitched up at the club's Annual General Meeting, which took place at the end of the football season. There were lots of fine words spoken, but they seemed oblivious to the issues facing the playing staff. I couldn't help myself and when I saw my opportunity I leapt to my feet and addressed the top table, expressing my concerns that I would need to get a job in order to supplement my football income. There were promises made but I wasn't confident they would be fulfilled, to be honest. Then, a gentleman called Laurie Betheldo, who was one of the directors and, incidentally, a Scouser, contacted me after the meeting to say he could give me work in his factory, which went by the name South African Woodworking Company.

'Great,' I said, 'where's this factory?'

'It's in New Brighton, George.'

My obvious reply was to inform him that a trip back to Merseyside wasn't an option, but luckily for me, New Brighton was also a district just outside Port Elizabeth. I had no idea what I was letting myself in for.

The factory was in the middle of a shanty town and believe it or not I ended up working as a security guard there for a couple of months. I'm 5 feet 6 inches, so I didn't exactly cut an intimidating figure. However, I didn't need to worry too much. Workers are the same the world over and the only time anyone bothered me was to ask me to tell them stories about football in the UK. My heart went out to them. I knew that they worked so hard for so little and went home to such extreme poverty.

I would regularly lend them money. Laurie found out and tried to stop me, telling me that I was being taken advantage of, and that none of them could ever afford to pay me back. That to me was yet another indictment of the system and acknowledgement of the injustice of poverty pay. I decided to ignore his warnings.

Industrial relations were like nothing I had ever experienced. Back in Binns Road, I had seen how workers needed to organise in order to defend their working conditions and pay, but they would never have to contend with an armed management. In Port Elizabeth, the secretary of the factory, a Mr Pienaar, kept a gun in his desk drawer. However, I can honestly say that I never felt in any danger during the few months I worked in the factory. Perhaps I was just being naïve.

Away from factory life, Carole and I were able to enjoy the sights and pleasures of what is a wonderful country. Just before Christmas 1967, and after winning the South African League Championship, we travelled the famous Garden Route for a week's holiday. This involved a 500-mile trip from Port Elizabeth to Cape Town via George, Knysna and Stellenbosch wine country. We drove past the Groote Schurre Hospital, where just a few days earlier the famous heart surgeon Dr Christian Barnard had carried out the world's first heart transplant on Louis Washkansky. Washkansky sadly didn't live too long, succumbing to pneumonia after only 18 days; however, Bernard's second patient, Philip Bleiberg, survived for a year and a half and was able to leave hospital. This was the start of what ultimately was a huge medical breakthrough.

Then, a few days later we took a cable car to the top of Table Mountain. There we were able to look across the bay to Robben Island, where Nelson Mandela was just beginning the third year of his life sentence. Mandela was to spend the first 18 of his 27 years in that jail. We were so young and just beginning our married life. Looking back now, I realise how little we appreciated how history was being made all around us and how the world was changing.

My lens was football. It always had been. And I did really appreciate the joy it brought to the people and felt happy to be a part of that. Such were the oppressive conditions these people were forced to live in, football had become one of their few outlets. Watching their team every other week was virtually the only thing they had to look forward to. In many ways, football serves that function in England too, but I have never witnessed such extreme deprivation as that which I witnessed in South Africa. Yet, despite all of that, they packed out every game and filled the segregated fan area behind the Park End goal in the Crusader Ground, waving their Union Jacks in recognition that we were an all-British team.

I have always felt so sad about the situation in South Africa, because there are so many visually beautiful places to see and visit across the country and in my time there I met some wonderful people who I'll never forget. For Carole and I, this was our first home together and my eldest son Gavin was born in Port Elizabeth and has since visited the city for himself. Sadly though, Carole and I have never been back since we left the country in 1968. That said, South Africa and the City of Port Elizabeth will always hold special memories for both of us.

Thankfully, the club moved to full-time football at the start of the 1967 season. In doing so we became the first full-time professional football club in the country. It also meant a significant improvement in wages, which meant there was no need to work in the factory anymore. The club also enjoyed huge sponsorship from the Ford Motor Company, who had a large factory in the city.

The growth of the club commercially contributed to success on the pitch. In 1967, my first full season there, PE City as they were known, were crowned South African champions for the first time ever. What a wonderful season that was. It went down to the last game. For the penultimate match, we travelled to the Rand Stadium in Johannesburg to play a team called Highlands Park. We desperately wanted to clinch the title back at St George's and if we were to do that, a win on the road was essential.

We had battled our way through that season to that point, and one game against Cape Town City stands out in my memory. It took place at their stadium, Hartleyvale, and was watched by over 20,000 fanatical supporters. I had scored what their fans thought was an offside goal, and in no time a riot began, with flares being fired and an attempted pitch invasion. The referee had no choice but to take all of us off the pitch until the South African police and their dogs had brought order back to the stadium. We somehow completed the game and hung on to our narrow 2-1 lead and were extremely grateful to have escaped injury. It was a frightening experience.

A Johannesburg team called Highlands Park had dominated South African football for the previous few seasons. They were blessed with some fantastic players, such as the brilliant wingers Willie MacIntosh and Bobby Hume; Willie had played for my old club Aberdeen and Bobby had been with Rangers. They also had a brilliant Brazilian striker called Jose Santoro. Charlie Gough – father of the former Rangers and Everton player, Richard Gough, was also one of their best players.

However, we were a very good team with a reputation for playing attractive football. Amongst our ranks were former Reds player Kevin Lewis and centre-half Terry Mancini, who later went on to play for QPR and Arsenal before eventually being capped by Ireland. Another great player in our team was John Fielding, who had played for Everton and Southport. Three players in that team scored three-quarters of all our goals. They were Kevin Lewis, Peter Kerr and me. Despite the obvious challenges of playing out in South Africa, in football terms, this was the greatest and most successful year of my life. I was playing at the highest level in South African football and with a great set of lads, in front of some of the most passionate and vociferous supporters in the game. And although I'd have undoubtedly swapped that for one season in Shankly's first team, it was a truly memorable experience.

So, as the season drew to a close, the sense of anticipation was growing. As players we could sense the expectation amongst the supporters and were acutely aware of what a league title win would mean for them. Travelling to the Rand Stadium in Johannesburg, we were also aware of the increased attention from the national media.

The game was watched by a capacity crowd of 30,000 wildly excited spectators. We would eventually run out 4-2 winners. We had been leading 2-1 at half-time, then our opponents levelled halfway through the second half. The game was on a knife-edge until the final ten minutes when two brilliant goals from Kevin Lewis and Peter Kerr won it for us.

The flight back to Port Elizabeth was great as we celebrated being one game away from the championship. We all knew the mood in the city would be at fever pitch, but we weren't prepared for the greeting we received. We were mobbed at the airport by over 10,000 fans.

We won our final game of the season 7-1 against a team called Olympia after being 1-0 down at half-time. It was an amazing turnaround and set off massive celebrations throughout Port Elizabeth and the Eastern Cape. I can't remember much of that evening, which was spent at a local night club. We celebrated long into the night along with the supporters, who treated us like kings.

In Port Elizabeth they held several events in 2017 to celebrate the 50th anniversary of that great championship-winning season. I'm immensely proud to be part of their history and only wish that I could have been there to commemorate it.

We followed up the success of 1967 with a runners-up spot in 1968. By then, though, a move back home was at the forefront of my mind. South Africa was so far from home and we had a baby son, Gavin, who was only a few months old. I had really enjoyed the football. It was played on hard and fast pitches and the standard was probably the equivalent of the English Second Division at the time. South African football was also growing in reputation. Many players who were coming to the end of their careers would increasingly see it as an option. For example, Ian St John and Roger Hunt would venture out there in later years.

As far as Carole and I were concerned though, our two-year contractual agreement was ending, and we were ready for home.

There was one incident that put the seal on it for both Carole and me, and it involved a break-in at our apartment that almost resulted in me being killed. I still remember the day vividly and it gives me shivers to think how close I came to losing my life. I recall that I had seen a guy hanging around the courtyard of the building, but I didn't think too much of it at the time. I simply went inside and was relaxing with a newspaper in the lounge area, when I heard a noise coming from the bedroom. Fortunately, Carole was out at work. I shudder to think what would have happened had she been there too.

I went to investigate and encountered the guy coming out of our bedroom. He had a hat pulled down over his face. I can't say I panicked or was afraid in that moment, though; I felt more confused than scared at seeing a stranger standing there in our apartment. So, I immediately challenged him and asked what he was doing there. He looked nervous and replied that he had made a mistake and entered the wrong apartment.

I knew this was rubbish and grabbed hold of his arm. I started marching him along the passageway outside the apartment, down some stairs into the courtyard. I then noticed that he was carrying a blanket under his arm. I'd have left the matter there, but then I noticed there was a gold watch strap hanging out of the blanket he was carrying. The realisation that he had been robbing us suddenly hit me, and I reacted instinctively.

I reached out and grabbed him by the lapel. My intention was to restrain him long enough for help to arrive. I looked around frantically to see if there was anyone else around and realised that Terry Mancini's wife, Pauline, was watching from her balcony. I yelled at her to phone the police. At that point I could see the fear in the man's eyes, and he reacted violently, pulling himself away from me. I resisted his attempts to get away, when suddenly a knife appeared in his hand. I recoiled in horror and he shouted, 'I kill you,' lunging at me with the blade. As I staggered backwards, I tripped and fell to the ground. Time seemed to stand still, and I recall looking up at him and that knife in his hand.

I was completely at his mercy, and in that moment, I felt sure that my time was up. Miraculously though, he turned and ran towards the gates to the apartment complex. I hadn't realised that, as I fell, he had swung the knife upwards at my midriff. It had cut through my T-shirt on its journey towards my face and torn the garment in two, before scraping my chin. I had come within millimetres of losing my life.

My grandfather would have explained this away, saying that my time simply wasn't up yet. Maybe that's true, but neither Carole nor I felt like putting our trust in destiny too much longer. It was time to leave. Of course, Carole was very upset and until that moment we had always felt safe in Port Elizabeth.

The incident became big news in South Africa, something that my team-mates loved. Footballers will waste no opportunity to wind each other up. One of them arrived at training carrying a sword to much laughter. Carole and I were obviously struggling to see the funny side of the incident, but it wasn't just the threat to our safety, it was the attitude of the South African detectives who visited us after the incident.

During the interview, the officer seemed incredulous that I didn't own a gun and told me bluntly that I 'should have shot him'. Then he coldly stated, 'If you had done that, it would have been much easier for us. All we would have needed to do was come and take the body away. Now, we will never find him, and we could just as easily have been coming to take your body away.'

I have reflected on why my attacker looked so scared, and why he fled in terror. Perhaps he understood that his life was worthless to the South African police. Certainly, given the conversation I had with them after the attack, it was clear to me that they didn't think his life was as important as mine. I found the whole incident so difficult to come to terms with and I still do to this day.

So, I wanted to leave, but Port Elizabeth weren't so keen to let me go. As Cliff Lloyd at the PFA had predicted, they suggested I had to stay. I had scored 38 goals in two and a half seasons.

However, I wasn't to be persuaded and I had an ace up my sleeve. The letter signed by Matt Crowe when he signed me. It promised I could leave after two years. The lawyer dealing with the case thought I would struggle to get away, until I produced that piece of paper. Once he saw that he knew I was good to go. Of course, I was hugely relieved, but at the back of my mind were nagging concerns about what I was going to do on my return to England.

The answer to that problem presented itself one morning in June 1968, when I received a letter from a man called Lou Kottler. Lou ran a famous curio shop in Cape Town and his letter felt like a gift from the gods. He wrote:

Dear Mr Scott.
Our mutual friend Mr Sidney Reakes, Chairman of The Liverpool Football Club, is on a visit to South Africa and he has expressed a wish to meet with you.

He will be leaving Durban by air at 9am on July 1st (Flight number 500).

Perhaps you could care to meet him at the Port Elizabeth Airport that morning. We hope this is possible.

Yours sincerely

L Kottler.

Director

Carole and I met Mr Reakes at the airport. It was a strange experience, as we were continuously interrupted by supporters looking for autographs. They were thrilled when I told them I was speaking to the chairman of the famous Liverpool FC. Sidney took it all in his stride and asked me what my plans were now that I was leaving South Africa, adding, 'You have obviously done well here, George.'

I had done very well, I thought, having played 62 times for Port Elizabeth and scoring 31 goals. However, it had also been a trying experience. I told him about the knife incident in our apartment and that we were desperate to get back home. He was naturally shocked and told me that I should get in touch with Bill Shankly as soon as I got home, saying:

'I'm sure Bill would do anything he could to fix you up with a club back in England. Bill told me to try to meet up with you on this trip. I know he thinks the world of you, George.'

That was a huge relief to me and Carole, and I was confident of continuing my football career in England. It took another month to sort out the legalities of my split with Port Elizabeth, but eventually they agreed to let me return to professional football in England. I then wrote to Bill to tell him I had met Mr Reakes and that I was coming back to the UK in October 1968, at the end of the South African football season. A week or two later, I received an envelope with the familiar Liverpool FC crest on the back and when I opened it the words jumped out at me.

Dear George
It was good to hear from you again and good to know that you met Mr Reakes.

He told me he had met you and had a chat.

You have certainly done well, and I'm glad. When you come home I will try to get you fixed up with a club.

Incidentally Gordon Wallace is with Crewe. I will give them all your best wishes.

We are still winning (the five-a-sides), no wonder with five referees in our team.

Yours sincerely
Bill

One of the most wonderful things Carole and myself experienced on our return to the UK was clearing customs and seeing the overjoyed face of Carole's mum in the arrivals area. She had travelled down from Liverpool by herself, as Carole's dad wasn't too well at the time. To see her holding our son and her new grandson, Gavin, for the first time was something to behold. He had been born just four months earlier. I'll never forget that. It was a great moment and it made me even more motivated to ensure that my return to the UK would be a permanent one. I wanted to build my home and family here.

However, first I had to somehow get back into professional football. And I knew that if I couldn't get a contract back home, my only other option would be for us to return to South Africa. I didn't relish that at all, and once again it felt like the pressure was on. It turned out, though, that there was one man who could help open that door for me. A man who had already played a significant role in my career. That man was, of course, Bill Shankly.

Chapter 11

The Long Arm of Shankly and Brian Clough's Colourful Greeting

AS WE flew back into Liverpool in October 1968, the words of Sidney Reakes were still ringing in my ear. I was a little nervous at the prospect of returning to Anfield to see Shanks. After all, I had left the club in tears just over three years earlier. Of course, I was a different person now. Britain had also changed while I had been away. The country was gearing up for decimalisation and new 5p and 10p coins had been introduced. Harold Wilson was Prime Minister, Enoch Powell was fanning the flames of racial tension and The Beatles were premiering *Yellow Submarine* in London.

In football, Manchester was in its ascendency. United had been crowned champions of Europe and City had won the First Division back in May. On Merseyside, Evertonians were licking their wounds after losing the FA Cup to a single Jeff Astle goal.

My experiences in Aberdeen and South Africa had changed me. I was a man now and I had tasted proper football; I had experienced life and the world, warts and all. Still Bill's personality cast a long shadow. It still does. I knew, Mr Reakes wouldn't lie. If he said Bill would love to see me, then that was the truth. After all, why would Shanks maintain such an interest in my progress halfway round the world, unless he cared and wanted to look out for me? I knew I had to go to Anfield and see him, whatever my reservations or pride were telling me.

Besides, I had no work. Carole and I had left South Africa without securing a contract at a British club. I would once more have to call upon the influence of the man who had tempted me away from the arms of my family in Scotland, whether I liked it or not.

Looking back, Anfield, for all its majesty, was an austere place back them. As I strolled into the car park behind the old Main Stand, the autumn sun casting shadows on the ground, I spotted a familiar figure coming towards me. It was Roger Hunt. Suddenly, I felt like the years had melted away. My time back in Aberdeen and my adventure in South Africa were like a dream to me. There was a comforting familiarity to Anfield. In every way imaginable, it felt like a straw to a drowning man. It represented home, in the football sense, but perhaps also in a spiritual sense.

'Hey George,' called Roger, recognising me instantly and a little surprised to see me, I suspected. 'What are you doing here?'

'I've come to see the boss.'

'Ah, okay. He's in his office talking to the press. Go in, I'm sure he'll be delighted to see you.'

With that he was off, waving to me as he went. I turned and looked towards the players' entrance. The door was open, and I felt my stomach lurch. Swallowing hard, I walked in. As I strolled down those old corridors, the ghosts came back to me. I could almost hear the laughter and the memories came flooding back. Then, I heard his voice. It was unmistakable and I felt the hairs on my neck and arms stand up.

Shanks was coming out of his office, and still chatting to a journalist, I'm not sure if it was Colin Wood of the *Daily Mail* or Dave Horridge of the *Daily Mirror*. Anyway, Bill was in fine form and whoever it was hung on his every word. Then, the boss caught sight of me standing in the corridor.

'Well, look what the wind blew in,' he said. I was trying to keep my cool, but I'm sure I was grinning from ear to ear. Bill seemed genuinely pleased to see me. The gentleman of the press was promptly dismissed, and I was ushered into the manager's office once more. It hadn't changed, but I had. So too had our relationship. I wasn't a kid anymore. Bill was no longer my manager. Yes, there was still an enormous respect for him, but I felt more confident around him than I ever had.

I sat down opposite him at the desk. He regarded me quietly for a few seconds, perhaps taking in the man who had once been a young boy crying in this very room, three years earlier. Then he spoke and any lingering tension I felt evaporated.

'Mr Reakes tells me your team have won the championship. And he says you have set South Africa alight, scoring goals.'

'It's been an interesting couple of years, Boss,' I replied. 'But I think I did alright.'

'Aye, lad. It sounds to me like you've done more than alright. So, what are your plans George?'

I told him that that I was married now, and that Carole and I had a young son, barely four months old. I made it clear that I wanted to play in the UK.

Returning to South Africa wasn't an option. Shanks listened intently, nodding occasionally. When I finished, he simply said,

'Where do you want to play son?'

The thought of replying 'right here at Anfield' never crossed my mind. I wouldn't have had the nerve back then to be so forward. In truth, I knew deep down that this door had closed and I just wanted to secure myself a contract at a professional club. I still felt I had a lot to offer and I was still a young man.

'Anywhere, Boss,' I replied.

Shanks nodded and screwed up his eyes as if deep in thought. Then he said, 'Aye, son. That'd be right. I'll tell you what George, how does Tranmere Rovers sound?'

Shankly's influence in football was enormous. On Merseyside, he was a virtual king and when he called, people listened and thankfully as far as I was concerned, they very rarely turned him down.

'Boss, that sounds perfect,' I said. 'It's a decent level and close enough to home.'

With that, he picked up the phone and immediately called David Russell, who was then the manager of Tranmere Rovers. Obviously, I couldn't hear what Dave was saying on the other end of the line, but this is Shankly's side of the conversation, as far as I recall it.

'Dave, Bill Shankly here. How are you? Aye. Oh great. Listen, Dave, I have a boy here. He's just come back from South Africa. Anyway, he was the leading scorer in their National Football League over there, and I'll tell you something else, he was the best player ever to play for my reserve team.'

Then he fell silent for a moment, listening intently. Dave Russell must have said, 'We can't afford to sign him,' because Bill suddenly barked into the phone, 'David, you can't afford not to sign him.'

Suddenly Shankly's expression changed, and he was smiling again and nodding. Then, in a flash, the receiver was back in its cradle.

'Have you got your boots, son?'

I told him I could get them.

'Right you are. Get yourself to Prenton Park, son. Good luck.'

In just five minutes, and based solely on Shankly's word, David Russell, had committed himself to giving me a month's trial at Tranmere Rovers. He had also agreed to pay me first-team wages. I should add here that in reference to my being the best player ever to play in Shankly's reserves, I'm more than happy to acknowledge that Bill was somewhat prone to exaggeration. Nevertheless, I'll take the complement gladly.

Later that afternoon, I arrived at Prenton Park and was greeted by Dave Russell. He looked me up and down, and just said, 'I hope you can play son.'

Without having seen me play, and purely on Shankly's word, he put me in the first team for Alan King's testimonial match against Derby County. This was a big deal, as County were a fantastic team who were destined to become champions of England in 1972. They had an array of stars such as Archie Gemmell, Kevin Hector, Alan Hinton, Alan Durban, John O'Hare, Dave Mackay and a young Roy McFarland, who Brian Clough had signed from Tranmere the previous season.

My fitness levels had dropped since the end of the season in South Africa, but I felt confident that I could make an impact. I knew that if I put on a decent display, I could earn a contract. My experiences in Aberdeen and abroad had given me the belief that I had what it took at that level.

On the night of the game, I recall walking down the tunnel at Prenton Park and the clatter of my studs on the floor. Out of the corner of my eye, I saw a figure standing near the entrance to the pitch. It was Brian Clough, and he was eyeing each of our players as they walked out on to the field. Perhaps, like Shanks, he was looking for signs of weakness, any niggling injuries that he could exploit. Or, maybe he was just trying to psyche us out. It was just a friendly, but men like Bill and Clough always wanted to win, whatever the level of game they were playing.

Clough stopped me as I went to pass him, looked me dead in the eye and said:

'I hear this is your debut, young man.'

'Yes, that's right.'

'Good luck.'

'Thanks.'

With that I ran towards the light and on to the pitch. Over my shoulder, I heard him utter the punchline:

'You'll fucking need it.'

I had a great first half. I remember spraying the ball around and generally enjoying myself and raised a great roar from the

Prenton faithful when I nutmegged the great Dave Mackay. I won't repeat what Mackay said to me when he finally caught up with me.

I wasn't sure if I could last the full 90 minutes but knew I had at least 45 minutes in me and was determined to prove myself.

During the second half of the game the greater experience and talents of the First Division team took its toll and they went on to win 2-0, but I had done enough in the first 45 minutes to convince the Tranmere hierarchy that I could be an asset to the club.

The local press reports the following day were very complimentary, with one reporter, Stuart Hooton, describing me as having a 'bright performance', while praising my ball control before proclaiming, 'Scott, I think, is here to stay. He can already teach his colleagues a thing or two about running off the ball.'

At half-time, the Tranmere secretary, Norman Wilson, had come into the dressing room, presented me with a professional contract there and then and asked me to sign it on the spot. It covered the next two seasons and, importantly, I would be on first-team wages and bonuses. I have retained that contract to this day. I feel it represents a crucial turning point in my life.

So often in life, you only get one chance to stake your claim. When one comes along, you must grasp it with both hands. With the benefit of hindsight that first half of a football match was one of the most important 45 minutes of my life.

I played regularly in the Tranmere Rovers first team over the next two seasons and I feel I gave a good account of myself. More importantly, the move enabled me to settle back on Merseyside with Carole. Although I was playing in the third tier of English football, the crowds were still decent. We would regularly see 10,000 or more turn out to see us on a Friday night.

I really enjoyed it at Prenton Park and one highlight was a great run to the fifth round of the FA Cup in the 1969/70 season – although I didn't get off to the greatest of starts in that competition. During a second-round tie against Port Vale, at Burslem, I managed to score an own goal. I remember during the game I was back defending, and a shot deflected off my leg and into the net. As a footballer, you hate moments like that. There's nothing you can do about it and even though you know that, it still hurts. In fact, that probably makes it hurt more.

Happily, I was able to redeem myself by scoring the equalising goal in the last minute of the game. That forced a replay, which we won 3-1. My goal would seal the tie and suddenly the pain of that own goal was erased. The cup tie was also memorable for me because I lined up against Johnny King in both matches.

Johnny is rightly a legend at Tranmere today. Johnny was a great competitor, who had featured 48 times for Everton in the 1960s. He would go on to be a wonderful manager at Prenton Park. I believe Bill Shankly was a great mentor to him during his early managerial career. Johnny led Rovers out of the Fourth Division at the end of the 1975/76 season and though he was sacked in 1980, he would return in 1987.

In his second spell he managed to move the club to within a whisker of the Premier League. It's little wonder that the club erected a statue in his honour. Sadly, he passed away in 2015.

However, he will always be remembered as having given so much to the game of football and to Tranmere Rovers Football Club in particular.

After victory over Port Vale, we were pitted against Portsmouth at Fratton Park. Our opponents were in the Second Division and the match attracted a crowd of 30,000. Our game was full of passion and commitment, and it didn't take us long to silence the 'Pompey Chimes' and run out 2-1 victors. The goals that day were provided by George Yardley and John McNamee.

George Yardley was a prolific goalscorer for Tranmere, whose career was badly affected by an awful back injury which he sustained after a tackle by striker Alf Wood in a league match at Shrewsbury. I was very friendly with George at Tranmere. He has since left us and he is much missed by all who knew him.

Playing for Portsmouth that day was Mike Trebilcock, who had become an unexpected Everton legend a few years earlier after scoring two goals for them in the 1966 FA Cup Final. Mike came back with us to Merseyside on the coach and regaled us with tales of how he had been shocked to find out from Harry Catterick that he was in the cup final squad just a few days before the trip to Wembley. And, that he only made it because of an injury to Everton centre-forward Fred Pickering. As I said before, sometimes in life you only get one chance and you must be ready to take it. Mike certainly took his chance that day and wrote his name forever in the history of Everton Football Club.

Victory over Pompey put us in the fourth round against Northampton Town. Unfortunately, we lost that game in extra time at the end of a replay. It was a huge blow made worse by the announcement of the fifth-round draw. Northampton had been given a plumb tie at home to Manchester United.

United won the game 8-2. It was a match that saw the incomparable George Best score six goals. I felt gutted that I had missed out on a chance to face him and that Manchester United team. As a footballer, no matter what level you're playing at, you dream of testing yourself against the very best.

I played at Tranmere for two years, making 44 appearances and scoring twice. By 1970, I was now approaching 27 years of age and was starting to think about the end of my career. Though three years off, the dreaded 30th birthday and worries about life after football were increasingly at the back of my mind. I had done nothing but play professional football since the age of 15, aside from my brief flirtation with the biscuit world, that is. I was still in love with the game, but some of the glamour was beginning to fade. I also knew that my ride was coming to an end. My attention was starting to drift to how I could continue to earn enough money to feed my family during the many years after football.

In those days, when a player reached the age of 30, he was on the way down. Most of us had left school with no qualifications and therefore the options open to us were extremely limited. I didn't fancy becoming a pub landlord and when I saw an advert for a sales job at Nestlé, the huge Swiss confectionary and grocery company, I thought I would give it a go.

The interviews were at the Adelphi Hotel, in the centre of Liverpool, and I attended in my best suit and tie. Football was all that I knew back then. I didn't have the first clue about business and my only foray into the world of work prior to this was hauling pallets around a factory in Binns Road. It was hardly a stellar curriculum vitae, I thought. What I was ignoring, of course, were the incredible experiences I had amassed in the previous 15 years. Sales is about forging relationships, acting with integrity, never giving up and sheer hard work. These were all skills I had accrued in the world of football.

I arrived on the morning of the interviews and was a bag of nerves. As I walked into the grand, ornate reception area and made my way to the giant ballroom, where the interviews were held, I realised that there were around 80 prospective candidates milling around the foyer and there were only two jobs on offer. I felt a tremor of anxiety rush through my body. I can't do this, I told myself. What do I know about sales? The sense that I was about to embarrass myself and that I was hopelessly out of my depth was overwhelming.

In what I can only describe as a fit of terror, I turned on my heels and walked back out of the building, down the stone steps and was halfway down Lime Street when I stopped in my tracks. I was furious with myself for backing out. I had never done something like that in my life. When I thought of the setbacks I had overcome, the things I had seen and the courage I had shown in the world of football, I knew I could never walk away from any challenge and still hold up my head. That just wasn't who I was, and it wasn't what I had been taught.

A thought popped into my head: 'What would Shankly do? What would he say, if he saw me fleeing from an interview like a scared wee boy?'

Years later, in 1975, Shankly would give an interview to a local lad who would go on to be a journalist at the *Daily Mirror*, about the importance of giving everything you have to be the best you can be, no matter what your occupation. That journalist was Brian Reade. Shanks would tell him:

'If I became a binman tomorrow, I'd be the greatest binman who ever lived. I'd have Liverpool the cleanest city on earth. I'd have everyone working with me and sharing out the success. I'd make sure they were paid a decent wage and had the best bonuses, and that we all worked hard to achieve our goals. Some people might say, ah but they're only binmen, why do we need to reward them so well for a job that anyone can do, but I'd ask them why they think they're more important than a binman. I'd ask them how proud they'd feel if their city became the cleanest in the world. And who would have made them proud? The binmen.'

Although, as I stood on Lime Street that day, I hadn't heard Bill utter those words, they didn't surprise me at all when I read them years later. That was the man he was, the way he lived his life and it was the attitude and value-set that he drummed into every player who pulled on the red shirt. No matter what you were asked to do, no matter how menial you felt it was or how intimidating it might have been, you should meet the challenge with the same effort and pride as if the fate of the world depended upon it.

I believe that's what he meant when he said football wasn't a matter of life and death, it was 'much more important than that'. He wasn't suggesting that it was literally more important than people. Shanks had huge regard for ordinary men and women. Particularly those who followed Liverpool. Their lives, their hopes and dreams meant the world to him and his one desire was to serve them well and make them happy, in the only way he knew, through football.

That's what he was saying, I believe. That football is more than a game, it's a means of giving service and just like any other occupation it has value and deserves your very best effort at all times. You don't shirk that responsibility, no matter if you're a professional footballer, a binman or attending an interview for a job that would help you to feed your family. Knowing all of that, I knew I had to go through with it.

So, I turned around and marched back to the hotel and sat down for the interview. I couldn't tell you what they asked, or what I told them, but I recall their reaction to seeing the reference from Shankly. I'm in no doubt that it was his words that sealed the deal.

I was at a crossroads now. I could have stayed at Tranmere, but Stan Storton, who had been a team-mate at Prenton Park and whose brother Trevor Storton later joined Liverpool, had already left the club to become manager of the Northern Premier League team, Ellesmere Port Town. Soon after being offered the sales job, I received a call from Stan who asked me to join him as a semi-professional. He was prepared to offer a three-year contract.

It didn't take me long to work out that working at Nestlé I would be driving around in a company car and combining the wages from sales and the contract at Ellesmere Port, I would be bringing in far more than I would if I stayed at Tranmere. As a man with a family and many years of work left in me, it was an incredibly easy decision to make.

The Tranmere players couldn't believe my decision to leave and go part-time. A few of the comedians in the squad were saying, 'You'll be driving round in a car with a huge Milky Bar on the roof Scotty.'

However, I know I had the last laugh, and in that moment I had become a part-time footballer at night and a Nestlé salesman by day. From that point on, I have never looked back.

Of course, Tranmere weren't happy about me leaving. I don't blame them. They had treated me well and had been there when I needed them most. The crowds who turned out in their droves to watch third tier English football were always generous to me and I enjoyed my time there. However, I had to make a decision that was best for my family, and I'm convinced that's what I did. I'm sure anyone placed in the same position as me back then would have done the same thing.

I had begun my journey away from football, and life as a full-time professional player. However, there were still six more very happy and competitive years of semi-professional football to enjoy in the Northern Premier League, with Ellesmere Port Town. I then moved on to the Cheshire League with New Brighton, before finally playing for Christleton in the West Cheshire League. I had the greatest of final hurrahs, linking up once more with George Yardley, my old mate from Tranmere.

Having played at a much higher level, George and I became marked men in that final season. The experience brought me to the realisation that that my football career was coming to an end. It took me some time to get over this, but sadly, at whatever level you play, it's something all footballers must deal with in the end.

I had already begun to build for a life outside the game I had loved so much. I was determined to put as much enthusiasm and commitment into my sales career as I always had in my football career. I knew that was the only way to be successful. My decision to focus on the next stage of my life was proven correct by the arrival of our second son, Craig, in July 1974. His arrival would complete our family and meant I was even more determined to do whatever it took to provide for Carole and the children in the years after football.

Craig's birth was a particularly joyous experience for us both, as Carole and I had experienced the pain of miscarriage a few years earlier. Both our sons, their lovely wives and families have given us so much pleasure. They have all been so good to us and we are very proud of them all.

My sales career was incredibly successful, and I seemed able to work my way up the ladder with relative ease. I loved every moment of it. I'm so glad I didn't run away from that interview at the Adelphi Hotel. As I look back now, I appreciate the helping hand of Bill Shankly in my onward journey. His reference, written in July 1966 has served me well over the years – not least of all in a lucrative sales career, with many adventures to be had before my retirement at 61.

And, although my playing career was over, Liverpool had now become my home. My love affair with Anfield had been cemented forever. I would follow Liverpool FC from now on as a supporter, and I had many new adventures to come.

Chapter Twelve

Denis Law, Elizabeth Taylor and Henry Kissinger

AS A young impressionable boy of 12, growing up in Aberdeen, I was aware of an incredibly talented lad some five years older than me. He was a schoolboy footballer playing for Powis Academy. He would also turn out regularly for the Aberdeen Lads Club, a team I would join in later years. That boy was Denis Law.

Denis was a young boy from a working-class background, whose father was one of those trawler men I would wave to from the pier in Aberdeen Harbour. Everyone in the Aberdeen schools football fraternity seemed to be talking about Denis. However, when I set eyes on him, I was really surprised at how small and frail he seemed to be, even though he was a few years my senior. He had blond hair and appeared to have a bit of a squint in one eye. This meant he wore the famous, or infamous – depending on your viewpoint – National Health spectacles. His appearance to me couldn't have been in starker contrast to his prodigious talent and ability.

He would be selected many times for the Aberdeen Schools Select team and, along with a fellow Aberdonian called Les Massie, in 1956 he was persuaded at the age of only 15 to join Huddersfield Town in Yorkshire, as an apprentice professional. Of course, the manager of Huddersfield at the time was none other than Bill Shankly.

I'm pretty sure that Shanks and his assistant, Andy Beattie regarded Denis as something of a prize. They had signed Les in order to ensure Denis wasn't lonely and didn't suffer from homesickness, although Massie would also go on to have a great career at Huddersfield.

Although still very young and somewhat lightweight, Denis was given his debut for the Huddersfield first team at the tender age of 16. He showed such fantastic ability that from that moment on, he was never out of the first team. He would quickly make a name for himself south of the border, in England.

I knew Denis's brother Joey quite well, and he used to tell me about how well Denis was doing and how brilliantly this manager called Shankly had treated him. Soon everybody knew about him, as the youngster began grabbing the headlines and started appearing on our TV screens. Then came the stunning announcement of his transfer to Manchester City for a British record fee of £55,000 in 1960.

After just one year at City, he was signed by Italian team Torino for £110,000. This was a colossal fee at that time. From there, he moved to Manchester United for £115,000 in 1962. The rest, as they say, is history.

If only Liverpool FC had found the money to sign him. My heart skips a beat when I think of him playing for Liverpool under Shankly. I recall him driving around Aberdeen in the close season, in his shiny red Jaguar. That would have been around 1962 and by then he was becoming something of an idol and role model for me.

The first time I met Denis officially was in 1960, while he was playing for Manchester City, who were in Liverpool to face Everton in a midweek game at Goodison Park. After training, earlier that day, Bill Shankly called me into his office. I was somewhat nervous as I walked along the corridor that led to his door, my mind racing and searching for what I might have done wrong.

When I sat down in his office, he told me he realised how much I admired Denis Law. He would be going to the game that evening along with Reuben Bennett and said that if I met him at the players' entrance at the end of the match, he would introduce me to Denis.

I was so excited. I couldn't wait for the evening to come. So, after the game I hurried down to the players' entrance and sure enough the boss came out and ushered me in. It had been a very cold and wet night and I imagined the players were keen to get into their hot bath. However, Shankly didn't hesitate to march into the Manchester City dressing room, leaving me waiting outside. A few minutes later, he emerged with a very wet superstar who was still covered in mud. He would introduce me to my idol with these words:

'Denis, I want you to meet a fellow Aberdonian who has come down to play for me. Just like you did. And he is going to be better than you.'

Denis simply smiled knowingly and shook my hand, saying:

'The best of luck to you son. You couldn't play for anybody better in the game. But I have to tell you he does tend to exaggerate.'

There was laughter, nervous on my part, and Denis disappeared back into the dressing room. The boss headed off to meet Reuben Bennett, who was his lift home. I was left, gobsmacked, to find my way home.

To be fair to the boss, he wasn't the only one to draw comparisons between myself and Denis Law. I still have an old newspaper clipping, written by a Scottish columnist in the *Glasgow Record*, called Waverley. He had travelled to Liverpool to watch Liverpool Colts play their Everton counterparts in the Lancashire Football League Division III. Obviously, he was particularly interested in what he termed 'the Liverpool Scottish', those who Shankly had scouted from north of the border. Of course, that included me.

I had lined up in that game alongside Gordon Wallace, Bobby Graham and Phil Tinney. A young Tommy Smith also featured in the game, which Liverpool won 3-1. Gordon got one of the goals. However, Waverley had spotted my performance and made a very flattering comparison with my hero, Denis Law. This is what he wrote:

'In Liverpool on Saturday, I saw the makings of another Denis Law, and like the blond bombshell, he is a native of Aberdeen. George Scott is the name and he is one of the teenage Scots who are members of one of the most fantastic outfits in football.

'With the exception of Monty Maclaren, from Auchterarder, a 6ft 2in 17 year old, the others are 16 or under; Monty's brother Scots are Bob Connelly (Dundee) right-half, Hamish McKenzie (Denny) centre-half, Philip Tinney (Dundee) left-half, Robert Graham (Motherwell) outside-right, Gordon Wallace (Glasgow) centre or inside-forward and the afore-mentioned Scott.

'Maclaren is a young brother of the ex-St Johnstone 'keeper now with Plymouth Argyle, while Wallace is a son of Dougie from South Africa, who used to star with Clyde.

'And believe me Gordon is developing physically in a way that will see him as strong as his father was on the field.'

It fills me with pride to have been compared to a talent as prodigious as Denis Law. I believe Shankly thought I could go that far when he convinced me to sign, and clearly others did too. However, football often has other ideas.

Nevertheless, that night at Goodison is still burned into my memory. I remember running across Stanley Park in the rain to my digs at 258 Anfield Road. I was on such a high that I thought I would never come down to earth. As an impressionable 16-year-old, my head was spinning that Shankly had said I was going to be better than my idol. Although, I would later learn that Denis was correct. The boss did have a penchant for exaggeration.

Our paths would cross a few times in the years that followed. Many years later, in the 1970s, when I was working as a regional sales manager for the American multinational company, Cheseborough Ponds, I was calling to see a large wholesaler client of mine in Manchester, called Rayburn Trading Company.

As I got out of my car, I noticed another drawing up behind mine. I was immediately struck by how familiar the driver was to me.

Sure enough, it was Denis Law. I immediately went over to shake his hand and the next minute I was sitting next to him in the passenger seat of his car. We were chatting away about the old days when we became aware of a crowd gathering around us. They were knocking on the windows and asking him to sign autographs. It got so hectic that we had to drive off around the corner, leaving my car behind.

Denis told me that he was working for Francis Lee – the ex-Manchester City player – as a salesman. He was selling a range of paper products, such as toilet rolls and kitchen rolls. It seemed we had a fair bit in common. I had a half hour to spare before my appointment, and I could think of no better way to spend it than chatting away to a hero of mine. I even gave up many customer leads to him, enabling him to develop his new career. I'm still amazed at the fact that an all-time great of the game had wound up selling toilet rolls.

A few months later, I was out on my travels again and this time I was calling on a toiletries wholesaler called Albert Harrison Ltd in Accrington, Lancashire. To my utter amazement, Denis once again pulled up behind my car.

'What are you doing in Accrington, Denis?'

He told me that he was using the page of sales leads that I had given him earlier in Manchester. Turned out they had been very useful for him and had also meant our paths would cross again.

'I know you are working for Franny Lee, Denis. But you've still got your BBC Radio punditry role as well, haven't you. I heard you the other night when United were playing down at Plymouth Argyle in the FA Cup. You were good.'

'Thanks George. But, you know, I'm really annoyed with United. After the game, I needed to get back to Manchester because I had an early meeting at Francis Lee's offices, in Wigan,' he told me. 'So, I asked them if I could fly back with them on their chartered plane. They told me there was no room for a classified member of the press.'

His face darkened as he retold the story. He was clearly still angry with his former club.

'Can you believe that, Georgie, after all I have done for them?'

I couldn't help myself, and with a wry smile, I said, 'Denis. You relegated them in 1974.'

His face brightened and erupted in laughter. I told him I had an appointment with the buyer and would have to take my leave. To my surprise, he said he would wait for me. Even though it was a quiet suburban street in Accrington, it wouldn't take long for another crowd to gather around his car. Denis just patiently got on with signing autographs as I entered the building.

I took great pleasure in telling the receptionist that her next cold call was a footballing legend. She wouldn't believe me. When I think back, I can barely believe it myself.

On another occasion, I was running a sales meeting at the Lymm Hotel, in Cheshire. A member of my sales team approached me and said that the Manchester United team were having lunch downstairs, prior to a game. I went to the restaurant in the hopes of finding Denis. To my delight, I bumped into him in the bar area.

We got chatting, when up walked George Best. Denis briefly introduced me to him, and although we only exchanged a few pleasantries, the expressions on the faces of my sales team were a sight to behold. There I was chatting to two of the greatest players in world football. I would dine out on that for quite some time.

My final meeting with my hero came a few years later, when I was working for a company called Bourne Publicity. I was attending the International Golf Show at the National Conference Centre in Birmingham, along with a sales colleague, Nicky Gold. Nicky was a scratch golfer and worked for me in Scotland.

As well as being a brilliant golfer, Nicky was also a football fan and a big supporter of Scotland. As we walked around the exhibition, I saw Denis in the John Letters exhibition area, talking to some of their executives. He had a film crew with him, and I realised he was shooting a commercial. Suddenly, he looked up at me, stopped what he was doing and crossed over to Nicky and me, a huge smile on his face.

'Georgie. How are you doing?' he said. 'What brings you down here?'

I introduced Denis to Nicky, who by now was completely star-struck. We stood chatting for what seemed like an age, when a voice interrupted us, 'Denis, we need you. There's a schedule to keep to.'

They say never meet your heroes, but every encounter I ever had with Denis Law made a mockery of that saying and this one was no exception. He simply turned his head and shouted:

'I'm talking to my friends. I will be there when I'm ready.' With that, he signed an autograph for Nicky and said, 'Bill Shankly told your boss he was going to better than me, you know. But what he didn't say was that he meant as a salesman, not as a footballer.'

After all those years, all his success in the game and the big clubs he had played for, Denis had remembered his encounter with Shankly and me outside that dressing room at Goodison Park. What a man, and what a footballer.

My first post-football job was of course with Nestlé. Though I probably wouldn't have believed it if someone had told me it in the ballroom of the Adelphi on the day I had my interview, my sales career was a tremendous success. I spent four very happy years at Nestlé. I worked my way up the sales ladder and was soon headhunted by Cheseborough Ponds, who would be bought out by the massive Unilever organisation. Unilever had its roots at Port Sunlight Village, on the Wirral. This was less than two miles from where I lived. The head office of the sales organisation, however, was in central London at Hesketh House, in Hesketh Square.

Lord Leverhulme, whose father had created the Unilever organisation and built Port Sunlight Village for his employees, would later become known to me when I joined Bromborough Golf Club, where he was president for many years. I would later be elected captain of the club, in 2009, something I still regard as a tremendous honour.

Once the Unilever takeover had been announced, I was called down to Hesketh House in London, along with two of my colleagues. When we arrived, we were informed that as part of the takeover deal, a division of the Unilever organisation would be responsible for the sales and marketing of Elizabeth Taylor's Perfume – Passion. It was the original celebrity perfume and it had been a runaway success in the United States and in the Middle East. Myself and my two colleagues, Peter Shields from Scotland and the late Paddy Hardy from London, were appointed as the three senior sales managers responsible for sales and marketing in the UK and the Channel Islands.

Peter was responsible for Scotland, Paddy for London and the South of England and I was responsible for the North West of England, the Midlands and Wales. It would be a job that would see me rub shoulders with a Hollywood A-lister and a former American secretary of state and diplomat.

It all started on a lovely summer morning in 1988. I was heading south on the M6 to fulfil a customer appointment, when the pager on my belt started buzzing. My first mobile phone was still a few months away, and it would be the size of a house brick when it finally arrived.

I pulled over at Sandbach services and simply couldn't believe what I was seeing on the pager. In fact, I was so convinced it was a joke that I had to ring head office for confirmation. As it turned out, it was no joke and I, along with Peter and Paddy, were being instructed to drop whatever we were doing, go home and pack for a trip to Paris, where we would be meeting Elizabeth Taylor, in person.

On arrival in France, we were greeted by a few of the European sales executives, along with a well-known music producer, called Brian Eno. The list of musicians that Brian has been associated with reads like a who's-who of the music industry. They include Roxy Music, David Bowie, Talking Heads, Ultravox, Phil Collins, U2, Coldplay and Genesis. He was, back in 1988, organising Liz Taylor's Paris trip.

We were scheduled to meet the movie star the following day at the Ritz Hotel. However, that evening we were treated to a sumptuous meal and the drinks were flowing, in a restaurant overlooking Notre Dame Cathedral. These days, the Ritz Hotel in Paris is probably best known for its association with the final hours of the life of Princess Diana. However, in 1988, it enjoyed a reputation as simply one of the finest hotels in the world. The opulence we observed when walking into the reception area took our breath away.

Our cases were whisked from our hands and we were led upstairs to what I can only describe as a palace. This was Taylor's suite, filled with beautiful furniture and ornate mirrors on every wall. Apparently, Ms Taylor was just 15 minutes away. Even after all this time, I remember vividly the nervousness and sense of anticipation I felt as the minutes ticked by. But, perhaps in keeping with her stellar persona, Elizabeth would keep us waiting. The 15 minutes came and went, then a half hour, before the door swung open and in walked two security guards, followed closely by the hotel manager and a lady I later came to know as Chen San, the star's personal assistant.

Then, in a moment that seemed to last an age, she arrived. She was dressed in an emerald-green satin dress, with a diamond brooch on her lapel. It seemed as big as my fist. My initial impression, as she walked towards us, was that although she had naturally aged, she was every bit as beautiful as her photographers would have us believe. Her hair was immaculate, and her eye makeup was an amazing violet colour. Chen San introduced her to my colleagues and me, before she retired to a very ornate chaise longue. A member of the hotel staff served us coffee and she then spoke to each of us in turn.

I must admit that I was a little star-struck. These surroundings were beyond anything I had been accustomed to. I remember thinking of my grandfather as I sat there, of how he had pushed that £20 note into my pocket and waved me off at that station all those years earlier. And I wondered what he would have made of where that journey took me. Here I was, in Paris, sipping coffee with possibly the greatest leading lady of all time. It had been some ride and I hoped I had made him proud.

She asked my name and then said, 'And in which areas do you sell my perfume, George?'

When she heard that Wales was part of my portfolio, she replied, 'Does that include Debenhams, in Cardiff?'

I replied that indeed it did and that sales in that particular department store were excellent. But I was curious as to what it was about that store, of all the others. I had to ask.

'Oh, George. I sometimes shop in Debenhams in Cardiff, when I come over to visit Hilda. But, sadly, I do have to wear a disguise.'

Hilda? I had no clue who she was referring to and my expression gave me away.

'Richard's sister of course. She still lives in the Valleys.'

She was referring to the man she married twice, Richard Burton. It was touching that though they had divorced for the second time, in 1976, she was still visiting his sister more than a decade later.

I was in something of a trance by this point and said a few things about how we loved selling her products and how they were flying off the shelves across the UK, and that it was wonderful to meet her in person. She then proceeded to give a little speech, thanking each of us for our hard work, before allowing each of us to take photographs with her.

Then, with her PA's glance at a stopwatch, it was all over. We were presented with a personal signed photo of her and, just as she was about to leave, the door swung open once more. In walked a hotel butler, carrying a silver tray that contained a single white envelope.

He offered the envelope to Elizabeth Taylor, who opened it, smiled and said:

'Of course, I can see him for a few minutes.'

We watched in amazement as the butler left the room only to return moments later accompanied by a very sophisticated gentleman, with a mane of curly hair.

'Elizabeth. Darling,' he said. 'What brings you to Paris?'

'Wonderful to see you, Henry,' she replied. 'I'm here to thank these gentlemen for the wonderful work they have been doing. They're making my perfume such a success in the United Kingdom.'

To our utter amazement, we were witnessing a meeting between a Hollywood superstar and the US Secretary of State and National Security Advisor, Henry Kissinger. He had been in Paris on official business and had just been negotiating with representatives of the Soviet Union.

He immediately turned to us and said, 'Gentlemen, it looks like you are doing a great job. She does not issue praise lightly. I must say, salesmanship is a wonderful profession. But I have to say, I prefer negotiation.'

Then it was all over, and they were both gone. We ran down to the hotel entrance just in time to see the flash bulbs of the paparazzi firing off, and her Bentley taking her to Orly Airport and onward to Los Angeles. It was quite an experience for a group of working-class lads.

I would meet my new 'friend' Liz one more time, this time back in England. Six months after our encounter in Paris, sales of Passion had continued to boom. I had negotiated and organised many special promotions in some of the top department stores in the UK. The part of my role I enjoyed more than any other was interacting with the senior perfumery buyers in the various national stores such as House of Fraser, Beatties and Debenhams. These women, who were the key buyers within the large department store groups in the UK and the Channel Islands, were known as the perfume dragons. They weren't the easiest of people to convince. However, the one common denominator was that, without exception, they all loved Elizabeth Taylor. Without exception, they were all very experienced buyers, but even they couldn't fail to be swept up in the glitz and glamour of Passion.

I used my association with the brand to gain their good graces and was even able to take them to see Michael Crawford and Sarah Brightman, in the original production of *The Phantom of the Opera* in London. It was a surreal experience, especially when I started handing out tissues to these so-called tough buyers, who had been overcome with emotion during the performance.

By the autumn of 1988, we were getting ready to launch the second product in the range, and I would once again get to meet Elizabeth Taylor in person. This time our encounter would be in the perfume hall at Selfridges department store in London.

The new product was called White Diamonds, and once again it was glamorously packaged and brilliantly marketed. Part of the marketing effort was to issue invitations to key customers and advertise a personal appearance by Elizabeth Taylor in the London press.

Again, my colleagues and I, who had been heavily involved in the Paris trip, would be leading the UK launch. We hired Richard Keys, the sports presenter who later went on to work with Andy Gray at Sky TV, to host and serve as master of ceremonies.

On the day, 2,000 women crammed into Selfridges perfume department and the scenes were reminiscent of a football homecoming or cup final. It was pandemonium. Of course, the guest of honour was fashionably late, and I still recall with some amusement, how Richard Keys struggled desperately to stall for time and keep order.

Mercifully, she arrived just 15 minutes after the advertised time, and a very grateful Keys gleefully gave way to the movie star. We all breathed a sigh of relief as she walked into the stage spotlight with the sound of Shirley Bassey's rendition of 'Diamonds are Forever' filling the air. Ms Taylor wore a fabulous purple dress with a large diamond clasp brooch and on her finger was the most amazing looking diamond ring.

At the age of 48, she still looked simply stunning. She had the crowd in the palm of her hands. I found her to be witty and entertaining and she showed great patience in the Q&A too.

The session ended with her signing some autographs for selected VIPs, whilst Eartha Kitt's 'Diamonds are a Girl's

Best Friend' blasted out from the speakers. This really was a spectacular occasion.

With the public portion of the event over, my job was to round up the top 15 sales representatives from UK department stores for a private audience with Elizabeth Taylor. This was to be their reward for meeting their sales targets. These women would line up, as if waiting to greet a member of royalty. In a way they were. Liz was the queen of tinsel town after all. They each took their turn to shake her hand and then moved on. I was given strict instructions by the celebrity's people that under no circumstances must any of the sales reps mention the name of Richard Burton, as it may upset the star.

One of the women in that line was one of my employees. Her name was Annie Hughes and she lived and worked in Cardiff, selling the perfume from Debenhams. Annie had a huge personality and was a wonderful person. She was also a huge fan of Liz Taylor. Annie had the most wonderful Welsh accent, and when it was her turn to meet Ms Taylor, she shook hands with the star for what seemed like an eternity. She seemed reluctant to let go and instead stood staring into those beautiful eyes.

I was starting to get a little nervous and then Annie dropped her bombshell, in that delightful South Wales accent.

'Miss Taylor, can I ask you a question?'

I watched, helpless and my heart sank.

Liz replied, 'Of course.'

'How did you persuade a Welshman to buy you a rock like that?' She was pointing at the ring on Taylor's finger.

We all looked at each other nervously. All mention of Richard Burton was strictly off limits. However, there was no backlash, and the movie star's response was as gracious as it was moving.

'Dear, that is a lovely Welsh accent. Where are you based?'

'I work in Debenhams in Cardiff, Miss Taylor.'

"Well,' replied Liz, 'he was a very special Welshman.'

Then, it was over, and the star of the show was heading to the door, when she spotted me and called out with a smile,

'Hello George, nice to see you again. I can certainly see why your sales in Debenhams in Cardiff have always been so good.'

Then, she was gone.

When I look back on my life, I'm struck by how rich my experiences have been. I have been blessed to have met some incredibly interesting people. To think it all began on a frosty morning, on a lonely platform at Aberdeen station, 60 years ago.

We never know where our adventures will lead. My grandad told me it was all mapped out ahead of me. I don't know if that's true, but I'm so grateful I got to take the ride.

Chapter Thirteen

Bill Shankly and the Legacy He Left Me

IT MAY seem self-indulgent to talk of a personal legacy in relation to Bill Shankly. In many ways, Shankly belonged to all of us, to football itself. In the incredible BBC documentary of the man's life before Liverpool, *Shankly: Nature's Fire*, an old colleague utters the line:

'Football belonged to Shankly. He just let the rest of us play it.'

It's a wonderful quip that goes some way to explaining his influence and, well, power. There are people who come along, perhaps once in a generation, who define the era in which they live. Then there are others who define future eras. Shankly, to me and so many others, was one of those.

But it was the scope and breadth of his legacy that's so amazing to me. He was someone who weaved his spell over the game, and was respected, even revered by his peers. Through sheer force of will he lifted Liverpool Football Club up out of the morass it was in and established it as a world power.

Yet, for all the grandeur of his achievements on the large scale, there are countless tales of personal interactions that have such special meaning to so many. In the Shankly Hotel, on Victoria Street in Liverpool, the walls of the dining room are festooned with letters to the great man, penned by children. Letters he replied to personally on an old typewriter in his living room. There are stories, now corroborated, of him attending weddings and christenings of supporters' children. And many of him playing football with local children on a patch of grass that now bears his name, in front of his former house in West Derby.

I don't wish to deify him, though. He was, after all, a mere human, blessed with the same frailties and flaws as the rest of us. But he was, nonetheless, a remarkable man.

The values by which Bill Shankly lived his life were based on common sense and they were easy to understand when communicated to us players. Determination, commitment, honesty, respect for others and unbounded enthusiasm were part of his lexicon. He demonstrated by words and deeds that the key to success was a relentless determination never to give up, no matter how bleak the chances of success seemed.

He is one of the most quoted men in football history, but for me there are two quotes that stand out above all. They became almost a mantra by which I have lived my life.

'The greatest thing in the world is natural enthusiasm, without it you are nothing.'

And:

'You get nothing for sitting still. Nothing happens unless you make it happen.'

Like Shankly, I never had the benefits of further education. I left school at 15 to play professional football. So, as I have carved out my journey in this world, I always kept those words at the forefront of my mind. They have served me well, both in the game I love and in my life after football.

So, in that sense I have always maintained that five years at Anfield, playing under Bill Shankly, was worth ten years at any university. No professor or lecturer could ever match the passionate way he communicated his messages. Nor could they have boiled down complex ideas and made them accessible in the way he could. I'm reminded of another saying of his, in which he was talking about how some people use fancy language to confuse or distance themselves from others. His approach, he said was different.

'Whereas somebody might call a man avaricious,' he would say, 'we would say he was bloody greedy.'

So, I always viewed the reference he gave me as an award. My diploma, if you like. While there was no graduation ceremony, this was my certificate and my passport into the world. It was a huge factor in me getting my first sales position after I hung up my full-time boots. In a small way, I owe my success in sales to the man.

When my career progressed and I began to manage sales teams of varying sizes, I always tried to apply Bill's style to the role. And, it was no surprise that it worked so often. I carried his messages into every team meeting and every encounter with a client. Always be enthusiastic, try to inspire by example, tell people what you will do clearly, and always do what you said you were going to do. I knew the importance of respecting those I disagreed with, but being true to myself and being honest with them. I knew my teams could never be successful without self-discipline and unless each member did their part for the greater good of the whole.

The genius of these approaches is in their timeless simplicity. In my sales career I won many awards by applying these methods, including Sales Manager of the Year, which I won four times at Unilever, in 1981, 1983, 1985 and 1989.

However, just as in football, in my sales career I would have to deal with setbacks too. I was made redundant at the age of 45, and again at 53. These weren't the best times of one's life to find yourself out of work. But time and again I wanted to embody that never-say-die attitude that Shankly drummed into me as a young man, and which I still see coursing through the veins of the football club today.

In the face of each setback, I would simply pick myself up and keep going. I got myself an even better job than the one I had lost and continued to work, until I finally retired at the age of 61, in 2005.

My first redundancy, by the Unilever organisation in 1989 when I was 45 was a huge disappointment. I knew that I needed to move on and ensure that I secured another position as soon as I could. I had, of course, received a very welcome redundancy payment, after 14 years' service and this helped to cushion the blow a little.

But it wasn't just the loss of income that bothered me. I would also miss the friends I had made and the security of believing I had a job that would see me into retirement. Unilever were very good, in that they registered me and other colleagues with an employment agency. The company was based in York, which meant travelling up there three times a week, printing off copies of my CV, making phone calls and filling in job applications. It felt a bit like a graveyard for redundant middle managers, but everyone there was in the same boat and a certain camaraderie was evident.

I recall how they would ring a bell and pop a bottle of champagne whenever anyone managed to get a job. The lucky individual would sign the cork and place it in this huge glass jar so that everyone could see that success was possible. Within three weeks, I got the opportunity of an interview with a company called Bourne Publicity who were based in Woking in Surrey. I was immediately offered the role of north-west England regional sales manager on a salary similar to the one I'd had at Unilever. They also threw in a slightly better company car.

I spent the next seven years at Bourne Publicity, and they were incredibly enjoyable and rewarding. Within two years I was promoted to national sales manager of the company and built a successful sales team using the same ethos I had been taught at Anfield all those years ago. The only downside to my new promotion was the sheer amount of driving I had to do. Trips to Woking twice a week and motivational meetings with my sales team all over the country would rack up around 40,000 miles a year.

Bourne were one of the largest promotional and business gift companies in the UK and it was a completely new industry for me. The range of items they supplied was endless. Everything that could be printed with a company logo on it, from golf balls, or pens, to Post-it notes, we sold them. I may have had limited industry or product knowledge, but what I did have was the ability to recruit, train, inspire and motivate sales teams. I had been doing that successfully for many years, and in Shankly I had the greatest role model.

It was hard work, but there were upsides to it. We worked hard, but we always ensured that people were rewarded for their efforts. Whether that was with trips to golf tournaments or other events it didn't matter. What was important was that everyone shared in the rewards at the end of the day. Where have I heard that before?

One of the most incredible moments at Bourne involved a trip to Israel as the guest of the Pierre Cardin perfume company. I vividly remember how it happened. I was driving home from Surrey when the phone rang. It was my managing director, Andrew Bourne. Andrew was a lovely man, but his only problem was he was a fanatical Arsenal fan and probably still is to this day. His father had formed the company originally and Andrew had assumed the role of MD on his father's passing.

He told me that all Pierre Cardin's European suppliers had been invited on this all-expenses-paid trip to Israel, which was to be a combination of training and leisure. However, due to other commitments, Andrew was unable to go. He then nonchalantly asked if Carole and I could go in his place. I can tell you I didn't need any persuading.

It was an amazing week. We flew out on a chartered plane. It was an experience like no other. On the flight to Eilat in southern Israel, we were entertained by magicians and jugglers, before arriving at what was a quite spectacular hotel. There were 300 delegates at this event, and they came from all over Europe. Every day we attended a themed breakfast, followed by a one-hour product training session in our various groups. Once that was out of the way, the day was our own to do as we wished.

They arranged a mini Olympic Games at which I won gold for the UK, in clay pigeon shooting and table tennis, no less. I even had to stand on a podium whilst they played the national anthem. Unfortunately, the medals weren't really made of gold.

One evening, the hotel put on a complete production of *Fiddler on the Roof* in the ballroom. It was as good as any West End performance. Then, there was the bus trip from Eilat to Jerusalem, to see sights like the Wailing Wall and to follow the stations of the cross all the way to the hill on Calvary, where Christ was crucified.

We crossed the border into Palestine to go to Bethlehem and entered the church which stands where, according to the Bible, Jesus was born. And, I even touched the very spot, which was somewhat worn by the hands of so many pilgrims who had visited over the years.

It was disappointing to see the spectre of commercialism alive and well in the Holy City. They were selling all sorts of souvenirs, and holy water by the bucket full. The Palestinian military lads seemed very young and they were positioned in the square where the church was situated. Some of them were amusing themselves by playing cards, while their guns were propped ominously against their chairs.

From there, we were off to swim in the Dead Sea, or rather I should say float on the Dead Sea – something I managed, whilst reading a newspaper.

Two days later we were driven across the Israel-Jordan border, to visit the famous pink ruins and the treasury at Petra.

These had been heavily featured in the film *Indiana Jones and the Temple of Doom*, starring Harrison Ford. On the way, we stopped at a Jordanian village for lunch, which consisted of a whole lamb that had been cooked in a hole in the ground. We sat in the square, eating our meal, and listening to the sound of local music and being entertained by an authentic Jordanian belly dancer, while the Middle Eastern sun beat down on us.

The site at Petra was amazing; a glorious temple carved into the side of a cliff. It's incredible that it was rediscovered in the 18th century. The cliff itself was a wonderful pinkish colour, a truly spectacular sight.

Then we had to prepare ourselves for the long coach drive back to the hotel. And, whilst it had been a relatively pain-free and quick crossing of the border on our way out of Israel, the opposite was the case on the way back. The security at the border was so tight that it took us over two hours to pass through.

On our last evening, we were treated to a poolside fancy dress party and huge fireworks display over the beach. For a boy from the district of Torry in Aberdeen, the whole thing felt somewhat surreal. I can only imagine what my old granny and grandad would have made of it, or indeed whether the great Bill Shankly with his strong socialist principles would have approved of all of the money spent on this extravaganza.

The whole week must have cost the Pierre Cardin organisation hundreds of thousands of pounds. Nonetheless, for Carole and me, it was an unforgettable experience.

We had no idea that in just a matter of months, I would be at yet another crossroads. With my adventures in Eilat behind me, it was back to the mundane world of work and a summons to see Andrew Bourne. He told me that the board of directors had met and decided that I must relocate from Merseyside to Woking in Surrey. They wanted me to be near the heart of the business. This was something I just couldn't consider. My roots were now on Merseyside, it was my family's home. I simply refused to do it and was fully prepared to receive a call telling me that my time at the company was over.

A week went by and nothing happened. I decided to fly up to Aberdeen for a quick visit to see my mum. On the flight, I just happened to be reading the jobs section of the *Daily Telegraph*, when I saw what appeared to be an advert for my job. I immediately called them and suggested that this was constructive dismissal. In the end, they agreed a financial settlement along with six-months' notice. That meant I had time to find alternative employment.

It was another bitter blow, as I had been at Bourne Publicity for seven years and during that time I had helped to increase the company's sales returns from £9 million in 1990, to almost £13 million when I left the company in 1997.

Bourne recruited my replacement from the London area, but it didn't work out too well for them in the end. Sales declined, people left, and eventually the business was sold to a competitor. It no longer exists.

I was now 53 years of age and out of work again, and that was no age to be looking for a new job. It would have been easy to despair, but as I had learned a long time ago, nothing happens unless you make it happen – you get nothing for sitting still.

I felt too young to retire. I felt I still had many years left in me and found myself once again studying the vacancy columns and business sections of the newspapers. I needed a job in the north-west of England and had also developed an interest in the pharmaceutical industry after my time at Bourne.

As has so often happened during my life, fate would serve up the right opportunity at the right time. I remember sitting at the breakfast table one day, when I saw an advert for a company called Donald Wardle & Son. They were based in Stoke-on-Trent and their business involved sales to nursing homes and pharmacies. I interviewed at their head office in Stoke, and, after hearing me talk about how I would bring my experiences to bear and help them turn their business around and move it forward, they offered me the position.

I'm often struck by how transferable the lessons learned and skills acquired in one field are, when you move to another. The job at Wardle & Son was, in many respects, similar to the job Bill had when he arrived at Liverpool, and I guess the same as anyone coming in to turn round an underachieving organisation. You get to know the company, the people who work for it. You decide quickly whose services you can't live without and then help those who won't help you take it forward to move on as quickly as you can. Then you identify the rising talent, the people with potential, and you nurture, train and encourage them. After that, if there are still gaps, you recruit people who specifically fit the company's needs. It's an ongoing process and it's exactly what Shankly did during his time at Anfield.

When I joined the firm, they were struggling and it was obvious to me that a great deal of work would be required if the business was to survive and prosper. The managing director, Andrew Wardle, and his family, were undoubtedly dedicated to the business. They had a brilliant financial director in Keith Bridgett. What they lacked, however, was strategic sales and marketing direction, and that's what I had been brought in to provide.

I immediately set about streamlining the sales and marketing operation by bringing in highly focussed training, motivational and personal development programmes. My idea was to eliminate weaknesses and build on the company's inherent strengths, which were many. I introduced annual sales awards, which became highly aspirational for the team, and results began to improve dramatically. I had learned, from my time at Anfield, the value of people understanding the basic principle that teamwork leads to individual benefits, as well as elevating the whole.

My achievements in the pharmacy division were beginning to be recognised by Andrew Wardle, and he soon asked me to take on the nursing home sector of the business too. I found the extra responsibility challenging. But providing support to the care sector was also very rewarding and some of the most gratifying years of my professional life.

During my eight years at the company, we were able to turn the business around, almost doubling sales revenue. I had achieved what I was asked to do and that gave me immense pride. When the family sold the business to United Coop Health Care Group, I saw that as my opportunity to bow out. I would leave the company in 2005 at the age of 61 and am confident that it was in a far better place than when I found it.

The managing director of United Coop Health Care Group was a man named John Nuttall. I had come to know him during the transition, and he knew that I had previously dabbled in after-dinner speaking. For that reason, I would be given the honour of presiding over the National Staff Awards event, as master of ceremonies, two years running. The evenings were a black-tie affair, attended by 600 people and held at Bolton's Reebok Stadium.

Although I joined the company during the sunset of my career, I have always looked back on those years at Wardle & Sons as the most successful and rewarding of all – especially given the age at which I joined them and the challenges we faced. Together, we moved the business from the 'second division' to the top of the 'first division'.

In my career after football, in sales and sales management, I met and worked with so many wonderful and talented people and many great characters. Since leaving the world of work, I have spent my retirement years playing golf and being immersed in family life. I have loved watching my grandchildren grow up and marvelled as their characters have developed. Of course, I still love watching the Reds from the Kop, which is still full of wonderful characters.

But that was never going to be enough for me. While I'm still alive, I'm determined to be the best I can be, at whatever I turn my hand to. I want to give something back to society and make my family proud. These, of course, are values instilled in me by Shankly, but also by my parents and grandparents. In many ways, the great man resonated with me so much, I think, because his beliefs chimed with those of my upbringing and the lessons my family gave me.

So, I have devoted a significant part of my retirement to raising money for Lymphoma research charities, a cause close to my heart for obvious reasons. I do this in the only way I know how, through my after-dinner speaking. And, of course, my Shankly stories are such a massive and wonderful part of that.

I first experienced after-dinner speaking as far back as 1979. I had played for New Brighton FC, who operated in the Cheshire League, between 1974 and 1976, and I had become good friends with a fellow player called Dave Greenhalgh. Dave's father, Norman Greenhalgh, had played for Everton, in the same team as Dixie Dean. And for many years he had been host at the Bromborough Hotel in Bromborough on the Wirral.

Norman was a very hard full-back and he was evidently given the name 'Rollicker' because he took no prisoners on the field of play. He always boasted that there wasn't a winger in the league who wasn't afraid of him.

In 1979, Dave had retired from football and was working in the building industry on Merseyside. I was still with Cheseborough Ponds. One day Dave rang me and asked if he could meet me to discuss a favour he wanted. It seemed that a great friend of his had been appointed as president of the Cheshire branch of the Scottish Caledonian Society. They would be hosting their annual dinner at the five-star Grosvenor Hotel in Chester, in a few months' time.

The society had arranged for the Lord High Sherriff of North Wales and Cheshire, Elgan Edwards, to do the Immortal Memory to Robert Burns at the dinner. However, he had called off unexpectedly and they needed a replacement. He asked me would I step in, saying:

'You're a good speaker, George. You have plenty of stories.'

Needless to say, I agreed to do it. It meant I would be spending the next two months researching everything I could about Robert Burns and what was expected of the main speaker at a Burns Supper, in proposing the Immortal Memory. I quickly realised that the similarities between Burns and Bill Shankly were amazing. Shankly loved Burns's poetry so much that he chose one of Robert Burns's great songs, 'My Love is Like a Red, Red Rose', when he appeared on BBC Radio's *Desert Island Discs*. Burns and Shankly were both from poor backgrounds and were born within a few miles of each other in South Ayrshire in Scotland.

On the night, there were around 400 people at the event. As I gazed out over the room, I was met with a sea of dinner suits. Many of these people were from the legal profession and there was also a sprinkling of captains of industry and people from the medical profession, including my own doctor. I decided to combine quoting Robert Burns's poetry such as, 'A Man's A Man for A That' with the many stories of Bill Shankly I had accumulated along the way. Of course, I would deliver this in the style of the man himself.

I can scarcely remember being more nervous than I was in the 15 minutes before that address, as I stood in the opulent surroundings of the men's cloakroom and toilet, rehearsing my lines repeatedly in my mind. Then I took my seat at the top table, glanced at the menu cards and realised that everyone sitting either side of me had more letters after their name than I had in mine. I was simply listed as George Scott esq.

Then, in a blink and a gulp, the master of ceremonies announced me and I was on my feet. I remember there was a very stylish member of the audience in the first row who had a handlebar moustache. It wasn't difficult to fixate on him, and fortunately he laughed heartily at my opening remarks. That gave me confidence, and when the laughter spread to the rest of the room. I was in my element. All those weeks of study and rehearsals were beginning to pay off. The speech seemed to fly by and as I finished, I was almost blown off my feet as the audience rose to give me a standing ovation.

I remember when I got home, my wife Carole – who knew exactly what it meant to me, not to let my friend Dave down – was waiting at the front door for me. I'll never forget the look of joy on her face when she realised it had all gone so well. It's always great to have someone in your corner, and I always know that whatever I'm doing, she is cheering me on.

It had been my first experience of public speaking outside of my work environment. The fact that I had been able to address so many people and receive such a great reaction gave me so much confidence. Once again, I had felt the influence of Shankly and had channelled it to achieve success.

Thirty years later, our whole family were devastated by Carole's diagnosis of grade 3 non-Hodgkin's lymphoma in 2009. Having watched her go through the most gruelling six months of chemotherapy, it's difficult to describe the feelings of elation we had when she was declared free of the cancer.

We knew only too well how fortunate we were to receive this wonderful news. So, when in 2015 one of the past captains at our golf club, Dave Faulkner, who was a wonderful character and is sadly no longer with us, asked if I would do a talk to the members of the Birkenhead Rotary Club about my time at Anfield under Bill Shankly, I was more than happy to do so, as long as the club made a donation to the Lymphoma Research Trust.

David, of course, immediately agreed, and the evening was a great success, raising £500 for the charity. However, in a moment typical of the area, at the end of my talk a group of Reds began singing 'You'll Never Walk Alone', holding aloft their Liverpool banners. Not to be outdone, however, there were a number of Evertonians in the room who immediately produced their blue-and-white scarves and began playing 'Johnny Todd' on their mobile phones.

That was the first of many such after-dinner engagements I have done over the years. As I write, I have raised over £11,000 for lymphoma charities. Many ex-players, particularly those who have been successful and are famous, can charge huge fees for speaking at various dinners. But for someone like me, who never achieved celebrity status, it's much more satisfying to be able to give something back to the wonderful professionals who fight on our behalf every day.

So, even now, I can say that my relatively brief encounter with Bill Shankly continues to shape my life and enrich it. Though I was never able to play for his first team, I still feel like a Shankly Boy to this day. And I continue to live by the values he taught me. They are as relevant in life as they are in football.

Chapter Fourteen

In My Mersey Paradise

I HAVE now made Merseyside my home. I'm a proud Scotsman and Aberdonian, but I feel comfortable here. I feel a close connection with the people of this region and their values are my values. Carole and I are so pleased to have raised our sons here on the banks of the Mersey.

There are few places in the world as in love with the game of football as Liverpool is. It courses through the veins of every Scouser. You struggle to find anyone in this region who won't engage you in conversation about the game and who hasn't nailed their colours to the mast in terms of which team they support.

In Liverpool, you're either Red or Blue, there is no other choice. That suits me fine.

That's also true of my sons, whose allegiances lie either side of the great Merseyside divide. Craig, my youngest supports Everton, while Gavin is a Red. I love that this is normal in this area, that so many families are divided down the middle and yet they can live together, work together and share their homes and lives without problems.

Gavin was a devoted Red from the moment I first took him to Anfield, at the age of seven. Kevin Keegan was thrilling the Kop back then. Gavin's two sons, my grandsons Callum and Charlie, have followed in his footsteps. The three of them go to every game at Anfield where they have season tickets in the Kop. Callum is now 18 and Charlie is 14.

Craig, however, chose a different path. He is a passionate Evertonian and has a season ticket in the Park End at Goodison. He never misses a match. Naturally, Craig's two sons, Cameron and James, who are now aged 17 and 10 respectively, are also true Blues, with Cameron attending most matches with his dad. And, as Craig married into a wonderful Evertonian family, you can imagine the banter has been both fierce and hilarious at times.

I have lost count of the number of times that, upon realising that one of my boys is a Blue, people have responded with, 'How on earth did that happen, George?' However, that's just how it is on Merseyside and our story is not all that unique. Long may it continue, I say.

It all started, I believe, while I was away working. Craig's Uncle Ken took him to an Everton reserve game. When I returned home, my son promptly approached me and asked if I could take him to Goodison to see the first team play. I must admit, although I was sort of on the horns of a dilemma, I could see how keen he was to go to see Everton. So, I took him. From that moment on there was no looking back for him and he has been a committed Blue ever since.

I continued to take him to Goodison whenever I could. I even sat with him in the Park End, and watched the Blues clinch the First Division championship on 4 May, 1985. He would have been 11 years old. Although my allegiances lie elsewhere, I'll never forget the look of excitement on his face at the final whistle.

I have often told Craig that I have always loved Everton Football Club. Even when I was a player at Anfield, I had so many friends across the Park. I'm always happy when they win, so long as they don't win the two derbies at Anfield and Goodison. As a loving father, the perfect scenario for me will always be Liverpool as champions and Everton as runners-up and the Reds winning the Champions League and the Blues lifting the FA Cup.

Over the years, Gavin and I have shared a love of Liverpool Football Club and have had some wonderful times following the Reds. Craig and I share our mutual love of golf. Craig's generosity to me has been very moving over the years. I'll always treasure the memories we have of going to see The Masters in America in 2017, when Sergio Garcia won. And, to Carnoustie in 2018, to watch Francesco Molinari win the Open Championship.

Thanks to Craig, we have played together at some of the greatest courses in the UK, including St Andrews, Turnberry, Royal Birkdale and Gleneagles. For someone who loves the game of golf as much as I do, these are unforgettable experiences. Both of our sons have been so generous to Carole and me over the years and we are very grateful and blessed to have such a wonderful family.

Of course, the relationship between the broader Liverpool and Everton support has soured in recent years, maybe not for all, but for many. That saddens me greatly. Whatever the reasons, and I don't wish to delve into them here, they have more in common than divides them and they have come together when it matters on so many occasions. Despite the enmity of recent years, that will always remain true for most of us.

Of course, there is no event that signifies this basic truth more than the Hillsborough Stadium disaster. The date of 15 April 1989 is seared into the hearts of everyone in the region, whether they support Liverpool or Everton. It certainly is in mine. I still recall the day vividly, not least because my son Gavin was at that FA Cup semi-final match.

I remember waking that day and going into Gavin's room to rouse him. He was going to the game with his mate Bryn, who lived just around the corner from us. They were both due on the coach at Birkenhead and I was worried he would be late. Both lads had been to Hillsborough the previous year, when the same two teams had contested the semi-final at the same venue. They were both looking forward to the day out.

While Gavin was downstairs eating his breakfast, I thought I would make myself useful and tidy his room. My eyes fell on the two tickets, sitting on his bedside table. Though they would have had little significance to me in that moment, I can still see the following words in my mind's eye to this day: 'Admit to Leppings Lane Enclosure'.

Gavin and Bryn were both season ticket holders on the Kop. They would always stand behind the goal at games along with their mates, and so it wasn't surprising to me that they had tickets for that end of the ground. I thought no more about it until much later in the day as the news of the disaster started filtering through.

After they left, Carole and I relaxed for the morning, before she decided she would like to take me shopping in Liverpool city centre. I would have much rather stayed home and listened to the game on the radio. But in the end, I reluctantly agreed to go with her and our youngest son Craig. I would just watch it on *Match of the Day* later that evening, I thought.

As any Red will attest, trying to engage in any activity while aware there is a match going on is almost impossible. And, all that afternoon I would find it difficult to focus on the clothes, shoes and perfume Carole was enjoying looking at. My thoughts were far away in Sheffield, wondering how the Reds were doing in the semi-final.

It must have been around 4pm, when we left Lewis's department store and headed for the car. On the way, I noticed a policeman and approached him to ask him what the half-time score was.

'The game has been abandoned due to crowd trouble,' he replied in an almost matter-of-fact tone.

It worried me a little, but I didn't for a moment think Gavin or Bryn would have allowed themselves to get caught up in anything like that. So, we got in the car and carried on through the Mersey Tunnel and headed for home on the Wirral.

Of course, the radio was on as we drove. I was a little distracted, daydreaming and probably thinking about when the replay would be, when the news bulletin shocked me out of my daydream. The newsreader was talking about there being fatalities at the Liverpool game, he mentioned the number 60, and he definitely said 'Leppings Lane enclosure'.

Of course, Carole's immediate response was to ask, 'Oh my God! Where is our Gavin, and Bryn?' Craig sat silently in the back seat, engrossed in his own thoughts and worried about his brother.

I was in turmoil. I was visualising those two tickets, and the words 'Admit to Leppings Lane enclosure'. All I could think to do was try to reassure her, even though I was worried sick. I blurted out something along the lines of, 'Don't worry love, he is in the Main Stand.' But it wasn't true, and I knew that. I felt sick.

It seemed to calm Carole down a little, and that's all I had wanted to do. Both of us fell silent for that eight-mile journey, lost in thought. Carole no doubt relieved, while I desperately hoped our son was safe. All the while, it felt like that fatality count rose with every mile we drove.

In my mind, I ran over what the odds of Gavin being involved in the crush might be. I reasoned there would have been thousands in that enclosure. And I prayed selfishly that destiny had been on his side and that he would be okay.

When we arrived home, I could hear the beeping of the answer machine in the lounge and ran across the room to play back the waiting message. We will always regard that message as the greatest sound we have ever heard, and the relief we experienced was overwhelming. It was Gavin, telling us not to worry. He wanted us to know that he had made it out of the crush and that he had found Bryn.

They were heading back to their coach pick-up point and hopefully would soon be on their way home. Back in those days there were no mobile phones and they had relied on the generosity of locals in Sheffield, who were letting people use their house phones to ring home and leave messages.

As it turned out Gavin had been in Pen C, right behind the goal in the Leppings Lane end. He had managed to use the crush barriers to protect himself, but still lost his friend Bryn in the melee. They were separated for an hour. Bryn had been lifted into the stand above, and Gavin eventually found his way out sideways, into the next pen.

Both suffered relatively minor physical injuries compared to others that day. However, when the newspapers came out the following Monday, with terrible pictures of supporters crushed up against the fence, we could see their faces, just eight rows back from the front of the pen.

Both lads had learned from their experiences the year before. There had been crushing at that time too, and when they found themselves in the same stand in 1989, they would both make sure they stood directly in front of and not behind the crush barriers.

Gavin was interviewed by the police as they collected witness statements during the initial investigation into the disaster. He would have to repeat the process again many years later, in 2014, when the Independent Police Complaints Commission held its Hillsborough Enquiry, following the publishing of the findings from the 2012 Hillsborough Independent Panel review process. That review process had concluded that no fans were responsible for the disaster and that its main cause was a lack of police control on the day.

Gavin has never really spoken to us in detail about his ordeal and the scars he must have carried after Hillsborough. And we have never pressed him on it. He still carries his original ticket from that that game, inside his season ticket wallet. It goes to every match with him and I suppose it serves as a reminder to be thankful for his luck all those years ago.

We, as a family, were just so grateful for his safe return. We know so many families had to cope with the most appalling of tragedies on that sunny April day. It began with such hope, joy and excitement and ended in terrible despair. One such family were the Devonsides. Barry is a good friend of mine. He is a great Liverpool supporter who sadly lost his son Christopher that day. I know he has never gotten over it. How could he? Barry is a great collector of all things Liverpool. I first met him at one of the Liverpool FC ex-players Christmas parties. Barry had driven Laurie Hughes, former Reds captain and England centre-half to the party.

That night Laurie was sadly taken ill, and Barry had to leave the festivities early, but not before we had a great conversation, in which I agreed to pass on some signed memorabilia to him. Hillsborough changed Barry's life forever. He has been a leading light in the fight for justice for the 96. I know he attended virtually all the court proceedings over the last 30 years. He fought steadfastly on behalf of his son, as so many others have.

I received a letter from Barry in January 2020, in which he said that even 30 years after the event, Hillsborough had taken its toll on him. And during the last two years he had suffered major health problems. Amazingly, he would end the note by telling me that he was 'doing okay'. It's impossible for anyone not involved in these tragic events to really appreciate the physical and emotional effects on those left behind on that tragic day.

In October 2017, I received an invitation through another wonderful Liverpool supporter, Chris Wood, to do an after-dinner talk for the members of the London Branch of the Liverpool FC Supporters Association. They were celebrating their 50th anniversary at the Shankly Hotel in Liverpool.

Chris is a brilliant historian of all things Liverpool, a long-serving member of the supporters' group and, I believe, had even served them as secretary during those years. Just before the Shankly Hotel had opened, Chris Carline (Bill Shankly's grandson), the director of the hotel, had asked me to do an interview for their in-house television channel. It was an incredibly emotional interview, and I considered it a great honour to be asked. Further to the interview, Chris told me that he wanted to collect the best Shankly-related stories received from supporters and ex-players. These would be inscribed on the ceilings of the hotel rooms when it opened. Carole and I once stayed as guests of the hotel, in room 117, and it was a source of immense pride to see mine written out on the ceiling there.

The evening of the 50th anniversary celebration was a huge success. I must confess to feelings of apprehension as I noted I would be sharing the top table with none other than Liverpool CEO, Peter Moore. However, we were all in celebratory mood and I thoroughly enjoyed the night. It's always a great privilege for me to tell my stories about Bill Shankly. The evening also raised £1,200 for Lymphoma Research and that made it even more special.

After finishing my speech, I returned to my table without realising that I was about to experience one of the most emotional hours of my life. I noticed that the chair directly across from me was empty. Sitting next to me was Fred Sephton, a long-standing member of the London Branch, and I asked him who was missing from our table. The seat had belonged to Jenny Hicks, the mother of Sarah and Vicki who tragically lost their lives at Hillsborough. Jenny and her family had been members of the London Branch of the LFC Supporters Association and she had been unable to make the trip at the last minute due to illness.

Fred told me a very poignant story. He said that he had travelled to Hillsborough with the Hicks family on the day of the game. He had been in the stand above the Leppings Lane Terrace. His abiding memory of the girls was of them turning, waving and making funny faces at him. Fred had been so traumatised by what happened at Hillsborough that he left the UK for a while, making a new life for himself in the Mediterranean.

I was still reeling from Fred's account, when I was approached by a lady who said, 'Can I please give you a hug George?'

She told me that listening to the part of my talk where I had referred to the tragic events of Hillsborough, she had been moved to tears. She explained that her name was Becky Shah and that she had been 17 years old at the time of Hillsborough. She had been unable to obtain a ticket for the game but her mother, Inger Shah, who was 38 at the time, and her 13-year-old brother Daniel had gone to the match together. Sadly, Becky's mother, her only parent, had been killed in the disaster. She told me of her quest for justice and of her anger at the authorities and *The Sun* newspaper, in particular about the treatment of her younger brother, Daniel, who had suffered a gruelling interview at the hands of the police. How awful must that have been, given he was grieving for the loss of his mother.

Becky wanted me to know that Inger had given tireless service at the Royal Free Hospital in London. She was a pillar of society and was neither a drunken hooligan nor a bad mother. Her death was a shocking blow to all her colleagues, many of whom attended her funeral. Becky told me she was the best mum anyone could hope for. It may surprise many to know that as a result of the death of their mum, Becky and Daniel had to be taken into care.

These are the hidden consequences of Hillsborough. The details that lie behind the numbers. I can't imagine the pain experienced by these children. To this day, that conversation with Becky Shah remains one of the most emotional experiences of my life.

A week after the Hillsborough disaster, the playing surface at Anfield and the barriers on the Kop were a sea of flowers and scarves, which had been placed there by Liverpool fans and indeed supporters of many other clubs. Football had truly come together. No one showed more support for Liverpool FC than our neighbours across the Park, Everton.

My younger son, Craig, and I went to Anfield to pay our respects and lay flowers on the pitch. So many others had the same idea and the surface was a blanket of bouquets and mementos. After we had left our own floral tribute, we made our way on to the Kop for a period of quiet contemplation. Craig, who has been a proud and devoted Everton supporter all his life, wandered off down to the bottom of the terrace and made his way towards the back of the goal, where he tied his Everton scarf to the net. Attached to it was a note. He just stood there silently for a moment, before returning to join me on the steps.

Before leaving the stadium that day, I couldn't resist wandering over to the goal and looking at the note he had attached to his blue-and-white Everton scarf. As I read his words, my eyes welled up with tears. It simply said:

'Thank you, God, for keeping my brother safe.'

In the years that led up to the Hillsborough Stadium disaster, it had seemed to me that the club was set for many more decades of glory. The magic set in train by Bill Shankly in 1959 was showing no signs of fizzling out. However, the years that followed were characterised for me by slow decline, particularly during the 1990s. It seemed like the club was struggling to recapture its identity. With the departure of Kenny Dalglish from the manager's role, the thread back to the Boot Room days had been broken. Graeme Souness took over and wanted to modernise the club. That was possibly the right thing to do, but maybe there was a sense of too much too soon.

When Graeme became the manager, I was genuinely excited. He was a wonderful and iconic former captain of the club. However, I did feel a little worried that we would be losing some of the ethos that had been in place for so many years. Continuity at a football club is important, I believe, and change should be gradual.

Graeme had been heavily influenced by the conditions and coaching methods he had observed in Italy whilst at Sampdoria. He set about introducing many of these facets into the club during his time as manager. He gave everything he had to the role and I felt he deserved to succeed. Unfortunately, the progress that everyone longed for – none more so than Graeme himself – failed to materialise.

Instead, it seemed like the club was struggling to recapture its identity. Roy Evans attempted to re-establish the old principles, but by then I felt we had fallen too far behind the likes of United.

At the turn of the century, we saw flashes of success with Gérard Houllier and Rafa Benitez at the helm. That glorious treble season of 2000/01 and of course the journey to Istanbul for the UEFA Champions League Final in 2005 are amongst the most iconic seasons in the club's history. However, at least in terms of the domestic league, what Shanks called the 'bread and butter', we were always playing catch-up.

However, the memories of Istanbul are quite the consolation prize. On 25 May 2005, 45 years after my arrival at Anfield, I found myself alongside my oldest son, Gavin, in the grandstand at the Ataturk Stadium in Istanbul. We sat in disbelief at what we had just witnessed, elated and exhausted. We had just watched Liverpool return from the dead. After being 3-0 down at half-time, against the best team in Europe, they had come back to level the score in the second half and had won the cup on penalties.

Naturally, in such moments, thoughts drift back, and we think of those who aren't there to share in the glory and the celebration. I have heard many fans describe this feeling. For me, I thought of the ex-players who fought for Liverpool and of course my old boss, Bill Shankly. The fighting spirit that led to our triumph, that still runs through this club like a vein of gold, was produced all those years ago under his guidance. How I wished he had been there to see it.

However, being a Liverpool supporter, you know that along with the sunshine, there's always going to be a bit of rain. It is of course the storm that makes the golden sky at the end so much more beautiful. Two years after that glorious day in Istanbul, we came up agonisingly short in another Champions League Final, in Athens. That was a terrible night for two reasons. After suffering a painful defeat, we found that the flight we arrived on had left and hadn't returned to take us home. We now faced spending the night in Athens, sleeping on the tarmac outside the airport building. And to make matters worse, we would be serenaded by the victorious Milan fans on the other side of the airport. Thankfully, Gavin, always resourceful, pulled a favour from one of his contacts in the aviation industry. Amazingly he got both of us a seat on another plane. That was our glorious comeback.

Sadly, we missed out once again 11 years later, in Kiev. But by then the storm that had raged for years was finally coming to an end. In 2019, in Madrid, we became six-time winners of the top European trophy, after beating Tottenham. I'll always have this wonderful image frozen in my mind, of my son Gavin celebrating the Divock Origi goal that clinched the win for us. Origi is at the corner flag milking the acclaim of the delirious Liverpool supporters, and there is Gavin in front of him, arms outstretched to the heavens. What a wonderful memory.

The memories of Kiev and Madrid have all but erased the torment endured after the destabilisation of the club under Tom Hicks and George Gillett. Along with the trips to Wembley during the brief return of Kenny Dalglish, I think those European adventures have helped to remind us what the club was all about. It has never been about balance sheets, profit, loss and debt. It was always about trophies. That's what Shankly understood. Liverpool exists to make the people happy and win silverware.

I was sad to see Kenny moved on, but I guess if he hadn't gone, we would never have found our way to Jürgen Klopp. I think Bill Shankly would have loved Jürgen. They share so many qualities: passion, enthusiasm, humour and a wonderful relationship with Liverpool's great support. Just like Shankly, Jürgen appears to me to be the perfect fit for Liverpool, and in exactly the right moment in the club's history.

There are many aspects of the modern game that Bill Shankly wouldn't have liked or been comfortable with. Bill was a very strong socialist and he believed passionately in the power of the team over the individual. He still admired the gifted and brilliant individuals of course, but he believed they could never truly succeed without a team around them. He loved Tom Finney, but if he'd have managed him, he'd have ensured he worked hard for the team and that everyone did all they could to support him too.

That, as far as I can see, is very much the Klopp way. That's one of the reasons why I believe Shankly would have adapted to the current game. Although a very different leader, Alex Ferguson built his philosophy on much the same ethos as Shankly. Though he also admired the gifted superstar, for him too, the team was always more important than the individual.

I'm not sure how Bill would have dealt with some of the ancillary things surrounding modern football. For sure, the media would have loved him. However, he might have struggled with the incessant nature of social media and satellite TV channels. I also shudder to think how he would have dealt with agents. Shankly always wanted to be in total control of the signing of players. The size of the modern transfer fees would have been incomprehensible to him. Having said that, he wouldn't have baulked at breaking transfer records. After all, he did that a few times himself with the capture of Ian St John and Ron Yeats, for example.

There are many similarities between Bill's great teams and Jürgen Klopp's current team. For Roger Hunt, insert Mo Salah. In place of Ron Yeats, we now have Virgil van Dijk. Meanwhile, Bobby Firmino fulfils many of the functions of an Ian St John, in my view. And, for sheer destructive power, Jürgen has Sadio Mané, while Bill had Kevin Keegan. Sure, these are all different players in many respects, but to my mind, both Shankly and Klopp have built their teams on similar foundations.

As I write, these building blocks are beginning to once more bear fruit. Under Klopp, Liverpool's army of supporters have rediscovered their bond with the players and their manager. The 'holy trinity' is as strong as it was back in the 60s. It interests me that Jürgen saw that as his first task; to turn doubters to believers once more.

Of course, Bill had the same idea. He wanted to harness the power of the supporters and their culture. Klopp has done exactly that, and he is aided in so many ways by the same charisma Shankly used to such good effect and his amazing ability to articulate simple ideas without pretension.

Under Jürgen, the Reds have played in three European finals, winning their sixth European Cup in Madrid. They have also contested a League Cup Final, missing out on penalties to an incredible Manchester City team. They have won the European Super Cup and have at last been crowned World Club Cup Champions. None of that seemed remotely possible when Jürgen took over.

In so many ways, the rebuilding job undertaken by Klopp was as monumental as the one Bill embarked upon in 1959. The results are similar too. While I and the rest of the world sit at home on lockdown in the spring of 2020, hiding away from a deadly virus and eagerly awaiting the resumption of Premier League football, Liverpool sit 25 points clear at the top of the league. They will surely be champions again.

When that happens, it will close the circle for me in so many ways. Sixty years ago, I embarked on a journey from a small train station in Aberdeen. It took me south and to Liverpool, where my destiny was forever entwined with the fortunes of this great club. Though I returned to the city of my birth, and even crossed the ocean to South Africa in pursuit of the game I love, this city on the banks of the Mersey was and remains my spiritual home.

Though these are difficult times, my wife and I are happy. Our children are successful and continue to fill us with pride, and we find great joy in our grandchildren too. Life is good now.

My association with Liverpool and the great Bill Shankly has led to me forging many friendships with people I would never have met otherwise. I'm proud to count among my friends some great ex-footballers and supporters from all over the world, such as Andy Beijer from Sweden. Thanks to Andy, I'll treasure my memories of visiting the Swedish Supporters Association in Stockholm, with my good friend Gordon

Wallace, and meeting Liverpool CEO, Peter Moore. There are many more people who have enriched my life beyond measure – too many to mention.

But mostly, to be able to live out the remainder of my life in this place, seeing the club I love, built by a man I continue to hold in the highest regard, restored to its rightful place feels like a fitting end to my journey. Who knows what the ride has left in store for us? All I know is I look forward to it with enthusiasm. Because without that, you're nothing.

Journey's End, At Least for Now

I WILL be 76 in October 2020. My surgery is complete, and I'm once again healthy. Carole and I have so much to be thankful for, and the wonderful treatment we have received from the National Health Service has been second to none. We literally owe our lives to the dedicated professionals who work, day in and day out, on our behalf.

Of course, now more than ever, given their herculean efforts during the Covid-19 crisis, we realise just how important their jobs are. For that reason, as I write these words, I do so in self-isolation in order to protect them and save lives. It's spring and the sun is shining in my garden. Life is good.

I may be approaching the final stops on my Anfield journey. But what a journey it has been. My grandfather would have us all believe that each moment along the way was preordained, that my fate had already been mapped out ahead of me. Who am I to argue? It has, at times, felt that way to me. Whenever I have needed it, that helping hand of destiny has always been there to guide me on to my next challenge.

However, I would like to think there is a little space for the good choices I have made, my determination and never-say-die attitude. That said, I can't escape the fact that my abiding sense that things will work themselves out has always been a great source of comfort to me. I must thank my grandfather for that.

I like to think, also, that I made him and my parents proud. That I honoured the debt I owed them and that I made good use of the opportunities they provided for me. I believe that I have.

I'm left with so many glorious memories, spanning 60 years of a life in football and beyond. I have crossed paths with so many fantastic players: Yeats, St John, Lawrence, Thompson Callaghan, Smith, Byrne, Lawler and Hunt. It was an honour to have shared a career with them. And of course, I have been blessed to have learned from some of the greatest footballing minds in history. Shankly, Paisley, Moran, Fagan and Bennett have inspired me so much and continue to influence my life and my thinking to this day.

I have also been fortunate to have watched the careers of some of the greatest players to don the Liverpool shirt. Keegan, Toshack, Heighway, Dalglish and Souness, Hansen and Lawrenson, Rush, Owen and Fowler have lit up Anfield. And of course, the club has continued to be blessed with great talent throughout my life, with the likes of Gerrard, Carragher, Alonso, Mascherano, Torres and Suarez. Thankfully, it looks set to continue too, with Alisson, van Dijk, Salah, Firmino, Mané, Alexander-Arnold and many others too numerous to name here.

I have also lived through so many fantastic games, moments that live in my dreams and fill me with joy. This club has given me so much. I still recall with pride our promotion to the First Division in 1962, with Kevin Lewis scoring two goals at the Kop end, in the pouring rain and the mud, against Southampton. Winning the First Division for the first time under Bill Shankly in 1964 and of course that FA Cup triumph in 1965 are among the highlights.

To have been around the club in these formative years remains a huge source of pride to me. I have been blessed with a ringside view to the making of history. In the 127 years our club has been around, we have lived through its most glorious days. And to have been involved on the inside for at least some of that success is a privilege. As is knowing personally the many architects of that success. For that I'll be eternally grateful.

Of course, I also got to play for my boyhood team, my first footballing love – Aberdeen. And I tasted success on foreign shores before carving out a successful life for my family and myself. It has been a wonderful life, and though nobody can know what is left in store for them, I'm happy now. And that's all any of us can ask for.

Finally, to the man who has inspired me so much throughout my journey – Bill Shankly – I would like to record my thanks. Bill, what you gave this club, the city it serves and me personally, is beyond measure. It has certainly been a special journey. How lucky I have been to witness at first hand these amazing six decades.

The magnitude of what this club has achieved since I stood at Lime Street station in January 1960 has been little short of unbelievable. All that has followed stems from those early moments, the decisions you made and the work you did. It's truly an honour to have witnessed it.

Even now, I can still hear your voice, Boss. I hear you telling Johnny, my stepdad, on that afternoon at Anfield in 1961, as we stood in the centre circle:

'Your boy is lucky to be here Mr Scott. This place will be a bastion of invincibility. They will all come here and be beaten.'

You were right, Bill. I was, it is, and to this day they still come here to be beaten. And, although I didn't make your first XI, I was lucky to be the twelth-best. It's the honour of my life that I was a Shankly Boy, who, as a man, has lived by the standards you set. Thanks for the memories, Boss.

So, until we meet again, Bill, I'll raise a glass once more to your memory.

You'll never walk alone.

George Scott, 'the Twelth-Best Player in the World'.

1 May 2020.

Collinge
STYLIST
F.C.